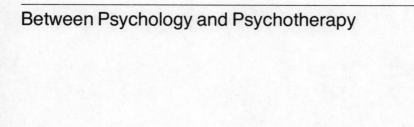

Between Psychology and Psychotherapy

Between Psychology and Psychotherapy

A poetics of experience

Miller Mair

R

Routledge

London and New York

First published in 1989
by Routledge
11 New Fetter Lane, London EC4P 4EE
29 West 35th Street, New York, NY 10001

Printed in Great Britain by Mackays of Chatham PLC, Chatham, Kent

British Library Cataloguing in Publication Data

Mair, Miller, *1937-*
    Between psychology and psychotherapy: a
    poetics of experience
    1. Clinical psychology related to
    psychotherapy
    2. Psychotherapy related to clinical
    psychology
    I. Title
    157'9

    ISBN 0-415-00021-1 (hbk)
        0-415-00022-x (pbk)

Library of Congress Cataloging-in Publication Data

Mair, Miller, 1937-
    Between psychology and psychotherapy.

    Bibliography: p.
    Includes index.
    1. Psychotherapy—Philosophy.   2. Psychology—
    Philosophy.   3. Poetics.   I. Title.
    RC454.4.M33   1989   616.89'14   88-32329

    ISBN 0-415-0 0021-1
    ISBN 0-415-0 0022-X (pbk)

for my parents and my children

Contents

Acknowledgements

Various people encouraged me when I most needed them. Those I want specially to thank are my friends and colleagues, Helga and Ian Cameron, Derek Dewhurst, Robert Hobson, Simon King-Spooner, Angus Macmillan, Roger Poole, David Smail, and Anna Smith.

Don Bannister gave me courage through his own example of caring and daring. Even as he died so tragically in 1986 he undertook to read the manuscript of this book and recorded his beautifully thoughtful comments in the last days of his life.

Special thanks are due to those who have come to me seeking psychological help. You have taught me more than I can say. In so doing you have made the whole problem of 'saying' a central theme in this book.

Introduction

This book is meant for anyone who seeks to understand themselves and others and what is involved in coming to such understanding. In that it draws largely from my work as a psychologist and psychotherapist, however, it is directed initially towards my colleagues in the 'helping' professions (clinical psychologists, psychiatrists, social workers, ministers and priests, counsellors, 'carers' of many kinds) who may recognize some of the matters which disturb me. In that I seek to move towards literary and artistic modes of expression, it may also be of interest to some in these wider disciplines. In that my aim is to reach through these various issues towards a different way of 'doing' psychology, of being a psychologist, there may be something of relevance here for those with interests in the whole topic of 'knowing' and 'being known'.

My focus is on ordinary human experience, not some special category of events called 'poetry'. My concerns are, however, with the powers of 'poetic diction' and with a 'poetics' of experiencing. This latter term, 'poetics', may be unfamiliar to some readers. In spite of having the ugly sound of some made-up modern terms, it has an ancient lineage. Aristotle used the term in his study of the ways in which poetry works and is constructed. His *Poetics* set the stage for centuries of work on metaphor and many aspects of the use of language. Like all disciplines, poetics has changed over time. A useful, recent contribution within the field of literary criticism is subtitled *Contemporary Poetics* (Rimmon-Kenan 1983).

My concern is with the crucial importance of a poetic approach in psychology and psychotherapy, as well as in everyday life, to complement the more pervasive 'prosaics' of how we normally speak and write. I am concerned with the fundamental significance of a poetic awareness and attentiveness in relation to any pursuit of understanding of ourselves or others. I believe that we persistently boil down our experiencing to dull 'normality', while our unspoken selves long for a voice of more passionate precision.

'Poetics' is not just the study of the use of language and other devices (like rhythm, pace, ordering). The term is also used more widely in other disciplines than those concerned directly with poetry or literature. Though writers in 'poetics' can be quite unpoetic in how they express their often analytic concerns, this is not always so. It is with those whose interest is to explore and understand the nature of their subject through an imaginative freedom of language that I wish to be associated. One such is the French philosopher of science, Gaston Bachelard. Two of his later books concerning *The Poetics of Space* (1964) and *The Poetics of Reverie* (1969) broke new ground in subject matter and in the manner of their composition. Within psychology a recent publication for more general reference is *Psychology and the Poetics of Growth* (Pollio *et al.* 1977).

At this point it may be important to say that there are people of poetic vision in all disciplines, in nuclear physics, mathematics, computer science, history, philosophy, and even in psychology (William James was surely one of these). Certainly in the many strands of psychotherapy there have been significant poetic explorers of relationship and mind. Amongst the obvious examples are the classic figures of Freud and Jung, and the more recent 'new voices' of Carl Rogers and George Kelly. There are also, in the border world of both psychology and psychotherapy, many who employ and value voices of poetic power. Among those who immediately come to mind for me are David Bakan (1966), Rollo May (1975), Robert Hobson (1985), and David Smail (1984, 1987).

Although poetry is not my concern here, but the issues that are essential for a psychology of psychotherapy, it is to poets and their care for experiencing and words that I want first to turn. Consider some comments on poetry and poets that bear on what I hope to undertake in more humble ways. Owen Barfield (1928) suggested that 'the meaning of life is continually being dried up, as it were, and left for dead in the human mind by the operation of a purely discursive intellectual activity'. He went on to suggest that 'without the continued existence of poetry, without a steady influx of new meaning into language, even the knowledge and wisdom which poetry herself has given in the past must wither away into a species of mechanical calculation'. Great poetry, he believed, is 'the progressive incarnation of life in consciousness'. It is this poetic imagination, the creative edge, that I am concerned with here, as a certain manner of being, a mode of action within any aspect of an ordinary life.

T.S. Eliot has said that there is precise and imprecise emotion, just as there is precise and imprecise thought. This is important to recognize in both psychology and psychotherapy. Some of Eliot's concerns are indicated by Stead (1964) in *The New Poetic*. They are worth mentioning here. What he says for the poet is equally true for the psychologist, psychotherapist, or person in the park. Eliot speaks of the necessary release of the poet from his own rational will and suggests that the mind of the mature poet is different from that of a more immature one, not in coming from a more interesting person, but in 'being a more finely perfected medium in which special, or very varied, feelings are at liberty to enter into new combinations'. He spoke of a state of negative capability, 'a passive attending upon the event'. In pointing out this crucial concern, Stead indicates that Eliot's 'escape' from personality was not a running away from oneself, but rather going deeper into the self, 'below the levels of consciousness'.

Eliot suggested that it is 'the poet's business to be original, in all that is comprehended by "technique", only so far as is absolutely necessary for saying what he has to say; only so far as is dictated, not by the idea — for there is no idea — but by the nature of that dark embryo within him which gradually takes on the form and speech of a poem.' He goes on to say that the poet cannot, when he is composing, simply will that a duck's egg should produce a cygnet. The quality and nature of the 'dark embryo' has been established by what the poet has made of himself and what his society has made of him. He notes that 'at the moment when one writes, one is what one is, and the damage of a lifetime ... cannot be repaired at the moment of composition'. All of this is relevant to all of us at any point of creative necessity.

Remembering that the 'poet' is present in all of us to varying degrees and in every context of our lives, it is also worth noting some words of a different Eliot, George rather than T.S. In *Middlemarch* she indicates that to be a poet 'is to have a soul so quick to discern that no shade of quality escapes it, and so quick to feel, that discernment is but a hand playing with finely-ordered variety on the chords of emotion — a soul in which knowledge passes instantaneously into feeling and feeling flashes back as a new organ of knowledge'. Realistically, it is noted there, as all of us will know too well, that 'one may have that condition by fits only'.

Stead also indicates something else relevant for poetry (and, I would say, every other aspect of life), in pointing out that 'style' is the poet's way of knowing the world. Style is not an optional extra or an added decoration. It is a way of recreating a world of experience. 'A failure of style', says Stead, 'whether the work is a simple description or something more complex, is a false report, the creation of an image which misrepresents "things as they are".' This, along with much else, will be an important issue in what follows here.

This is a book concerning human experience, but most particularly it concerns some of *my* ways of experiencing, my ways of composing what I know and seek to know about. It is a very personal book, concerned with *personal knowing*. Much thinking in psychology is shaped towards the hardening of 'objective knowledge', supposedly separated from any particular hand or mind. For me this is a major flaw, a basic fault, in the psychology we seem mainly to be striving for. In psychotherapy, and every other encounter of a more intimate, personal kind, impersonal knowledge will not do. We are there in the midst of knowing what we dare to know, being shaped towards blindness by what we fear to see. Here it becomes startlingly clear that we have to help ourselves and others to know 'in our bones' and for ourselves, not take second-hand opinions or beliefs that others claim. This is a very different kind of 'knowing' from that which is still mainly focussed on in psychology and in most psychological research into psychotherapy. There again, it seems mostly to be impersonal knowledge *about* psychotherapeutic process or outcome that is sought. It should be no great surprise that we thereby pile up dead words, and the dangerous immediacy of lived experiencing, in poetry and in life, slips by and disappears.

It is not just that personal knowing is more vital and elusive than the lumps of fact we often value, it is also that knowing personally is always something undertaken by someone, in some relationship to self and world. Our personal ventures in seeking to know, or variously to ignore, are necessarily entered by someone, somewhere, in relation to some ends. None of our knowing is floating free in the air, as often seems to be the implicit claim for the facts and theories that fill our psychological tomes. Here again I feel another basic flaw. In what follows my concern is to seek my own voice, located in my place and time, no more. If what I say reaches out to anything of you, it may be because of what we share in the ongoing conversation of our place and time. I mostly manage to believe Carl Rogers' dictum that when we speak most personally, we speak most generally too.

As a clinical psychologist who has, for over twenty-five years now, been actively involved in psychotherapy, this presentation is an attempt at turning round to conjure up the psychological concerns that now speak strongly to me. My perspective now, however, is *from* the world of psychotherapeutic meeting, and from there, within the fought-for knowing of many lives in pain, I wish to speak into being something of the psychological world I need. This has led me, over the years, towards a different 'model' of psychological inquiry, which seeks to stand somewhere *between* the present worlds of 'psychology as a science' and 'psychotherapy as a mode of professional care'. It is towards a 'conversational psychology' that I reach, a psychology of a different kind from what we presently know. In reaching towards this still uncertain goal, I am heartened by the good companions who have fought their separate and different ways towards a somewhat similar trail. Amongst these is Robert Hobson, who has already formed and tested the outlines of a conversational model of psychotherapy (Hobson 1985). Rom Harré recognizes the primacy of 'conversation' in all his explorations into 'social' and 'personal' being (1979, 1983). In a different context of human learning, Laurie Thomas and Sheila Harri-Augstein (1985) have published a significant book subtitled, *Foundations of a Conversational Science of Psychology*. Surely it is not just chance that these latter and myself both derive much of our seemingly dissimilar psychological inspiration from George Kelly's remarkably fertile mind (Kelly 1955, 1969).

This present work is not the kind of book with many references to buttress every claim. Being a personal venture, I have sought to speak with my own voice even when what I say may well have been said better by many others before me. I do not make much use of the terminology of behaviourism or psychoanalysis. This is not always done in ignorance of what others say. It is because everything here has to be personally owned and if it carries anything of value towards you, I hope it will be undertaken then as a personal question, worthy of being personally explored and known by you.

Probably what is attempted here will fail. It is certainly easy prey to many criticisms which it will deserve. While this is so, it is my hope that some will seek to *participate* in what is said rather than reach first for the angry marker pen. What is presented here is not an argument from first to last. Almost everything invites you to enter in, start anywhere, follow what *you* think and feel. This book consists of many new beginnings, many different attempts to say something of what and how things feel for me. It is a digging up of ground, hoping to renew and prepare for what may yet be sown. Any fruits that are ready for picking here are small and growing still, perhaps less and other than they may still become.

What follows is in three parts, like a sandwich or a musical composition, perhaps. Almost everything in Parts 1 and 3 came to first flower in the broken, 'personal story' of the middle movement, the filling between the, hopefully, nourishing bread. What is offered there was not written as verse or poetry. Almost all of it was written as it is, but in more rambling physical forms. In order to give it some protective shape, I chose to present these pieces in 'short lines' to allow them some chance to say what they have to say. In ordinary 'prosaic' shape they might more easily have been killed at birth, left to die for lack of documented proof.

Part 1 contains a series of essays in and around psychology and psychotherapy that were mostly given first as talks. They were each under-taken as a sensed and necessary part of something I was trying to reach towards knowing in and through them all. There is some overlap between them, but each leads on, seeks to sing its own particular song within the wider theme that my own 'dark embryo' sought to say.

Part 3 was written most recently, though with many pieces culled from scribbling over many years. My concern here is to begin to reflect on all that has gone before. No happy ending is achieved, but some intertwined elements of *a discipline of discourse,* within which both conversational and experimental psychology may have a mutually challenging and sustaining place, are described.

Perhaps I should end my beginning by coming clean. My hopes are not modest even though my expectations are more bleak. My aim is to challenge much that is accepted as the way things have to be done in psychology and in the psychological scrutiny of psychotherapy. No direct attack is mounted though. My aim is radical revision, not casual complaint. It is a questioning of roots, not fruits.

Much that is important in what we do is ignored because of our wide-spread insistence on objectivity and impersonal knowledge as prime concerns. We lose track of what we are up to in our silent shuffling beyond the little patches from which we claim illumination. I'm not suggesting that anyone give up anything or stop doing what they value. I am suggesting that we take something more on board, so that our acts of knowing are owned as well as whatever objects we create from them. It is a widening of attention that I'm suggesting, so that we sense more of what we already do.

Without doubt this is a biassed book. It does not present an even-handed view. This is intentional since I want to try to correct the gross imbalance of another kind already present in much current thinking in psychology. We tend to banish what is tentative and growing in favour of what is solid and simply seen. So much that we are encouraged to do is prosaic and safely derivative, hiding us safely in the modest skirts of our professional norms. Too little of what many psychologists say seems to be personally important, vibrating with our lives in time.

All of this may seem aggressively extreme. It is, of course, a pretence, but not a lie. Everything that I want to speak of here is young and easy to disown. If I don't nail my colours to the mast now, I could so easily leave obscure what I clearly hope towards.

I am already defending myself in being too forceful, and then in my seeming willingness to withdraw. This may be because almost everything spoken here is vulnerable and weak. I am afraid of what you will think and say. I only hope that you will be both kind and true; no sentimental response will do.

Part one

A poetics in practice

Chapter one

Caring to know

We live in a situation of accelerating technological development with
increasing divisions between those who have and those who are in obvious
need. We have to 'grow' individually and socially if we are to stand a
chance of coping with the dangers we are creating. There is, of course, no
easy way in which this can be done. No single achievement by any individual or group will do the trick. It is going to be a touch and go business,
taking much imaginative effort by many. We do not have much time to
spare, and need to seek whatever help we can in increasing our local and
wider understanding of ourselves in relation to our world.

No particular discipline has any claim to special attention since all will
have their parts to play. As a clinical psychologist I have to do whatever I
can within its particular context. As part of the wider discipline of
psychology, whose main focus of concern is on developing reliable
knowledge of human development and functioning, I believe I am somewhere in the thick of this struggle towards greater awareness of the human
condition.

There are not many in society, however, who would see the discipline of
psychology as playing much of a role in this connection at the present time.
It might even be true to say that few within the discipline of psychology
itself would see themselves as doing much either. Psychology has defined
itself as a 'science' and works hard at training all its members in the rigours
of objectivity, measurement, impersonal experimentation, and the statistical manipulation of data. As a general discipline it has been decidedly
reluctant to take up social causes or wear the ordinary hearts of its practitioners on any of its official sleeves. Psychologists, and even clinical
psychologists whose job it is to care for those in distress and personal
conflict, have generally been taught to keep themselves and their own
personal concerns well out of sight so that an impartial 'scientific' stance
can be adopted even in the midst of immediate need.

This kind of disciplined self-denial has probably been necessary, in our
kind of society, for psychology to establish itself even as a halfway serious
undertaking. It has certainly allowed useful exploration of sensory func-

tions and many aspects of human development. Within the context of clinical psychology (which is currently viewed mainly as an 'applied science', applying to the problems of human 'maladjustment' and distress knowledge and scientifically tested procedures from general psychology), many ways of alleviating problems involving anxiety, depression, sexual disability, and suchlike have also been developed.

While accepting all this and wishing to encourage further exploration within the 'pure science' of psychology and the 'applied science' of clinical psychology, I want also to draw away from the conventionally accepted beliefs and procedures to raise some other possibilities. I want to suggest, instead, the outlines of a somewhat different way of conceiving of issues concerning human understanding, and different ways of being engaged in their exploration.

The basic bet

I must stress that I am not trying to create a situation of either/or. I do not believe that all right is on the side which I wish here to emphasize, and that all wrong is on the other. It is more like an argument 'within the family'. I want to try to encourage colleagues and others to give generous consideration to an alternative perspective which may complement what is already done. What is suggested in the course of this book is not 'scientifically attested'. Neither is it something which can be easily stated or set out in simple logical form. It is a different way of thinking from that which is most familiar within both psychology and our wider society. It suggests a different 'world' which has to be entered and lived a little from within if it is to be known at all.

The question I am seeking to raise here is 'what kind of psychology is more likely to help us develop knowledge *and* understanding of ourselves and others?' Clearly I do not know the answer to such a question, but do want to lay my 'basic bet' on the table.

Put simply, I believe that intimate knowledge is likely to teach us more than distant knowledge. Personal knowledge is likely to change us more than impersonal knowledge. Knowledge gained with our eyes, ears, and imaginations wide open is likely to be more valuable than that acquired when we are conceptually and procedurally blindfolded. Knowledge which takes continuing account of the social and cultural contexts within which the questioners and the answerers are located is likely to be more valid than that gained from snippets of formal meeting, shorn of their individual and historical relevance. Knowledge acquired through the patient process by which the questioner takes time to be trusted and to show care for the answerer is likely to be more significant than that gained by the 'hit and run' merchant who only wants to make a quick psychological 'buck'.

At the present time the 'basic bet' of scientific psychology (and clinical psychology as an applied science) is on the pervasive usefulness of the *experiment*. I want to suggest that a better 'basic bet' is on something like the activities we, at present, call *psychotherapy*. I will go on from there to suggest that a 'conversational' rather than an 'experimental' psychology should concern itself essentially with *all* aspects of *conversation*, and not just with the narrow categories of conversation we now refer to as 'experiments'.

Again I must emphasize that I am *not* arguing against the usefulness of experiments and experimenting. Far from it. I consider the crucial contribution of both the clinical psychologist and the psychotherapist as being in their willingness to experiment. Like the clinical psychologist George Kelly (1955, 1969), I don't believe, however, that professionals are uniquely gifted with the powers of constructive experimentation. Kelly suggested that it may be more useful to view people as if, in some important respects, we are all like 'scientists'. He suggests we are *all* involved daily in making sense, experimenting, and evaluating outcomes, since our lives depend on just these kinds of activities.

Within the psychotherapeutic situation, it is very clear that many obvious and more subtle experiments are undertaken and encouraged. Being for or against 'experimenting' is not the issue. Rather is it a matter of how rigidly experiments are to be structured and at what level of abstraction the discipline of psychology is to be conceived in relation to them. At present, psychology is both grounded *on* and grounded *by* too lumbering an adherence to formal procedures of experimentation (however valuable in their place), and too concretistic a procedural commitment to defining reliable knowledge as that which emanates from these set-piece engagements with a sawn-up world.

My concern here, though, is not to argue the details of this case since it is not a rejection of formal and informal experimenting that I wish. What I am concerned with mainly is to indicate the 'drift' of my interests so that what follows in later chapters can be set in the wider context of at least *my* intentions. Neither is my aim to suggest anything as foolishly concretistic as the wholesale undertaking of 'psychotherapy' whenever we want to develop any useful understanding and knowledge. Much in what is called 'psychotherapy' is quite as unpalatable for me as much in what is called 'experimentation' within psychology.

I am concerned rather with some of the *strengths* in the psychotherapeutic encounter and with some of the *limitations* in experimentation, in the genuine hope that new powers of inquiry can grow within a psychology which speaks more widely and deeply to our urgent needs to know and to care. It is not to 'psychotherapy' as a way of *treating* human problems that I wish to attend here, but to the *kinds of relationship* involved in psychotherapeutic meeting, viewed as a *vehicle of psychological inquiry*.

Part of the problem with psychology (and with psychotherapy, though I will say less about this here) is that it is a product of our culture. This is inevitably so, of course, but the danger is that in seeking to develop knowledge of human experience and functioning it blindly adopts assumptions, manners of inquiry, central concerns, and postures towards people which are expressive of that culture, rather than being more radically questioning of its hidden biasses. I believe that this is also true of clinical psychology (and, of course, many other disciplines too) and will try to show something more of the direction of my concerns by looking quizzically at my own discipline from the perspective of psychotherapy.

The myth of an applied science

Some would say that clinical psychology *is* an applied science. It is certainly described as this in lots of official reports and in almost every training course for clinical psychologists in Britain at least. I would suggest instead that the idea of clinical psychology being an applied science is a *myth*.

In saying this I'm not being disparaging since myths are of great importance in any culture for any group to shape and sustain their identity. In beginning to *see* that it is a myth, I am participating in the already weakened state of that myth. While it was young and vigorous, clinical psychology was lived with total commitment *as* an applied science. The persistent focus of concern was on finding ways of carrying across from general psychology methods of inquiry, theories concerning human behaviour, and experimental results to 'apply' these to problems of human unhappiness and disability which had previously been conceived differently within a medical framework. As a discipline (or a tribe) develops through time, however, it is likely to continue to *speak* its allegiance to the central myth which shapes its consciousness, while some of its practices and its emerging beliefs have strayed elsewhere.

From within a myth certain ways of doing things are quite invisible, being accepted, without being noticed, as the way things are. While claiming allegiance to a set of mythically important beliefs or actions, it is difficult to recognize that what is being *done* and what *claimed* may not always coincide. When inhabiting a world created by a particular mythological story, certain characteristic qualities of life, or manners of acting, asking, and answering, will be incorporated as virtues and values of unquestionable worth. Those who do not live in these ways can then immediately be recognized as children of a lesser god.

The myth of 'clinical psychology as an applied science' has been (and no doubt will continue to be) of considerable importance. It has given this vulnerable little discipline the culturally powerful cloak of protection of *science*. Just as almost anything had to be 'religious' in times past, so now almost every discipline which wants to make its way in the world has to be 'scientific'.

Similarly it gained for a small group of adventurers the more immediate potential protection of the 'Big Brother' of psychology, who could be used as a threat when bullying psychiatrists or others were becoming too overbearing. Beyond even this, there has also been an indirect immunity in claiming to be 'scientific' since this often allows us to act without taking full responsibility for what we are doing (claiming that we are just doing what the scientific literature says) or justifies us in not getting involved too closely in human affairs (claiming that we cannot, in all honesty, step beyond what the scientific evidence prescribes).

Clinical psychology is a relatively recent invention, having been operating in something like its present form in Britain for less than 50 years (though for quite a bit longer in America). In this short time it has changed the focus of its concerns quite substantially. From a beginning place as the 'psychological scientist in the clinic', concerned mainly with research and the measurement of intelligence and personality, the clinical psychologist has become one of the influential 'therapeutic' specialists in health settings. Here again, the main initial thrust was towards the development of methods of therapy (behaviour therapy and behaviour modification) which were relatively clearly based on principles established by experiment and derived from general psychology. More recently, much wider involvement in therapeutic work has become common for many clinical psychologists. Some have become experienced in various psychotherapeutic approaches which derive their justification and credibility from clinical imagination and practice rather than from scientifically tested theories.

A psychotherapeutic meeting

In general, the psychotherapist (there are many different varieties, deriving from many different ways of understanding and conceptualizing the important issues in creating and resolving problems in living) enters into some kind of conversation with the client with the intention of facilitating some degree of greater understanding and encouraging new ways of acting which may break the deadlock of past rigidities. The psychotherapist has to develop ways of listening to what the client is saying and what they are pointedly *not* saying; noticing what the client is *doing* while he is claiming something different; encouraging the client to begin to acknowledge and face his own fears and vulnerabilities; supporting him as he tentatively risks undertaking what his own family, group, or tribe has so far disallowed. In coming to know the client, the psychotherapist has to be patient; has to listen and come to understand the language and concepts of the client; has to be available on a continuing basis for a time to allow the development of sufficient trust. In this way the client may come to risk the disclosure and eventual displacement of long hidden fears or long cherished ways of acting which have become more of a hindrance than a help.

It is just this kind of attention that I now want to turn on the discipline of clinical psychology itself. Imagine, if you will, a walking and breathing embodiment of this 'myth of an applied science' coming through the clinic door to seek some help in understanding some of his recent troubles. In listening to him we may recognize some of the blind spots of the present myth and look towards some of the issues which a different approach to human understanding might allow.

The *first* thing I, as the psychotherapist, notice with this new client is that he keeps claiming that you have to think things out first (develop a good theory) and then test these thoughts in controlled, practical ways. Almost all his knowledge seems to be 'in the head'. He insists on doing only those things that have been tested in approved ways. He clearly believes that if he thinks things out and then gets some 'scientific' evidence that he is right, that will always carry the day. He keeps being amazed, horrified, shocked, dismayed by the ways in which others seem to disregard this obviously correct manner of proceeding and allow other 'emotional' or 'subjective' or 'political' issues to affect the matter. He does not seem to realize that undertaking some new way of thinking or acting takes more than just knowledge in the head.

To achieve and defend space so that some forms of life can be nurtured takes courage and often involves confrontation, attack, endurance, testing in the fires of battle. Many die and are broken in the trench warfare of committees and organizations. Many of us retreat to where we can at least survive, rather than continue to struggle to build and sustain the habitations, encampments, tribal villages which may have been of special concern to us, but which demanded too much when we tried to build them in the front line of practice.

Those of us brought up in the mythology of psychology as an essentially *theoretical* discipline, tested in formal and oddly baroque rituals, come as lambs to the slaughter very often when plunged into the realities of practice in the field. We expect, as we have been taught, that if we can make a logical case and if we have the right amount of 'valid' and 'reliable' evidence (the kind we have been taught to regard as the very best kind to have), then we should win through. We are liable to be traumatized by our first bruising encounters with those more experienced in the mysterious and brutal ways of the organizational world.

Our puzzled client finds that the world of *practice* is very different from the world of *theory*. Some of his 'members' have reacted to this discovery by becoming the toughest of 'organization men and women', claiming that nothing matters other than changing organizational structures. They are liable to abandon careful work with real people in favour of battling with 'the system'. Others have preferred to shrink into the organizational woodwork, hoping they will not be noticed. From there they have tried to do as best they can what they have been taught as their proper task. By being obedient to what others want they sometimes become quite highly regarded, posing as they do no threat at all.

Our client here has not noticed that he has simply 'bought' the prevailing cultural assumption as regards the way in which knowledge is acquired. Knowledge, he assumes, is essentially *theoretical* and has to be acquired by impersonal methods of formal experimentation in which the rules of proper checks and balances have to be insisted on. From this perspective, launching out into *practice* without having the properly attested theoretical knowledge is a gross heresy, a sure sign of failure in the 'applied science' game.

But, as I hope to suggest and illustrate in this whole presentation, it is possible to take a different stance. It is possible, as Shotter (1984) has also argued, to seek to found a psychology *in practice* rather than *in theory*. In such a psychology we would be assuming that we can and must learn from our own spontaneous and imaginative actions, launched into and undertaken sometimes before any detailed reflection has been possible. Our problems would then be of a very different kind. We would have to find and develop ways of learning from what we had already done, rather than *prescribing* our actions in advance as our present 'applied science' mythological friend claims to do.

If we approach knowing and understanding from a starting place in *practice*, knowing personally through our own engagement in affairs, we will quickly find that knowing of this kind takes endurance, it feels risky, it calls for delicacy as well as 'guts', and needs both space and time. We have to bear the pains and the joys of knowing in our own experience, its guilts and excitements. In this we will quickly recognize that *ignoring* is an integral part of any knowing, since we have to turn away from what we cannot bear or fear to undertake. We are likely to come to recognize that our ways of ignoring have been developed to an even greater extent than our still timid ways of involving ourselves in the dangerous seas of knowing for ourselves.

Our client has been trying to live by thinking everything out, trying everything out in artificially obedient contexts where the real world is all but excluded. He then *applies* these 'solutions', with eyes at least half closed in case he should see more than he wishes to recognize or is prepared to understand.

A *second* thing I notice about my unusual, cultural client (this 'myth of clinical psychology as an applied science') is that he (it is a *he*, though many of his members are *she*) is very keen on being seen as 'hard' and 'tough', 'precise', 'logical', and 'unemotional'. He really does go on and on about what a 'macho male' he is. Goodness knows what he does to his enemies, but he certainly frightens some of us who are supposedly on the same side!

Why does he make such a big thing out of being so 'hard headed', 'tough minded', and 'tightly controlled'? Well, I suppose any psychotherapist is going to suspect immediately that there is something here he *fears*. There is something he is avoiding, keeping well away from, by this determination to 'keep a grip'.

As I listen to this small mythological expression of the wider cultural myths of our society, what can we suppose is being so studiously kept at bay? Surely it is just what our culture as a whole is so frightened of, all that is soft, warm, feminine, intuitive, intimate, vulnerable, open, uncertain in our natures and our social lives. Surely this little discipline of clinical psychology has again adopted a heightened version of the wider values and fears of our distance-keeping, objectifying, emotion-fearing, appearance-saving, vulnerability-hiding culture.

When I look beyond his protestations concerning the crucial importance of hard-edged method and control, I quickly realize all is not as he makes it seem. I notice that more than half of his members *are* female and that many of them (as well as many men within the profession) take the traditional female role of quietly doing very different things from what the defining male mythology suggests they should. Many members are not happy with the hard, unfeeling claims that are made on their behalf. Many act in sensitive professional ways they do not often speak about. They care for what is apparently regarded as too 'soft' for the 'he-man' image they still shelter under. Mostly they do this because there is no acceptable way of speaking of what they know or of giving suitable form to what they are tentatively feeling towards.

Our mythology leads us to defend a place which encourages hardness and distance and gives us no support at all in coming to know the close and the uncertain. In this pursuit of distance there are those who, for the best possible motives of greater service to the culture from which they speak, argue that since there are so few clinical psychologists they should not waste their precious time in unvalidated practices like psychotherapy. They say we should, instead, withdraw still further from intimate contact with individual clients to teach the teachers, instruct the carers, guide those of a lesser kind who may be professionally less fastidious as regards immediate contact with those in need.

Perhaps this mythology drives us even further. May it be that it leads us to project our 'weaknesses' onto those others who come to us with their problems. So often we see our clients as having those fears and difficulties which our own professional methodology fears and has difficulties with. Might it be that, in creating our methods of behaviour modification and control, we are passing on to others the defensive structures which have worked so well for us. By so doing we undoubtedly help many, but also hinder some who seek to *know* rather than control their fears.

In all this we seem to deny much that is of great importance to ourselves and others. The realms of feeling and sensibility, by which all close relationships are enriched and all science and art are created, are somehow being swept away. This mythology speaks much of 'applying', little of 'creating'.

It is this rich realm of 'creating' which an alternative approach to psychological understanding needs to retrieve. Starting in the necessary intimacies of *practice* we may yet learn to use, trust, and glory in the sensibilities we are each capable of developing. This is not an open road towards psychological decay, though any such approach will not bring instant solutions. Equally certainly, it will bring difficulties of its own. Yet surely it cannot be to the eventual diminishment of genuine psychological understanding if we begin to allow and nourish strengths which we have decried as weaknesses and subtleties of mind which may be strengthened to take us to places where no hard-edged formality could go.

A *third* thing becomes apparent about our client. There is much talk from him of *research*, but again, as a psychotherapist, I am left feeling that all is not as it is claimed. 'Research', our 'clinical psychology myth' tells us, is the jewel in his crown. This, he claims, is what is basic to everything he is and does. Nothing, he says, amounts to anything if it is not guaranteed by research methods and backed by the findings of research.

And yet I have to say that while his claims have some substance, there is something too emphatic in the way he keeps making them. He is not altogether comfortable about something.

Once again, by looking beyond the mythological claims, a very different impression is to be gained. I begin to remember that few of his members seem to *do* any research, certainly not research which is published. Clinical psychologists do not, in fact, seem to be very enthusiastic publishers in general. While a lot of research and publication noise is made by a few (those specially sanctioned servants of the myth), most clinical psychologists do little or nothing which would normally be called 'research'. Beyond this, I suspect that few clinical psychology departments do much research (though there is usually at least one myth-serving member to keep the flag flying). Almost no time is given to research. In some departments, members are even told that they are not to waste their precious clinical time on research activity.

Is this a sad tale of our dearest wishes being thwarted by the cruel pressures of circumstances? That certainly is what many say when questioned on the subject (the myth still has sufficient power to make its members guiltily aware of their continuing failure to live up to its demands). Yet I suspect that this is not really how it is. As clinicians we would certainly have other thoughts if the husband of one of our clients just happened to be too busy with other pressing matters whenever his wife was ready to go to bed.

Might it just be that we are 'voting with our feet'? Perhaps we don't *want* to do 'research'. Mostly what we have been taught to regard as 'research' seems to many to be lumbering or thoroughly unsatisfying. Mostly we don't believe it 'works' or produces enough to justify all the time, energy, and pain which is involved. Perhaps, sometimes, we are rebellious and resist 'research' since it often seems, by its formal methods, to disqualify much of our own experience.

Might it not, therefore, be that the members of this myth-governed body are positively making space for what they do really value (mostly this is more personal contact with clients in the course of ordinary clinical activities), and letting the rest go by. Even though the myth of clinical psychology as an applied science places its basic emphasis on research, most clinical psychologists do not do it. They suffer, instead, the nagging sense of failure which this entails. 'Better' they seem to say, 'a time of guilt than continuing enslavement to a way of life which has so little life for me.'

Again I have to wonder if there is much more inquiry going on than is recognized by the formal term 'research', or more that would be done if some different, more clinical, more available manner of seeking could be found. While not wishing to propose some form of inquiry which would replace the experimental methods we presently employ, I do wish to offer 'another way' which might appeal to some. This alternative will be rooted in the kinds of intimacy which are made familiar in psychotherapeutic meeting. Perhaps because of this it is unlikely to be widely popular since it demands disciplines of thought and action which our present mythology neither recognizes nor values.

My seemingly self-confident client has many other problems, governed as he is by a myth which no longer quite fits what 'he and she' sometimes wants and often needs to do. Only one other, a *fourth*, point will be made.

Scarcely is he through the door than my client is trying to teach me how I should be doing my job, what concepts I should be using to think of psychological change and how I should be assessing outcomes in what I do. He is determined to teach others since he seems convinced that his ideas and methods are better (quite naturally, he assumes, since they are based on 'research' findings, backed by at least some scraps of 'hard' data, based on clearly stated theory, even though these sound rather simplistic to anyone who has not been trained to approved levels of limitation).

This myth, speaking as it does within the wider cultural tradition of Protestant doubt and questioning, has given birth to another missionary breed. Clinical psychologists have been taught from the beginning that a basic part of their duty is to teach and, by and large, they have been obedient to this calling. They have gone forth and taught. Their teaching has been introduced to all sorts of courses, from nursery nurses to architects, psychiatrists to prison warders, and few have been allowed to get away.

Not all of this has been a happy experience, either for the psychologists or those who have been on the receiving end of this professional generosity. Amongst clinical psychologists there seems to grow a pervasive sense of frustration and unhappiness with much of the teaching they have to do. Hordes of mystified nurses and uncaringly bewildered psychiatrists have had to sit through hours of grim instruction on the wonders of Pavlov's dogs, Eysenck's dimensions, and Skinner's pigeons. Not all of it has made much sense either to the recipients or the jaded deliverers who, in dutiful fulfilment of another teaching chore, may wonder if they *must* keep on with this when they themselves use little of what they feel obliged to give away.

Now, of course, not all psychology teaching is like this. Much that is truly useful and exciting is also, sometimes, said. But in my present role as a therapist to this somewhat difficult, intellectualizing, 'macho', pedantically obsessive, self-advertising client I have again to notice the disjunction here between the myth-given duty to *teach* and the sense of mystified irrelevance which still filters out of so many lecture rooms.

There is so much emphasis on *teaching* others and so little emphasis on *learning* for ourselves (except through the defensive structures of research design). Perhaps again, this client of ours is living in the head, by rule, in some self-protected way. He seems again to have arranged his priorities and time so that he is the high and mighty one, the giver and teacher to others. It is they who are in need, not he. He is strong and knowledgeable and always right. He keeps telling me how everyone else, and the system in general, seems endlessly to frustrate his best and most cogently correct intentions.

As clinical psychologists we have, it seems, defended a space for ourselves as holders and bringers of 'good news' to others. We have *not* defended much space for learning for ourselves. We do not recognize and encourage continuing learning for ourselves from clients, colleagues, or even ourselves. Naturally we approve of the idea of learning, in theory, but mostly we do not seem to value ongoing, daily learning as a crucial part of what we *do*. We are, indeed, quite remarkably careless, I would say, of those clients who come to teach us daily from what *they* know.

But then, it would be against the ruling of the myth if we were to acknowledge our own *ignorance* and seriously make space to learn. We do not daily remember William James's still accurate observation that 'our science is a drop, our ignorance a sea'. It is perhaps the greatest weakness in the 'myth of an applied science' that we do not even suppose we have a continuing need to learn from those we meet. The myth seems to let us assume that all the real, imaginative inquiry has been done somewhere else, and all we need to do is to think out ways of applying the fruits of someone else's creative labours. As a result, we do not seem often to bear the demands of coming to know personally. We do not often seem to struggle with the strange and sometimes terrible experiences of coming to know for ourselves.

It is here, at the very core, that we have become grossly careless, uncaring, ignorant of how to care, of how to learn through deeper conversation with others and ourselves. We have shuffled off learning under the heading of 'research'. By so doing we have become embarrassed amateurs rather than careful professionals in the painful refreshment of facing our own ignorance. We so often do not allow new beginnings of understanding in so many opportunities to learn from our daily work and meetings.

It is here again that the approach to knowing that I wish to suggest has, perhaps, something different to bring to our ways of caring and knowing. It offers a view of psychological life which allows us to see beyond the reach of 'application', moving us towards a more original involvement with the world we seek to know.

A personal approach to knowing

If you are to come to know *personally*, it means starting from and repeatedly returning to your own ways of experiencing, rather than resting content with some more conventionally constructed position. This is not to say that our own ways of experiencing are not also socially constructed, but in reaching towards personal knowing these lived 'templates' need to be both owned and questioned.

This kind of approach to knowing means taking a position of responsibility for what you are coming to know, rather than shuffling off any responsibility onto rules, conventions, or impersonal necessities of various kinds. It means taking the *activities* of experiencing very seriously, rather than resting content with what is communally claimed as the 'correct' procedure.

In all this, the term 'personal' does not mean 'individual' or 'idiosyncratic'. It refers to a more profound perspective on events, explored from a position of full participation and repeated reflection thereon.

It is probably not very 'cost effective' to take persistent note of a person's viewpoint and to help them towards their own decisions. It is far easier, more time- and labour-saving, to direct, manipulate, or otherwise guide them towards what is likely to be 'best' for them. To be 'personal' is more troublesome, time consuming, and demanding of many virtues which are in short supply.

I know that I am not very personally developed. I also believe that this is true for most people around me, even though we often hide our limitations behind the camouflage of the expected. I also suspect that the future of our society depends on whether or not we become more able to be personal and less reliant on the blind following of injunctions, prescriptions, and conventional social roles.

More widely, I believe that our civilization has been and still is experimenting in massive ways with some of the many possibilities of being personal (more often exploring the subordinate possibilities of impersonality in different guises), what it might mean to be personal, how it can be borne, how it can be eased. The first great shifts in values concerning 'the personal' were enshrined in 'religious' terms, then in art and politics, and now, more diffusely, in many kinds of social protest. We must, I think, try to remember what has been learned (and is still being learned) under these earlier and alternative guises and resist the temptation to assume that everything that matters has been created in recent 'scientific' terms.

To be personal is a choice which cannot be forced. It can always and readily be abandoned. It is the easiest thing in the world to desert a personal position and take refuge in 'objectivity' rather than understanding. Being personal, or allowing others to be personal, means taking time, your own or the other person's time. It cannot be rushed to fit the demands of external requirements.

Trying to take a personal approach to knowing *includes* rather than excludes any or all *impersonal* procedures, since all such procedures are the actions of persons in relation to events. This means that a personal approach is a more comprehensive way of working, not a more limited one than the adoption of narrowly 'objective' or 'impersonal' methods. We can undertake relatively more or less of what is involved in the range of possibilities for personal knowing.

In psychology there has been particular care for the narrower, more impersonal, and objective ways of coming to know. These have led us to a reliance on tight, limiting methods to a point where dangerous inadequacy is apparent in many psychologists (as well as many others) as regards the wider, more intimate, and demanding aspects of personal knowing. Gentleness allied to subtle, flexible strength is required if we are to care enough to know more than the surface of ourselves, others, and our worlds. There are so many ways to body forth, touch with light and shade, emphasize and hint towards what may yet be known. There are many ways of telling other than the dull conventions in how we often speak. Our often banal tradition of psychological expression leads us to claim that we are simply being dutiful to what is simply there. But for ourselves, for any understanding of human experiencing, we need to remember that the world is much more varied than our simplest conventions allow us easily to see. Not only this, but it has an 'inside' as well as an 'outside', and if we are to speak truly what we know, we will require more than is offered in the current methods of simplistic understatement.

It is towards a mode of human inquiry which recognizes that we need to take care if we are to know even a little of what matters most deeply to ourselves and others that I seek to move. In taking such care we will have to free ourselves enough to imagine how things may be beyond the ways we have been taught not to see and not to say.

Chapter two

Pretending to care

Some of the differences between the formal, experiment-based, 'scientific' approach to the study of human action and the more informal, free-flowing, 'conversational' approach which I will explore in this book, can be highlighted by referring further to the practice of psychotherapy.

'Psychotherapy' can be seen as various forms of conversations within which the 'client' struggles for new ways of understanding and acting in relation to issues in his or her life which have been experienced as distressing and disabling. In this they are helped by the 'therapist' who seeks to create and defend the space needed for this undertaking as they speak together in words and deeds.

The term 'psychotherapy' is in almost every respect an unsatisfactory one in that it carries, for instance, overtones of 'medical treatment' where the 'therapist' has the 'medicine' which the 'patient' has to 'take' if the 'cure' is to be effected. The notion of 'treatment' or 'therapy' is a very misleading metaphor here. The engagement between the participants seems to depend most on the active involvement of the 'client' who has to 'work' at the issues which trouble him or her. The 'therapist' here is not handing out 'treatment' from a position of independent expertise, but has to engage with the person who seeks help and act variously as a guide, encourager, supporter, and companion in learning.

Since, however, there is no widely understood alternative to the term 'psychotherapy' I will continue to use it here as a traditional shorthand rather than a cryptic description of what goes on. In a similar way I'll continue to make use of the terms 'therapist' and 'psychotherapist' rather than add further sources of confusion to a presentation which is likely to be sufficiently tangled.

As usual in this book, I'll speak mainly from my own experience, while hoping that there will be enough commonality of issues to allow me to speak to others from different walks of life. My own professional activities led me from an initial training in clinical psychology towards being involved in psychotherapeutic practice. While focussing attention on some of the difficulties of this move from 'scientific' psychology towards the more personal issues of psychotherapy, I hope to highlight also some of the ways in which imaginative pretence seems often to be as important as (or even more important than) well attested pieces of formal knowledge.

Movement between these two worlds of psychology as a science (or clinical psychology as an applied science) and psychotherapy has sometimes been for me a confusing and threatening progression. I've been tussling with the many personal and professional difficulties involved in this transition, just as psychiatrists, priests, social workers, general practitioners, and others have to do when they make a similar move from their initial disciplines of medicine, theology, or whatever towards the different kind of demands in psychotherapy.

I believe that the current practice of trying to carry across the methods of exploration and research that have been developed in general psychology to apply these in the psychotherapeutic domain is essentially a hopeless task. It may be akin to trying to colonize and subjugate a spirited and distinctive race, with only superficial similarities to the aspiring master-race of scientific psychology. To the degree that the transfer of concepts and methods from one domain to the other is achieved, some understanding will be gained through imposing on the unknown realm the shapes of known conventions. Much of the native culture, however, will be driven out, underground, or out of sight. In this situation, the experience of the psychologist moving from one domain to the other is likely to become even more confusing. It will seem that we are gaining more knowledge, while actually obscuring the major issues and leaving the psychotherapeutic territory largely uncharted. Rather than acquiring living knowledge, habitable understanding, we may eventually find that only 'native' or 'naturalized' guides are then able to help us find our way around.

I believe it should be a major task for a psychology of psychotherapy to develop sensitively delineated maps and conceptual guides to these still relatively mysterious, psychological lands. Such a psychology should help us to a useful understanding of the landscapes, and of the manners, customs, rituals, and challenges of the people we may find there.

In addition to attending to a few of the questions that I've been able to formulate, in retrospect, about this journey from being a psychologist to becoming a psychotherapist, I want to stress the importance of becoming a psychologist again, at a different level and in a different way. The kinds of human struggles for understanding and freedom which constitute the realm of psychotherapeutic practice are of much wider importance for individual and social life than is often recognized. Because of this we need to try to make conceptual as well as practical sense of it. We need to reach through our journeying towards a more adequate psychology of psychotherapy, and of the issues of human experiencing that psychotherapy points towards.

Caring and knowing

Psychotherapy, in its various forms, is an expression of our current understanding of what is involved in caring; in caring somewhat more fully for 'persons' rather than 'patients', or some more limited social role. But psychotherapy is itself still limited, and is in many respects a strangely ritualized cluster of ways of giving expression to social caring.

In addition to being about helping and caring, the activities that we normally refer to under the broad label of 'psychotherapy' also have a focal concern with knowing and being known. It is an arena which highlights issues to do with 'knowing'; involving both ontology (ways of being) and epistemology (aspects of knowledge). It is a context, or a cluster of contexts, in and through which we engage in whatever is involved in coming to know ourselves and others. In psychotherapy, we struggle both with the issues of knowing in its many modes and the many ways in which we seek to ignore, avoid, manage not to know. We are here thrust into the midst of knowing, but also the higher domain of seeking to come to know something of what it is to know and not to know, to be known and not to be known. This is a vital realm of human inquiry, concerning central aspects of our ways of living with ourselves and through each other. This reaches well beyond the social rituals we presently call 'psychotherapy'.

Our society is changing rapidly in so many ways. Our ways of engaging in the diversifying activities we consider to be 'psychotherapeutic' are changing too. Everything is in motion. Not only will we see major changes in what we understand as 'psychotherapy' (even its melting back into many other things), but we may see major changes in what we understand as 'psychology'. As we learn to draw more fully from our developing experiencing in the psychotherapeutic realm, and conceive more adequately what there we find and make, so we may find that we are creating a transformation in what we understand of what it is *to know*.

I will attend here briefly to three related topics. First, I'll sketch out a few points concerning 'knowing personally', with coming to know for yourself and relying on your own experiencing. Second, I'll note a few features of the psychotherapeutic situation, especially as regards the 'pretences' that often characterize much of what we do. Third, I'll try to draw attention to some of what may be psychologically involved in undertaking more of what is entailed in coming to know for yourself and relying on your own experiencing; in developing a psychology of psychotherapy, or more generally, a 'psychology of personal knowing'.

Knowing for yourself

For me, the move from being a beginning practitioner in the science of psychology, towards being a fledgling psychotherapist, involved a range of particular adjustments, as well as quite general changes in attitude.

You are likely to find yourself, increasingly, having to rely on yourself, rather than on the results of experiments, or other formal pieces of knowledge. In psychology we are taught to rely on specific knowledge, of results or method, and then find that we are in the midst of much that is less clearly labelled. Often, as beginning psychotherapists, we try to buttress ourselves against vulnerability and pain. We create safe forward encampments for ourselves by dressing carefully in the armour of some particular theory, or by bringing with us the rolling stock and armaments of specialized techniques. By such means, we can keep ourselves protected for a time, till we begin to get a *feel* for where we are, and can then begin to dare some sorties out beyond the pallisades of our previously prepared positions.

In this situation, there are at least three general questions you may, explicitly or implicitly, have to ask and answer: 'Who or what are you to trust?' 'How can you enter more fully into your own, or someone else's, experiencing?' and 'How much of yourself, or of other people, are you willing to know?'

(i) Who or what are you to trust?

As I've already said, you may start, as you are likely to have been taught as a psychologist, by trusting the 'protective clothing' or 'armaments' of factory-made methods. But soon you will have to ask yourself if you are only going to do what your protective armour allows. Even while this armour may shield and encourage you, it will sometimes cramp your movements, and sometimes your client will be too quick and slippery, leaving you helpless, like a knight who has fallen off his horse.

Unless you begin to improvise on your own account, start from and repeatedly return to your own experience, you are going to be endlessly dependent, waiting for the next supply train from back at base (the psychological laboratories of the world). Unless you come to recognize that *you are the only instrument of knowing* you will always have with you, you will remain a bit-part actor in the psychotherapeutic drama. Of course the instrument of your own sensibilities is crude and fallible, but with discipline and loving care, it can be elaborated and refined.

All this, however, takes you in the opposite direction from most of your early psychological training, which often seems intent on undermining who you are and what you may already have begun to sense and know. It also involves you in a gradual education of your capacity to feel, to touch, and understand when nothing can be seen and no certified signposts tell you officially what supposedly is so. And it means that you must begin to care as much for clues and hints and signs, as for those more formal friends, 'evidence' and 'proof'. You have to learn to live on the move, rather than rely on fixed positions and externally fortified encampments.

(ii) How can I enter more fully into my own or someone else's experiencing?

How can we reach beyond the common-sense view of things, the way things obviously are? We learn our prescribed, and often willingly accepted, parts. We gradually undertake to present ourselves as this or that kind of person; undertake to appear, to ourselves as well as those around us, as relatively consistent in many aspects of our lives. When the consistency becomes too much, the rigidities too real, psychotherapeutic help may be a means of struggling with such roles that have become too thoroughly engrained. And within the context of psychotherapy, we have to experiment again. We may have to undertake many other parts of who we are, that we do not yet clearly know we are, or might yet be. This undertaking of other parts is similarly required of you as therapist. Since you may, through your own flexibility, encourage change in those who seek your aid.

Put briefly, as therapist or client, you will need recourse to imaginative play, make-believe, possibilities, fictions of what may yet be realized. And this brings you immediately into the realm of the possible and the unproven. It takes you away from the established and the safely respectable. We find ourselves in a theatre of uncertainty, surprise, new possibilities in being. We are taken to a place where everything we securely know is put in question. Everything becomes relative, insubstantial, other than we may have been assured it was.

Through metaphor, new possibilities of meaning, of living, can be entered and explored (Mair 1977a), new costumes, new plays, new parts, new access to the scripts we did not know we were being spoken by. The person, locked in inarticulate loneliness, may become a thriving, bustling, 'community of selves' (Mair 1977b) when they begin to explore themselves *as if* they are more than an isolated island, a unitary soul.

We are here at the meeting place of many disciplines, many ways by which we may enter into knowing what we did not know or scarcely knew we knew. Painting, poetry, sculpture, theatre, computing, astronomy, physics, music — every vehicle of human expression is potentially useful for some particular searching to enter and know as a living thing. The previously secure world may tremble beneath your feet. Your familiar masks may become more flimsy than you thought they were. You, yourself, may be in the vestibule of change.

(iii) How much of yourself, or of other people, are you willing to know?

It is easier to deal with bits of people than with all of them. It is easier to deal with people in terms of particular problems, than to probe more widely. It is easier to deal with people in terms of prepared procedures rather than allow more fluidity and flow. All these easier ways may be useful, may often be enough. But sometimes they will not do. Sometimes they will not touch and hold and heal that which is closer to the heart of the matter.

It will become necessary to listen to the person in the context of their whole life, rather than bits and pieces only. This may well require you, with almost all of who you are, to meet almost all of them.

Again, you may then be drawn beyond where you have been prepared to go, prepared to know. This is new territory, wilder and less charted than the formal farm-steadings of psychology-as-a-domestic-science had prepared you for. What may be required of you is something stranger than the conventions of ordinary social meeting that you familiarly know.

We are all nurtured and strangled, sustained and starved, liberated and trapped within the moving web of our own experiencing, of our place and time. We are endlessly in relationships. Everything is between here and there, this and those, self and other selves. Multiple meetings of many kinds constitute who we are. We are in it together. We cannot step out and start again. And almost everything between us, which constitutes the relationships we are constituted by, is invisible and unmarked. We have to learn how to develop and use radar-scanners of our own, tuned especially to the moving patterns of intention, the force fields of action and reaction, the pressures and vacuums of approach and veering away, many kinds and places of meeting, many ways and means of parting. Here again, we are not in a place we have been professionally trained to know.

No wonder many find this realm too threatening, too strange, too undefined, too intangible, too difficult to catch by the heavy-handed ways we have, as psychologists, been taught to use.

The psychotherapeutic situation

In moving from psychology, or many other formal disciplines, towards psychotherapy, you need to know something more of who you are yourself. You do not, overnight, or even after a weekend workshop, become a 'fully functioning person'. Most of us do not get far in the course of years, or over our whole lives. With our inadequacies, we have to do the best we can. I want to say a little about that and about myself here to suggest ways in which private and professional concerns can complement and contradict each other.

I do not get on easily or comfortably with people, do not find it easy to fully care for people, as some around me seem to do. I do not find much of what many people seem mostly concerned with of much interest to me, in relation to what I seem to need and be. I do not find it easy to let myself be known, nor reach across, in ordinary life, to care enough to know those I daily meet in intimate, professional ways. And yet I do seem to need, or want, to know intimately and be known. It is not just lack of interest or concern — quite the opposite, perhaps.

So I find the conventions of the psychotherapeutic role a powerful help to me. I am protected in a diving bell, provided with the loose, protective clothing of a role. Together, my client and I, we inhabit the oxygen tent of a protected world in which things are different from the outside world (different and yet so much the same). Life and death are issues here, battled for in specially supportive air.

Here I can *pretend* to care. I can pre-tend, can reach beyond and in front of myself as far as caring is concerned. My intention (what I hold to in my life) is to care, but here I can pre-tend, stretch forward to something of how it may yet be for me, and them.

Who, here, is more in need is not always an easy thing to say. Here I am, gentle, firm, loving, understanding, knowledgeable, a helper — the good guy, the saint in thin disguise, the ideal man, ideal son, lover, husband, friend — if only — if only it were true! We are in the land of make-believe, of figments of the mind, of fictions, other ways to be. The rules of ordinary gravity do not quite hold. We are allowed to play.

This is an invention of our own. This is how we can be other than we ordinarily are. Here we reach beyond, to how it might yet be.

It is, this invention of ours, this place of adult play, bought at a price. It requires its own laws. There are limits and rules (different limits and rules, but rules there are!). As therapist, you bring all of you, but you will not be known (how fine for those who fear to be known, and are struggling to find a way, but not quite yet!). You meet only a little and from time to time (how fine for those who cannot sustain the enveloping messiness of ordinary meeting — not yet at least!). You come out of the sun at whatever angle may usefully startle and sustain (how fine for those who cannot easily be real within the ordinary rules!). You accompany another in their search, only hint at and gently touch your own (how fine for those who fear to venture far from home!). You rest within the prosthetic womb of being less, and also more, than who you know you are (how fine if you are a psychological cripple whose deficiencies just fit the place of make-believe!).

How fine, till you must face your world alone!

We reach beyond ourselves to reach into who we and they yet may be. But we may succumb to the prevalent industrial disease of supposing we are already someone other than we are; believe we are good and kind and caring, trusting, noble, fine! We may be in danger of believing this when we have not yet reached beyond being someone who merely needs to believe, and needs to be sustained by those who need to believe, that we are the paragon we long to be.

We are in a place of opportunity and personal danger (just as GPs are with the drugs that they prescribe). And *limits* may be of the essence of this other world. Rollo May (1975) suggests that creativity itself requires limits, 'for the creative act arises out of the struggle of human beings with and against that which limits them — a psychology of creation must also be about *limits*'. Confronting limits, he says, may actually turn out to be expansive, 'limiting and expanding thus go together'. Form provides the essential boundaries and structure for the creative act. 'Persons in therapy — or anybody for that matter — are not simply engaged in knowing their world; what they are engaged in', suggests May, 'is a passionate reforming of their world by virtue of their inter-relationship within it.'

Thus it may be that out of our own limits and the limits we both impose and endure in the psychotherapeutic world of serious pretending, something of broader human use may yet be made.

Caring to know

What I have said suggests that there is much that may be new as you move from the realm of psychology in its conventional, academic forms towards psychotherapy as a world of purposive make-believe. For some, it will be enough to move from there to here and do no more. They will want to settle, put down roots in the new soil, learn to live in a different way, never return.

That is not enough for me, and I want to suggest that it should not be enough for you. A psychology of personal knowing will require much more than we have yet achieved; and the wider, more personally involving modes of knowing that are part of the psychotherapeutic world, hint at how far we still have to go. Although there are many theories we still have no adequate psychology of psychotherapy, and I believe that we will need some quite different conception of science if we are to encompass the personal knowing and seeking-to-know of those who are engaged therein.

We do not have any adequate mapping of the territories of human knowing and what variously is involved; the different modes and manners of knowing and seeking not to know. Every way of knowing is, at the same time, a way of ignoring, of turning a particular blind eye, of seeking not to know. We are for ever in the uncertain process of deceiving ourselves by seeking mainly what we seek to know.

Personal knowing must include both subjective and objective knowing; to seek to know objectively is itself a personal act.

As we move into the psychotherapeutic situation, we realize more fully that we know so much more, through our intuitive sensing, than we can spell out or clearly say. We need to understand so much more of what and how we know. We live still in the belief that we should move from the firm ground of fact, but in the psychotherapeutic situation people sometimes learn 'to fly'. They find that fictions are as useful as, if not more useful than, fact in helping us create and recreate something of our worlds.

We have generally been taught that knowing is somehow separate from who we are. Yet in the psychotherapeutic world we see so clearly that knowing has to be lived and owned and undertaken as our own if it is to help us change. If we, or our clients, do not come to know in this living way, we simply act a part, remain apart, knowing only in the head, do not *really* know.

All this highlights that in psychotherapy we are engaged in the huge issue of *responsible knowing*, of really undertaking what we know as an imaginative and moral choice. In seeking to understand more fully what is involved in such surprising, courageous action in the conversation of our lives, we will need to develop a different kind of discipline. Our technical knowing has already far outrun our powers to undertake the moral weight and pain of what we have created for our world. So far, we mainly know *about*, do not know more fully for ourselves.

Through psychotherapy, and other ways of seriously pretending towards what we still only dimly sense, we may be able to compose a moral science of action, in and between and amongst ourselves. Unless we come more fully to know ourselves and each other, care enough to know more of what it is to know and to be known, to know and not to know, then we may not create the means by which to care beyond the limits of our present often careless and quite uncaring ways.

Chapter three

Some personal impressions of psychotherapy

Psychotherapy is, therefore, a personal rather than a technical undertaking. Even though 'technique' and 'technical knowledge' are significant at times, these have to become uniquely part of someone (the therapist) in the particular relationship-of-the-moment with someone else (the client). In this situation where we are really trying to undertake what we know, feel, and imagine, it is important for developing therapists to work towards some personal integration of what is involved for them in this role they are undertaking, this part of their own lives.

There is, however, no simple way to come to know what we are doing or even what we believe we are doing. Some understanding of ourselves and our actions has to be struggled towards again and again. It is because of this that members of the psychology department where I work are required to spell out, from time to time, something of their present understanding of their personal approach to psychotherapy. Difficulties immediately arise for each one of us. How am I to begin? What kind of 'line' am I to take? What is important for me and what should be left out or merely hinted at? What relationships between my own history and the formalities of my training should be noted? What place should be given to broader values or individual preferences? What dare I admit to of my fears and weaknesses? What dare I say to this particular group of people at this point in time and in this particular context?

In considering such an undertaking here I've found that I don't want to speak directly. In trying to convey something of what matters to me in psychotherapy I want to be more oblique. In reading what follows, I'd like you to suspend any expectations you may have concerning an 'adequate' account of psychological aspects of psychotherapy. Perhaps instead, as you read, you could think about your own experiences in therapy, counselling, or any similar helping relationship. I don't want to present an argument, but rather to give some impressions from my own experience, and the wider concerns within which my work in psychotherapy finds a place.

Spelling out the mystery

Please begin by trying to feel your way into the following 'short lines'. They
say something that matters to me.

> We should start our spelling out
> from the centre of our
> deepest mystery
> not from some simplified
> side effect
> or snippet

> We cannot build mystery
> from fragments
> of what we assert as known

> Our problem is to
> grasp and bear
> the mystery
> not in the sense of holding it
> but holding ourselves
> within it
> when we sense
> where it may be

> Every movement
> from the mystery outwards
> will be less than
> the all
> In opening and explaining
> we deepen the mystery
> or our awareness
> thereof

> The aim of science
> is to deepen our sensing
> of the mystery
> To deepen and extend
> our awareness
> of the mystery
> of the universe
> To find answers raises
> undreamt of
> questions

Our lives enter more deeply
into the mystery
as we think
we see the light
To live in what we know
and claim to know
is to avoid
the mystery
To live in our ignorance
which is much more difficult
is to dwell
in the outer edges of the mystery

You cannot spell out beforehand
the mysteries
from which you speak
or give clear specification
of the parameters
which shape
and hold
and give life
to your very words

To know the answer beforehand
is not possible
if you would give voice
to the unknown
from
and in which
you live

This is for me a starting point, an assumption, a proposition of what matters — though perhaps not for you.

Approaching from a different direction

Many psychologists, in approaching the discipline of psychotherapy, are led to start their inquiries from the perspective of science, or at least the science of psychology. They come, therefore, with a particular cluster of moral and procedural values. These initial metaphors that shape our fledgling understanding are mostly 'digital' rather than 'analogical'. We are accustomed to cutting things up, breaking them in pieces. We are frequently tied to numbers, and to words.

Here I want to invite you instead to pay attention to some snippets from the history of art rather than science. The points I want to make are taken from a well known introduction to the subject entitled *The Story of Art* by E.H. Gombrich (1972). Whatever this book's virtues as a history of art, it is certainly of value as an introduction to psychology, providing as it does a simple, yet grand sweep through much of Western man's developing and changing relationship with the world.

The period I've chosen to attend to covers part of the eighteenth and nineteenth centuries, a period leading up to and overlapping with important formal developments in what we now recognize as psychology and psychotherapy. It was a time when there were some striking breaks with tradition in painting, and more widely in the arts (and sciences too). Initially I'll say a little about William Blake (1757–1827), John Constable (1776–1837), and William Turner (1775–1851). I want to draw your attention to a few of the things Gombrich says about these people, and various others following them. As I do so, I'd like you to try to keep translating what is being said into something of possible relevance to 'psychologists' and 'psychotherapists' rather than 'painters'.

'The Romantic Rebellion'

Gombrich refers to this period of change in art as 'The Romantic Rebellion'. In commenting on William Blake, Gombrich describes him as 'the most outstanding example of this new approach to art'. Blake, it seems, 'despised the official art of the academies, and declined to accept its standards'. Some people thought him mad. Others dismissed him as a crank. Only very few of his contemporaries believed in his art, and thereby saved him from starving. Gombrich goes on to say that 'Blake was so wrapped up in his visions that he refused to draw from life and relied entirely on his inner eye'. It is easy to point to faults in Blake's craftsmanship, but to do so, Gombrich says, would be to miss the point of his art. 'Like the medieval artists, he did not care for accurate representation, because the significance of each figure of his dreams was of such overwhelming importance to him that questions of *mere correctness seemed to him irrelevant*' (my italics). (Please think here of this statement in relation to the giving of significant accounts of psychological/psychotherapeutic issues.) Gombrich then concludes by indicating that Blake was 'the first artist after the Renaissance who thus consciously revolted against the accepted standards of tradition, and we can hardly blame his contemporaries who found him shocking. It was almost a century before he was generally recognised as one of the most important figures in English art.'

So here is someone who reacted against the tradition of 'accurate representation' of the outer world. In order to give significant form to what he experienced and knew, he could not bind himself to 'mere correctness'.

Gombrich then says something about William Turner, a very different character who was, indeed, obsessed with the problem of tradition.

'Turner too', says Gombrich, 'had visions of a fantastic world bathed in light and resplendent with beauty, but it was a world not of calm but of movement, not of simple harmonies but of dazzling pageantries. He crowded into his pictures every effect which could make them more striking and more dramatic, and, had he been a lesser artist than he was, this desire to impress the public might well have had a disastrous result. Yet he was such a superb stage-manager, he worked with such gusto and skill, that he carried it off and the best of his pictures do, in fact, give us a conception of the grandeur of nature at its most romantic and sublime.'

Gombrich suggests that we compare Turner's picture entitled *Steamer in a Snowstorm* (now in the Tate Gallery, London) with a seventeenth-century painting of ships in another storm at sea (painted by Simon Vlieger, entitled *Mouth of a River*, in the National Gallery, London). He points out that if we compare 'this whirling composition' with the seascape of Vlieger, we can sense how bold was Turner's approach. He points out that the Dutch artist of the seventeenth century did not only paint what he saw at a glance, but also, to some extent, what he knew was there. The artist knew how a ship was built and how it was rigged, and, looking at his painting, we might even be able to reconstruct these vessels. In contrast, Gombrich points out that nobody could reconstruct a nineteenth-century steamer from Turner's seascape. 'All he gives us', he says, 'is the impression of the dark hull, of the flag flying bravely from the mast — of a battle with the raging seas and threatening squalls. We almost feel the rush of the wind and the impact of the waves. We have no time to look for details. They are swallowed up by the dazzling light and the dark shadows of the storm cloud.'

Again Gombrich is (and I am) talking here about the *manner* in which somebody chooses to express something. Turner's manner was quite different from the seventeenth-century Dutch painters who tried to reproduce appearances of almost photographic precision. In thinking again of accounts being required in relation to some understanding in psychotherapy, the dramatic stage management of a Turner may sometimes be more apposite than the hard-edged crudities that, too often, we employ.

Gombrich next talks a little about John Constable. Nowadays, when some of Constable's pictures are sold in Boots and Woolworth's, as the epitome of conventional art, it is difficult to realize that in his time he broke with tradition in so many ways. Some of his work was regarded as so different from accepted conventions that it was almost shocking. What he broke away from was a whole series of conventions as to how reality should be conveyed.

This theme of the breaking of convention in relation to the representation of reality is itself a recurrent reality in the history of art. By analogy, we should perhaps expect something similar in psychology as we struggle for conventions, again and again, through which to catch and explore something of the realities involved in, for example, psychotherapeutic encounters.

'Permanent Revolution'

Gombrich proceeds to talk next about the Impressionists, and heads his chapter 'Permanent Revolution'. He outlines some of the changes in painting which were so dramatically developed in the nineteenth century. For our purposes it is useful to remember that this was the century in which our modern versions of both psychology and psychotherapy were given their shape.

For the first time in history we find a huge expansion in the choices which an artist had as to how he would paint. So many of the conventions concerning how things should be done were being swept away. A great flowering of different ways of doing things meant that painting in particular, and art generally, became the means by which people could express something of themselves. In earlier times, painting had rather been a means by which certain traditions were re-exemplified. So, with the new century, there came this great *expansion of expressiveness* on the part of the artist.

A second thing that markedly changed was in relation to the conventions which governed *suitable subject matter* for painting. So there was, for example, Courbet, beginning to paint pictures of common peasants in common, inglorious contexts.

A third change at this time was emphasized by the Impressionists. Painters like Edouard Manet and Claude Monet took over and extended Courbet's concerns for common life. Gombrich indicates that they 'looked out for conventions in painting which had become stale and meaningless. They found that the whole claim of traditional art to have discovered the way to represent nature, as we see it, was based on a misconception'. (Again this begins to sound like so many modern writers questioning much that has been conventional in psychological and psychotherapeutic research into matters concerning human understanding and change.)

At the most, they could concede that traditional art had found a way of representing things under very artificial conditions. Painters let their models pose in studios where the light falls through the window, and made use of the slow transition from light to shade to give the impression of roundness or solidity. The art students at the academies were trained to base their pictures on this interplay between light and shade. (Compare again the analogous disquiet experienced in some psychological circles, in more recent times, about having the traditional experiment as the necessary centrepiece in anything worthy of the name of science.) The people had become so accustomed to seeing things represented like this that they had not recognized that in the open air we do not usually perceive such graduations from dark to light. In the outside world there are harsh contrasts in the sunlight. Objects taken out of the artificial conditions of the artist's studio do not look round, or so clearly modelled. The parts which are lit appear much brighter than in the studio, and even the shadows are not uniform because the reflections of light from surrounding objects affect the colour of the unlit parts. 'If we trust our eyes', says Gombrich, 'and not our preconceived ideas of what things *ought* to look like, according to academic rules, we shall make the most exciting discoveries.'

What Edouard Manet claimed was that the effects created in artificial conditions are often completely different from the things which happen in the open air, in the ordinary circumstances of life. What he did was to try to present something of how things appear in everyday circumstances, not what 'ought' to be, as traditionally defined by studio conditions and conventions. Gombrich points out that 'such ideas were first considered extravagant heresies' and suggests that this is scarcely surprising. Throughout the whole story of art, Gombrich reminds us that we have seen how 'we are all inclined to judge pictures by what we *know* rather than by what we *see*'. He points out that through the centuries different discoveries were made which eventually allowed artists to conjure up a convincing picture of the visible world. No one, however, Gombrich says, 'had seriously challenged the conviction that each object in nature has its definite, fixed, form and colour which must be easily recognisable in a painting'. (Similarly, in psychology, we have been, and are still embedded, in similar traditional views concerning people having identifiable and enduring characteristics or personality traits, or mental illnesses, etc. In contrast, a different and more recently emerging perspective on people has gained some ground. This alternative views people as being quite significantly affected by, tinged with, and shaped differently by the people and events with whom they are associated and by whom they are described in their ordinary living.)

It may be said, therefore, that Manet and his followers brought about a revolution in the rendering of colours which is, Gombrich suggests, almost comparable to the revolution in the representation of forms brought about by the Greeks. They discovered that, if we look at nature in the open, we do not see individual objects, each with its own colour, but rather a bright medley of tints which 'blend in our eye, or really in our mind'.

So it was that Manet, and many others who were eventually to be called 'Impressionists', though also very different from each other, 'all wanted to create the impression of solid bodies, and did so through the interplay of shadow and light'. As a consequence, Gombrich suggests, as we stand before one of Manet's pictures 'it looks more immediately real than any old master' (and again, for me, there is the suggestion here that to capture and represent reality more surely, adventurous breaking of familiar conventions of what we take to be known and given may again and again be necessary).

A fourth change was also emphasized by these painters. They were not

29

only concerned with the treatment of light and colour, but were sometimes similarly concerned to catch and give convincing expression to *forms in movement* (and once again, I at least am reminded of persistent searchings in psychology and psychotherapy to find ways of describing, conceiving, and conveying something of the essence of psychological *movement.* How difficult we still find it in practice to come to terms with, for instance, George Kelly's (1955) suggestion that we view *man as a form of motion.*)

Gombrich here goes on to say that 'the painter who hopes to catch a characteristic aspect, has no leisure to mix and match his colours, let alone to apply them in layers on a brown foundation as the old masters had done. He must fix them straight on to his canvas in rapid strokes, caring less for detail than for the general effect of the whole' (and again, one is reminded of the struggles of so many to find some way to catch and convey, alive, something of the essence of what is happening in psychotherapy; and also the dreary history of failure of our traditional research methods to do much other than deaden and dismay many who care passionately for whatever human realities are fleetingly and powerfully at work in the various human relationships we call 'psychotherapy').

It is sobering to read of how the paintings of Manet, Monet, and others were so completely ridiculed as being incredibly (not just mildly) inaccurate. Their appearance was taken as a sign of incompetent idiots being at work, resulting in daubs of paint littering untidy canvases. Gombrich indicates, however, that what the Impressionists aimed to achieve was something entirely different from, for instance, the Dutch painters of the seventeenth century. 'They were', he says, 'trying to care for the way light and colour presented themselves in the eye, not to represent some features of the "thing" they knew was there.'

Some psychological impressions

It seems to me that there are some quite striking resemblances between the concerns which the Impressionists, for example, had and the concerns of people presently struggling to develop new paradigms for relevant psychotherapeutic research, and seeking to understand anew something of what goes on in the fluid realities of the psychotherapeutic encounter. Perhaps in psychology and psychotherapy we are nearing a stage of 'permanent revolution', and moving out of our 'classical' period (though for us, that phase has been in no way comparable in its beauty, power, or grandeur, to the classical period in art) where there were known and accepted ways of studying and presenting the nature of how things are.

The point that I am labouring here is that in the history of art we have, in detail, a spectacle of a whole range of struggles of people coming to grips with the nature of the world around and within them. We see clearly something of the repeatedly changing beliefs and battles about assumptions and approaches. There is also something else that is relevant to my understanding of psychology and psychotherapy. We see here, not just changing traditions, but also such incredible differences in style, texture, tone, composition, expression, materials used, and ways of approaching matters of concern. What we often seem to do in psychology is to assume that we have a discipline that is to be approached and understood by certain kinds of methods, and that there are certain kinds of techniques which, if you learn and use them, will ensure respectability, acceptability, and officially approved access to the truth.

Just as in art, within the scientific tradition it is often difficult to break out and recognize how legitimate it is (and how often it has happened before) for people to struggle to develop new and personal styles, caught as they will also be within the conventions of their time. But here as elsewhere, styles and conventions have changed, and in doing so have changed also our understanding of what may be going on in our worlds, visible and invisible, open to touch or accessible only to feeling.

All this is, for me anyway, an argument to think in terms of some understanding of human experience through artistic modes of expression, just as much as through scientific ones, or journalistic ones, or poetic ones, or whatever else you will. This is a 'first assumption' that I eventually came to after years of being brought up in, and then struggling to be free of the narrowing effects of, the scientific tradition as so far defined within psychology. I have come to the belief that the currently dominant scientific approach is strikingly and persistently hostile as a mode of approaching a whole range of human experience. In saying this, I am using the word 'hostile' in both its everyday sense and in the way it is used by George Kelly (1955) — that is, of trying to extort validational evidence for its own ways of approaching things when there are plenty of grounds, if you look for them, for recognizing that these 'scientific' ways of trying to make sense of issues concerning human experiencing and action aren't adequate.

Psychotherapy seems to me to be about important things to do with style, colour, how you approach your subject, passion, vision, sensitivity, courage, conventions, and the breaking of conventions. There are endless ways of being engaged in it. There are, of course, conventions of our times that we are trapped and sustained within, but these are all potentially breakable, and most will be broken and changed beyond present recognition. What may at present, to some traditionalists in psychotherapy, seem wishy-washy or crude in the approaches of others may, after a little time, be seen as being about something rather different from the ways in which the undertaking has so far been viewed and valued.

Something of the sensibility that Gombrich leads us to, of recognizing style and manner in and between people, seems to me to be an important matter for psychotherapy and any adequate psychology thereof. So it seems important to approach the business of psychotherapy from within more than one tradition, not just from the perspectives of science. It seems to me that when someone enters psychotherapy as therapist or client, there should be doors thrown wide open to allow them to recognize that all kinds of traditions of understanding and engaging with people are relevant and potentially of value.

Having said all this, however, I have to admit that I am still caught, up to my neck, in the scientific tradition in psychology. This is part of the ambiguity for me. As for many others, I can say and believe certain things, but still be tied to my history. It is difficult to detach yourself from what you are trapped and yet sustained within.

Personal concerns in psychotherapy

In what follows, I want to try to turn and look at a few of the things I have been able to notice about my concerns in psychotherapy. I've decided not to give my account of what I think I do in therapy — and I'm not trying here to give a complete or even a balanced account. Rather than trying to paint a seventeenth-century Dutch picture, I want only to give some impressions of my approach to therapy.

The first thing that struck me in coming to think about it was that *my approach varies. I vary* from person to person and time to time. Sometimes I feel touched and quickened by people, and sometimes my engagement with them is just dutiful. I am sometimes doing just the minimum to get by. I respond to people differently, and they respond differently to me. It really isn't the same all the time.

What I find I can say at one time about what the psychotherapeutic situation involves for me is just very different from what I am able to say at another time. There are times when I feel able somehow to penetrate quite a bit more deeply into how it seems to be for me. There are other times when I simply can't, when I see and feel nothing beyond the surface of an obviously mundane and pedestrian activity. Only sometimes can I get a startling sense of some sort of mystery, excitement, and beauty in it.

This may have a bearing on aspects of research into psychotherapy. I am aware that if I were asked questions about psychotherapy on one day, I would be able to say a lot more, and differently, than I might if I were approached at a different time. So I don't think we are dealing with something that is static, that you can just dip into and find out about.

But, perhaps, the central obligation that I place myself under in approaching psychotherapy can still be stated quite simply. *I must try to listen to the person in the context of this, their one and only life.* Quite often when you look at a person *in the context of their life,* suspended between their birth and their death, you can recognize more acutely than usual that this is their first time of facing everything. You can often see and feel and sense people's anxieties, panics, lostness, and much else, however well groomed, well dressed, big, tough-looking they seem to be. To gain this sharp perspective on where they are standing at this point in their life seems important to me. Sometimes it is easy to do, and sometimes all but impossible. Some people seem, almost, to have radar-jamming protection around them which throws my scanning system completely haywire and I can get no sense of where they are. Then sometimes, if you keep at it, suddenly it's there, a clear sense of how they are arrayed, of how they are standing and moving in relation to their lives.

This sensing activity involves imaginative participation in your own feelings and in the life and being of the other. For me there is *important magic in imagination.* I don't want to try to define what I mean by 'imagination' here, but I *don't* mean just having little fantasy thoughts in your head. I'm not talking of imagination as the playing of unreal games, but as a stepping back to allow some new vision, and then a stepping into that vision in order to understand anew from within. To speak from within is far more than to speak from recollection or from far off. To invite someone to envision something often means giving them, first of all, the means of beginning to do it. You can then invite them actually to enter their vision, and feel it and speak within it. This is an entirely different undertaking from sitting and talking in ordinary ways, or doing other things. It is at a different level. Often, again, this can't be done — not yet anyway — perhaps never.

The next point that strikes me is a further reach of the imagination. In thinking of ourselves and others, what 'guiding model' will be specially helpful? The title of a book by Krishnamurti (1972) provides, for me, the clue. One of his books is entitled, *You are the World.* The notion conveyed to me in this title is important in therapy. 'I am the world', 'You are the World', 'We are the world'. I'm referring here to *the pervasive importance of metaphor.*

It seems to me to be necessary to recognize that everything we know about the world may be relevant to our understanding, or our developing an understanding, of someone with whom we are in relationship. At different times someone's confused experiencing may be clarified by considering what they sense in terms of 'jungles of wild animals', 'battles across the plains', 'football matches', the smallest matters concerning 'cell division', or the largest imaginable issues concerning 'the creation and destruction of galaxies'. Anything we know about the world may be a vehicle by which we can give form, shape, and expression to something in somebody's experience. In this way, the exploration of the outer world and the inner world can be intimately related.

A different kind of issue now. *Every now and then I find myself required actually to move in my own life in therapy,* not just stand aside, or prod somebody else. At times, you may find much more than your professional stance being called upon. You will sense that you, personally, will be affected. For somebody as cowardly as me, this has been quite frightening sometimes.

To ask someone a verbal question is one thing. To undertake a quest of some kind with them is something different. Mostly, I think, we get off with sitting on the sidelines, but every now and again somebody actually pulls you in. You have to be on your guard for it, and be prepared to take some part, outside the conventions you usually allow.

Feeling, and giving form to what is between us, seems crucial. I find it worthwhile to use, and to remind myself of, the notion of *invisible worlds*. That is to say, most of what happens between us is invisible. Often in therapy we need to have the means whereby we can body forth something of the invisible world that is felt between us. Almost all our social conventions lead us away from this; away from noticing the things that are being done and worn and said, and what *feels* as if it is happening between us. This invisible world, rather than the more superficial world of public convention and polite blindness, is often difficult to attend to, and difficult to convert into something that is visible, substantial, sharable.

In every culture, I suppose, there are conventions about sensibility. In ours, there is *embarrassment about sensibility*, embarrassment about gentleness that is shared. There is, I think, a tremendous lure in our culture towards brutality of various kinds. A collusive dismissal of certain kinds of feelings and thoughts; subtle ways of belittling, disallowing, or devaluing your experiencing or someone else's experiencing. In psychotherapy it seems important to find ways to remember that sensibility, gentleness in the sense in which I am talking of it, may be embarrassing. But that's too bad! The sooner I, and you, get over that feeling the better it will be for whoever we are working with. To flee from embarrassment into many forms of subtle brutality is a major wrong.

Related to sensibility is another point. It seems again and again necessary to *listen for the turns of phrase, the telling image, the give-away line, the afterthought*. Often people can speak themselves without knowing that they are doing so. Often we speak us, speak ourselves, without knowing how to speak *about* it. It is so different when someone speaks from themselves, from a bit of their living world, as opposed to speaking about things only. This kind of speaking, speaking from the centre, seems especially important for the therapist to respond to.

Still on sensibility, I'm not suggesting that 'it' exists in some single form. There are sensibilities of different kinds and degrees, and lacks of sensibility in many forms. One of the realms of sensibility relevant to psychotherapy has to do with *timing*. I don't mean calculated timing, but rather the business of responding to the movement of the dance, even if it is sometimes a hesitant dance that is happening between you.

On the negative side of sensibility, I have the impression that *I repeatedly impose with an iron pervasiveness my own limitations on therapeutic situations, on people.* I pretend it is not so, but over and over again I limit what is happening by what I don't understand, what I am embarrassed with, frightened of, disinclined to bother with. There are large worlds of experience I don't have, just don't know about. Such realms can't, therefore, become available for me in relation to somebody else. This is why it is so necessary to find ways of recognizing that the other person may, in some elaborated sense, know, feel, sense a lot more and differently from yourself. They may teach you the beginnings of sensibilities you simply do not have, if you can somehow avoid restricting them too much within your own limitations.

Thinking of ways of understanding something of the flow and movement of therapy, I have often found the metaphor of *hide and seek* to be quite useful, for therapists as well as clients. There seems often to be an elaborate game of hide and seek going on in the invisible world between. It is often a serious and frightening game, played for high stakes, the terror that being found will lead to loss of face and loss of life itself. Sometimes people hide and all the other parties walk away and don't notice that someone of special significance is still hiding, waiting to be found, longing to be found. They may even walk away and thank each other for being so helpful.

But what on earth could it mean in relation to psychotherapy for some- one to be '*getting better*'? This is surely not always obvious beforehand, but it is something for therapist and client to explore and even battle over. No single image seems adequate. Obviously, like everyone, I rejoice to see someone released from the grip of some tyrannical obsessional ritual, or become able to walk to the shops again, or otherwise enter the world again in mundane, practical ways. I'm happy with success like this; I'm also aware, however, that not everyone is like that. That isn't all that may be involved when we talk about 'getting better' or 'improving'.

What kinds of images might be of some use when thinking of 'getting better'? If you don't think of the therapeutic meeting as being necessarily to do with 'illness' and 'recovery', or the 'learning of particular skills', how else might you conceive of what is happening?

One of the things I find sometimes useful, though not in any way defini- tive, is to think about the criteria you would use for judging a good story, song, dance, poem, or painting. In what terms would you decide that a story was successful, better than another, as far as you are concerned? Is it exciting, involving, invigorating, is there a diversity of characters, is it about the weaving and interweaving of themes, does it have overall balance, is it to do with its style of open passion or gentle insouciance, is it a matter of honesty to experience, or what?

All these are also notions that can be used, along with many others, in evaluating and giving value to people's lives. I don't believe there are any universal criteria by which a good story can be evaluated as 'good'. Obviously it depends on who is reading it, or writing it, and many other things. The same is true in therapy.

But all metaphors have their limitations, and if you use this one for judging change and development in therapy, you should remember that there is a big difference between a story and an actual adventure. The story is written within the consciousness of somebody and is a contained world. Being on an adventure, writing a story with your life, is somewhat different. What you are involved within is 'total drama', and the images of drama can also be of use in refreshing your vision of process and outcome — temporary outcome.

And then there is the question '*what am I prepared to know and feel and get involved in?*' As mentioned in the previous chapter, it is sometimes easier and safer to have bits of people done away with, or shrunk into insignificance, rather than enter the deep waters that involvement with others may lead you towards. 'What am I prepared to undertake in actually caring enough to come to know somebody?' Sometimes, for me, more can be endured than at other times. But level of commitment remains a crucial issue. When you undertake to work with someone, what level of commitment are you undertaking? You can't often spell it out in detail beforehand, but I've been aware, at times, of beginning to work with someone new and noticing my heart sinking. I've then had to rally myself and recognize that if we are to continue, I have to accept that it may mean years of work, and that it is going to be a persisting battle against strong odds.

Sometimes I turn my back on that demand, but sometimes, too, I've noticed that it has been important to sense quite explicitly the extent and extremity to which I may be called. Without this early recognition, you may suddenly be caught unawares, thrown off balance, as the person lands you with some unbargained for demand, a sudden suicide attempt, or some other frighteningly testing question or assertion. Within the sensing of a deeper or longer term commitment, which can reach out to touch and hold the other person, there may be great security, like a climber's rope, that you can both hold to when times get difficult. Something of that already made commitment can be rested on, to prevent you both from falling from the overhanging ledge you are trying to reach together.

Finally, in this section, *we are all born into situations where certain maps of our world, psychological maps of our world, have been prepared for us.* Some are born into families where the maps of what it is to be an acceptable person are drawn to indicate that they have to be nice, polite, quiet, sexless, or whatever. For myself, there are still large chunks of terrain that I sense to be important for my life, that are missing or only sketchily drawn in the maps I was imprinted with. I've had to try, often painfully, to redraw the maps. That process, the need to elaborate or start again, seems to keep going on. It is a problem that crops up too in therapy. People are often living in worlds with maps that don't seem to fit.

Part of the business of therapy is to help people to become explorers and makers of new maps. This is, of course, much more demanding than being simply a psychological tourist, simply following the map already prepared for you.

Reflections on impressions

I don't think I can just turn, look, and see myself and what I'm doing. Rather is it a matter of getting fragments of information occasionally flashed back from other people. Often we are bad at picking up what others are conveying, often they are bad at providing us with the information we may need.

In trying to present something of my 'personal approach' I'm scratching around at what is essentially impossible for one person to do, of and for themselves. What I can try to do is to dig around and turn over the soil in the general area of my concerns, and help make the soil more fertile so that things that feel important can grow. I cannot turn and state clearly what I am doing in psychotherapy, or any other aspect of life. All that I think we may be able to do, every now and again, is to shine flashes of light onto what seem to be the moving forms of what we are engaged within. I started by saying that I think we are engaged, in psychotherapy and in life, in profound mysteries. I think we can get some sense of some of the things that may be going on, every now and then. Sometimes we can be clear and coherent about these, often not. You need to catch glimpses of a way in which the world has been seen, felt, entered into, known. Perhaps, in psychotherapy research, we need to find ways of 'painting', conjuring up, conveying something of what may be importantly going on for us *now*, rather than seeking for something that is supposedly generally going on, for everyone, all of the time. We still haven't, I suspect, recognized just how personal our engagements with others are. We keep trying to make a generalized science, a final solution, before really recognizing sensitively what may be happening in many particular lives.

The points that I have been trying to make are dots on a landscape, and by no means a complete picture. I've been trying to say some things that seem important to me. You may also be concerned with some of these, but your way of highlighting them, talking about them, approaching them, giving them form, will be different from mine, because you are different. Just as there are differences so manifest in the work of different painters, their subject matter, manner, concerns for colour, ways of approach, so also there are different ways of tackling the 'canvas' of psychotherapy. For me, everything becomes of special value if it can both exemplify and be itself. It seems important to have some creatively co-operative discourse between the manner and the content of our inquiries.

In part, we are building shells for ourselves in talking about — and so encapsulating, objectifying — what we understand of our personal approach. For me there is a moving mystery of some kind involved here, and attempts to try to spell it out are important, but need to be abandoned quite persistently. I think I should end up being as uncertain on the day I die as on the day I qualified as a clinical psychologist — even though it be uncertainty of a different quality and kind.

To suggest that I'm not able to turn and give an account of what I'm doing is not to say that I'm not able to do anything at all. But I am able to say only a limited amount in trying to make something explicit of what I am engaged in. However I turn, I am still not attending to where I am now attending *from*. Where we experience *from* seems inherently unattendable to. There is, so to speak, a self that is always unknown, and we are always objectifying some other self in order to catch glimpses of it. It's like seeing the moon, brilliant with light shone on it from somewhere else. You can get *some* notion of the sun by looking at the moon, perhaps. When people can talk a little from within the mystery of themselves, you will gain some impression of that from which they speak. But we cannot, it seems, approach that place directly, or know ourselves simply, face to face.

Almost everything about psychotherapy is almost an entire mystery to me. In saying this, I'm not trying to be obscure or trying to create a mystique out of what is simply not yet known. As psychologists, I do believe, we are still too readily inclined to boil down mystery and suppose it can be disposed of as small and manageable problems. Alongside the necessary work of explication and clarification we need also to ask a deeper question. 'How can we actually deepen the mystery, heighten our awareness of the mysteries in what is going on? How can we make more subtle our awareness of the mystery, enlarge our sense of what may be involved, so that we can find ways of conveying something of it?' What we so often seem to do is to start immediately to boil things down to small and manageable forms.

In every situation, there are limitations on what can be sensed, on what can be said, on what can be shared. This situation of writing for public presentation is a context which allows attention to some things, just as it makes more difficult the grasping and giving voice to others. More and different things can be sensed in some contexts of attending than can be risked or reached in others. At different times and in different relationships different understandings achieve the possibility of sharing, some cannot endure abrupt exposure to too harsh a light. This must surely affect quite radically what can publicly be known and shared about the essential intimacies of human meeting.

Chapter four

Psychology in an intermediary mode

Having looked towards my own experience in psychotherapy I want now to turn to look back towards psychology. In this repeated oscillation between practical involvement and reflection I hope to create new *space* wherein different kinds of psychological activity can be given more public credibility.

Over the years I've felt much dissatisfaction with the standard, hard-headed, distancing methods favoured in psychology. It would be possible to spell out quite a number of my particular unhappinesses in this regard but this critical activity is not what I intend here. For all the particular complaints I might be able to make, I've continued to be restless about something else that felt crucial but which I've not been able to grasp or say. Much in psychology has seemed as if it lacked something important or as if some important way of going about things had not been recognized. Always the issues involved have been unclear but persistently tantalizing.

The more personal, communicating, caring activities involved in psychotherapy have seemed to be much more in the midst of whatever it is that I have been seeking, and yet whatever it is has also seemed more ordinary and not trapped within some particular professional speciality. Surely, somewhere between psychology and psychotherapy there is a land occupied by tribes other than those which practise the beliefs and rituals of the 'scientific experimentalist' or the 'professional helper'. The poetic, dramatic, religious, and suchlike are surely enacted there in some different way.

George Kelly (1955) has inspired me with his liberating conception of ordinary people as experimenters, inquirers and sense makers, just like the psychological scientists who seek to study them. The surprise and humour in his manner of writing, especially in his later essays (Kelly 1969), seem to suggest greater possibilities of freedom in psychological inquiry (Mair 1985). Other writers, too, have given me hints, but none feel adequate in relation to whatever I have been struggling with in my personal darkness.

I have become aware, as indicated in Chapter 2, that issues like manner, style, composition, and tone in our ways of meeting, being, and doing are somehow important. How we speak or tell of what we know seems crucial, though the usual descriptions we give in psychology and psychotherapy are often lacking in whatever makes the difference.

Through all this time I have had a continuing feeling of unease in rejecting so much of other people's legitimate struggles in psychology. Every now and then I've become aware of throwing out a variety of babies as well as their various bath waters, all the while seeking to find and give some form to whatever it was that seemed to have me invisibly in its grip.

Some clarification of some of this powerful but misty problem has been developing for me. I will say a little about this here.

Put briefly, I have begun to realize that there are different *modes* of psychological activity and that these have different intentions, different forms, different hearts, different structures, different rules, different qualities and that the pursuit of different modes of psychological activity makes different demands on the inquirer and requires different kinds of heroism, requires different sacrifices, and offers different joys.

The experience of another psychologist

While I was working on this theme, a colleague in a psychotherapy supervision session articulated for me something of what I was seeking to say. As he spoke with thought-filled feelings about the experiences in psychology that had mattered to him I was touched , confirmed, and encouraged in the line I was pursuing. I was excited by his words. They carried, as he spoke them, the weight of his life.

As we talked, my colleague said a variety of things as he began to focus in on what seemed most important to him. In speaking of psychological knowledge in general he said: 'It's all there and it's only a matter of finding it out for myself;' 'there's nothing new to contribute;' 'I don't feel very inspired by clinical psychology;' 'there's a wealth of good ideas and a hyper-wealth of crap, and most research is in the latter category.'

To focus more sharply on the issues he was reaching for I asked him if he had read any psychological work recently that *had* any significance for him. After a little thought he listed four books or papers that had in full or part touched him deeply, spoken to him in some way he found significant. Relative to his own particular interests he listed and commented on David Smail's *Psychotherapy: A Personal Approach* (1978), Sheldon Kopp's *Guru: Metaphors from a Psychotherapist* (1971), Peter Lomas's *The Case for a Personal Psychotherapy* (1981), and my own paper entitled 'The Community of Self' (1977).

He said a little about each of these and I then encouraged him to try to say something of what these pieces of writing had in common as they spoke to him. These are some of the things he said and which I noted as he spoke: 'There's such *clarity* in them', he said 'and anything I would research would come out with the same ideas as these'.

'There's a basic honesty there. There's something human, even though it is not empirically tested. It still feels more like real knowledge than things you read in traditional modes.'

Speaking of Smail's book he said, 'It *resonates* with my experience of doing therapy, whereas behavioural papers on something like "Obsessions and Compulsions" seem dry, arid, meaningless, except for the clinical examples.'

'It gives something to *aim for*. There's a certain *eloquence* there. They are all very *articulate*. It's that that I would aim for.'

'At one time I would have aimed to be as good a therapist as whoever, but now I'm more aware that writers like these are very *eloquent* in what they say about therapy'.

'They actually *capture* the experience. There are bits in all of them where you say — "Yes, this has happened to me".'

'The usual way people write is at least one step removed. If you read "straight" papers you can grope around and fit experiences into them, but in reading these others that happens *spontaneously*. There's a much more solid association happens in me *which doesn't detract from the experience of the therapy*, but the usual way of writing does. The person remains a Mr So and So and doesn't become a such and such.'

At this point I asked my colleague if he could think of any other books he'd read in the past, within psychology, where something like this sort of response had been involved for him. Quite readily now he suggested another instance in recalling his reading of *Memories, Dreams, Reflections* by Carl Jung (1963). 'When I was reading this book', my colleague said, 'I was reading more than the words. Somehow the things spoken in these words *spoke at a deeper level*. It wasn't just pure excitement', he said, 'it was great! This is an idea I understand! It was much more a *bodily feeling* — I had to close the book — it had to be digested.'

I asked him what he was looking for in his work as a clinical psychologist now. He responded by saying that as a young child he was very excited by learning but that he lost this in grammar school. When he eventually became an undergraduate, he said it was like being back at primary school, filled with wonderful, exciting ideas and a big *thirst to know*. When he came to do his training in clinical psychology, it disappeared again and the academic side became, for him, arid.

'I want to get that *excitement*, that *thirst*, back.'

'It's almost like *blood* for me.'

'I think I'd die if it wasn't around.'

'When I'm depressed, my curiosity disappears. When I'm not I get that ... it's almost like blood or oxygen ... curiosity!'

With the kind of writing he'd been talking about, my colleague said, 'I want to read *more of the same*. It gives me a sense of *belonging*. When I read something like the *British Journal of Psychology* I feel an *outsider, I don't belong*. I feel *cut off, lonely*, and not *nourished* by it. But there is a whole area I couldn't live without that is nourishing.'

A longing for refreshment

As it happens, about the same time as I was coming to the ideas that are outlined in this chapter, and had been listening to my colleague, I happened to hear someone on the radio talking about and quoting from a nineteenth-century writer, Richard Jefferies. He was a Wiltshire farmer who became a writer and is especially remembered as one of the greatest nature-mystics to have appeared in Britain. A passage from one of his books was quoted which especially struck me and I sought it out. Jefferies struggled to find expression for his own experiences in relation to the world around him. He spoke from his particular experiences and within his times. As you read the extract which follows, perhaps you could listen to what he is saying and think also of your common experiences of or in psychology, and perhaps other aspects of your own life too.

> The story of my heart commences seventeen years ago. In the glow of youth there were times every now and then when I felt the necessity of a strong inspiration of soul-thought. My heart was dusty, parched for want of the rain of deep feeling; my mind arid and dry, for there is a dust which settles on the heart as well as that which falls on a ledge. It is injurious to the mind as well as to the body to be always in one place and always surrounded by the same circumstances. A species of thick clothing slowly grows about the mind, the pores are choked, little habits become a part of existence, and by degrees the mind is enclosed in a husk. When this began to form I felt eager to escape from it, to throw it off like heavy clothing, to drink deeply once more at the fresh fountains of life. An inspiration — a long deep breath of the pure air of thought — could alone give health to the heart. (Happold 1973)

Something again in this seemed to me to be speaking as my colleague had done and to be drawing attention to one of the modes of psychological activity, of knowing, which I will now refer to as the intermediary mode.

Modes of psychological activity

I want here to give a thumb-nail sketch of what I'm calling different modes of psychological activity. For the moment I will distinguish only three modes (though there are many others). I have called these the *investigative mode*, the *organizational mode*, and the *intermediary mode*. Thereafter I will attend particularly to the intermediary mode in this chapter.

Before proceeding I want to emphasize a number of points that seem important.

(i) I am not seeking to make *categories* but to draw *distinctions.*

(ii) I am not seeking to indicate *topics* within the amalgam of psychology, but *modes of activity in and across topics.*

(iii) I am not arguing *for* one and *against* others, but rather for greater understanding of all modes so that they can be lived and known more fully.

(iv) As I've already indicated, I'm not listing *all* modes that might usefully be distinguished.

(v) It is important to recognize that each mode interpenetrates all the others and to a considerable extent can be turned on the others, and can be drawn from by the others.

(vi) Each mode has to be entered and known in itself, because they are different ways of being and attending to being.

The investigative mode

As I see it, almost all the focussed attention in psychology is given over to this mode of activity. It has to do with a wide variety of ways of *finding out about*, with taking apart, breaking down into pieces, examining in detail, with creating shared conventions and common practices, with establishing grounds for belief in what is demonstrable.

The organizational mode

This mode could be called 'political', but I'd prefer not to use that term here. In psychology much time, *in practice*, is taken up in establishing and maintaining our place in a threatening and not always friendly world, with establishing safe havens, buttressed by social assertions and arrangements. This is the professionalizing aspect that some deplore and others see as essential.

This mode includes all the activities (or aspects of activities) that have to do with power, with making and sustaining a place in the world, with social cohesion, networks of support, inclusions and exclusions (the demands and rules of the tribes we live amongst), with sustaining the social organism against all comers, the cutting out of a place in the world and maintaining it against others who might threaten or overthrow it.

Sometimes in psychology, things that look like investigative-mode activity may better be seen as primarily organizational. Universities and departments have to maintain themselves by being seen to be productive within the conventions of their peers and much undergraduate research, at least, is not truly investigative but to meet the demands of the organization that something be produced, so that conspicuous production can lay an acceptable claim for departmental recognition within the local and national academic jungle. Much research is to maintain a place in the academic or public world rather than being primarily investigative, for the sake of that which someone truly seeks to know.

The intermediary mode

This mode is to do with very different things. It is about conjuring up, evoking, startling into new vision, taking to a different place, giving back to, describing from within, sharing, bringing to life, enlivening, removing the layers of dust and convention. It is to do with what George Kelly called 'transcending the obvious', which he considered to be the basic psychological problem of man. In talking of this sort of activity the poet Wallace Stevens suggested that for most of us reality becomes something of a cliché, covered over, conventional, too familiar, all but invisible. For him, and for others, escape from this cliché is by means of metaphor, the refreshing use of new transpositions.

What it is and what it isn't

The intermediary mode is to do with touching and being touched, personally. It is to do with those communications which refresh and bring a person to life, open them up to new possibilities. It is life sized, life related, life informing. In this kind of communicative activity a person feels themselves to be spoken to, confirmed, validated, somehow recognized, sometimes startled, stirred, moved, excited, challenged, surprised into an experienced knowing. It is to do with such matters as refreshment, discovery, creation, and conversion.

It is not to do with conclusions but with entering into the middle, into being in progress. It has to do with lived embodiment rather than particularized conclusions. It is founded in and returns to personal experiencing as a living engagement. It is rooted in someone's experiencing.

It is not to do with blobs of knowledge. It is not analytic nor systematic. It is not complete in itself and rounded off or defined with sharp boundaries. It is not general but has particular generality. It is not a poor relation to any other mode of psychological activity and it is not reducible to other modes. It is neither good nor bad in itself, but has great possibilities of both.

The role of the intermediary

To be an intermediary, or to act in the intermediary mode, is to be a messenger, a go-between, a negotiator. It is to be a membrane that vibrates, to be a hand reached out across some divide, to be the space between. It is to be a servant, a transformer. It is to give something fundamentally of yourself, to be a poet.

In psychotherapy, as one particular context of human relationships, the therapist acts largely and often as an intermediary, though also in other modes. The therapist (just as in other contexts, the parent, lover, politician, or poet) helps a person to go between his different selves, to learn what different parts of his own experiencing may be involved in and concerned about. So also between self and world, person to person, discipline to discipline. The therapist stands often at the crossroads of many disciplines transforming what may variously be known into what may now be of particular use, seeking to move between members of a family or group so that they can begin to speak and listen in such a way that they will be moved and known.

Some features of the intermediary mode

The shape and texture of a psychology that took particular note of the intermediary mode would be different from other modes of psychology. Different modes of psychology require different values, activities, passivities, methods, and validities.

Intermediary psychology can be as devastatingly misused as any other. It can become the worst kind of insidious advertising (reaching the parts other psychologies can't reach!), propaganda, emotionalism, sentimentality, self-flattering exhibitionism, anti-intellectualism.

But at its best, it can move and touch, challenge and confirm, meet and inform the whole being. It can lift and refresh the spirit. It can change you from who you are to become to who you are. It can sing.

It is closer to what we traditionally call art and the mysteries of religious experience rather than ordinary science. It is lived into knowing, lived from and through. You become the crucible and the chemicals of change.

Psychology in an intermediary mode is necessary for our lives together. It is to recognize and come to understand the changing moods. It is to reach for understanding by casting away, turning around, looking askance, lighting from a new angle. It is to understand within the texture of the sustaining fluid of the things themselves and not within the predetermined one-and-only-way things are to be understood. Its manner and methods of reaching are textured and turned, shaded and varied with the way things are to be and this means no final and fixed ways of being, no final and fixed methods of approach, no final and fixed rules of doing.

The parable and the painting, the poem and story, the play and the song are among the means by which this psychological mode can be explored. Since the medium is integral with the message (even if sometimes ironically opposed to it), we are in the realm of the 'analogical' rather than the 'digital' (Watzlawick *et al.* 1968) though any such distinction is only a

45

hinting and nudging rather than particular and precise.

What do we know of the means of such knowing? How do we care for and sustain this mode of psychological inquiry? One thing is sure, we see almost nothing of it in the main tunnels of psychological science.

What is involved?

Being an intermediary involves — caring to get the message right, so that it articulates what is being felt and so that it reaches and touches those to whom it is addressed. It is presumably a form of rhetoric, related to poetry and art, literature and religious expression, advertising and propaganda — and yet it is not specifically any of these. Unlike being an investigator or being concerned with survival in the organizational mode, it is not primarily concerned with impartial analysis and testing, nor with political planning and priorities.

What sorts of abilities matter here? Listening with all of you, feeling, being able to formulate and give expression to what is being spoken, felt, or shown in a variety of ways; being able and willing to give voice with sensitive pungency (not just accuracy in some literal sense) to what is being said in the living space of both the speaker and the receiver. The finding and creating of means of conjuring into effective reality, speaking it like it is, is important. Being willing to bear the pains and uncertainties of creative endeavour, rather than follow the set paths of formal testing; attending to and staying with the hints and clues along the way; knowing how to hunt around to find new hints of life in trails that seem to have gone dead; being able to wait and suffer through the lean time; and being able and willing to be given over to the terrible excitement and pain of holding and shaping and giving birth when the feelings and ideas flow.

Being an intermediary is fundamentally to do with communication, powerful or delicate or vivid or accurate communication, rather than primarily to do with testing the general credibility of something, of examining in controlled detail its parts, or to do with asserting one's rights and position to set up bulwarks against possible encroachment and defeat.

A wider look

There are many things to be said concerning the intermediary mode. All psychological theories make their first and basic appeal as they touch and resonate with the experience and concern of those who attend to them. Skinner no less than Rogers reaches out to pluck at the heart strings. Each of them speaks to individuals nourished and locked within the conditions of our time.

As with theories, so also with experimental designs, statistical proofs, and all other trappings of how we live. All speak to us of some style of being, as well as whatever else in practical usage. Just as there are many styles of chairs and teapots, so also the style, the line, colour, and beauty of what we respond to in our professional methods is crucial to our acceptance of them. Not only all these, our methods, but the very *facts* they offer up to us are tinged with their own brands of fact-appeal, especially enticing to some, less so to others. It is easy (and may even have some truth in it) to say that we are here concerned with 'valuing', but we are rather in the realm of the more sensuous, the aesthetic, the feeling/body closeness of our boundaries with the world.

This mode of psychological activity is not just relevant for some, but for everyone, though some will like it less and others more.

There are no set ways, and yet set ways will be found (in the organizational mode we know that everything needs some space to live and thrive within). There are no generalities, though some reaching beyond the particular is likely, in and through the particular, now.

So many of us are prisoners and exiles, rejects and oppressed minorities, even within ourselves. So much of who we are is in hiding, on the run, not wanted, quite ignored. So little is brought to life again, disinterred, brought into the sun. In dealing with ourselves as with each other we live the minimal conventions of our time — and then someone speaks to someone in us we have forgotten. Someone curves out a sense of something that we are (and know it in the shock of recognition now, though we could not have said we knew). This is the moment when we glimpse the islands and the sea beyond, the giving back, the entering into what we knew and never knew we knew. This is the lightning shaft, the intermediary mode.

A geography of knowing

What I have said here is a first attempt to conjure up something of the kind of distinctions I'm beginning to explore and question. Every human utterance, every act is multi-modal, potentially infinite in its range of meaning. Through context and convention, attention and contrivance we narrow down what we will take each thing to mean. But in psychological affairs at least (as distinct from chemistry, mathematics, and physics) every act is multi-modal, participates in many different 'worlds', even when we choose to ignore or simply fail to recognize that this may be so. If we are to build a psychology that respects something of our own complexity we may have to give credence to the many modes in which we know, the diverse modes of human action, otherwise we will endlessly confuse and contradict ourselves as we struggle to know what and how we know.

Any particular act participates in many modes, though some may be given greater prominence than others in any particular situation. Thus my writing here can be seen, in its detail as well as overall, as part of an inquiry of mine, to probe and specify, test and examine some important questions, issues in my life. At the same time, this same presentation may reach out to touch you, or some who read, so that they are moved, and somehow changed, confirmed, questioned or otherwise re-formed. Simultaneously this same act of writing, if it carries some coherence that may convince, can also be seen as taking part in the politics and warfare of the organizational mode of knowing. Someone may be able to use its arguments to buttress and protect their own struggles to develop their understanding within, say, the intermediary mode which so often gets obscured and dominated by those who have so far cared only for the credentials of what I have called the investigative mode.

If it proves useful to speak of modes of psychological activity, modes of knowing, it will be important to recognize that there are many modes and not just the three that I've tentatively given some temporary form. It might also be useful to attend to others which might be called the *conventional,* the *ritual,* and the *interpretative* or *hermeneutic* modes. Beyond this too, these modes are not to be made into watertight compartments since they endlessly interpenetrate and cohabit with each other and each can be turned upon each other so that some inquiry biassed to the intermediary mode may be examined and dissected (and often in itself destroyed) through action in the investigative mode. So also the opposite or any other combination of twists and turnings on the self may be explicitly pursued or remain implicit in how we compose and constitute ourselves.

In all this it seems to me important that we seek for more knowing of what it is to know, for some more explicit understanding of the landscape of human knowing and the ways in which that landscape is modified and moved by the many ways in which we turn our various modes of knowing on what and how and who we seek to know. Without some sense of the geography of knowing (though this metaphor in itself is quite inadequate to conjure up more than a little of what might be involved), we are likely to continue as we have been doing to persecute each other and ourselves because our modern and conventional maps of the terrain of knowing tell almost nothing of the world of knowing that we seek to know. I suspect we have, indeed, abandoned older maps that told of the diversity of what we are involved in in our quest to know. Ancient explorers who mapped out something of the landscape of knowing from their own explorations in the field may still be better beginning guides than more recent technocrats who believe we are simpler than we know we are.

Chapter five

A use of imagery in psychotherapy

It is one thing to talk *about* an 'intermediary' mode of psychological activity, it is another to try to *show* a practical instance of what is meant. This will be a showing. What is said here will not tell much about the use of imagery in psychotherapy as a general topic. Instead, I'd like you to listen to the story that will be told, enter the world that will be conjured up, feel what you can of the life being lived there.

Here it is not just a brief moment of meeting which is being considered, but a continuing way of speaking together as the experiencing of one person's life is changed. Try to take part and let yourself be attentive to whatever may be sparked in your awareness.

Attending to yourself

Before launching into the story I'd ask you to stop for a little to pay attention to yourself. Try to attend to your feelings. Are you scampering around somewhere else? Are you still brooding on an argument from last night? Are you feeling queasy and wondering if the egg you had for breakfast was a bit off? Try to notice what you are feeling and where you feel yourself to be now. As we go on, you may see that it is of some importance, if you are to hear something of what you may be able to hear, that you begin by knowing something of where you are now.

My concern is with feeling, our intimate engagement with the world, and how we can recognize something of the form of those acts of feeling that we are engaged in. It is part of a concern with metaphor and figurative thinking generally. We can give form to feeling in painting, sculpture, poetry, drama, dress, and so many other ways. Imagery is one of these other ways.

Before continuing, I would ask you again to pay attention to where you are now. This time, I'd like you to leave behind the eggs, or whatever. Pay attention to yourself wherever you are sitting or standing now, as you read this, at this moment, in the context of whatever your surroundings are. It might help to close your eyes. Pay attention to what you feel.

I don't want you to think too intellectually about this, but rather to let your attention float over yourself as you are existing now.

See if any words come to mind to help you identify, get hold of, some of your feelings. Are you, for instance, feeling a bit edgy, bored, sleepy, irritated? See if you can get hold of something of what you are feeling. Can you catch it in any words at all? If you can I'd like you to notice them and then let them go again, get rid of them.

Now see if you can be a bit more loose, unrealistic. Pay attention again to what you are feeling. Try to express it in some other way. 'It feels as if ... I was sitting in a field with lots of rabbits all around me ready to scamper away....' It's no good if you start thinking too much about it. See if you can conjure up for yourself in some more elaborate, perhaps less realistic way, a form of words that catches how you are feeling just now.

If nothing comes at present, it doesn't matter, though it's worth trying, just in case.

A particular client: Janet

This will not be a formal case history. I want simply to convey something of the imagery Janet produced and used during a short segment of the longer therapeutic process that she was involved in with me. I'll give an account of the sequence of images she produced over the course of a month. Try to put yourself into what she is saying. Try to conjure it up as much as possible for yourself. Try to be present to the images. This may not be easy, but may be aided if you have already managed to be a little more present to yourself.

At the time Janet was 31 years old. Soon after qualifying as a teacher she became withdrawn, ground to a halt. This was closely related in time to the death of a close friend and the death of her elder brother, resulting from cancer.

She had been in hospital for a year when I first met her. A variety of diagnoses were tried at different times. Certainly she was seen as depressed. To begin with, and for a long time, she was almost totally uncommunicative. She had had ECT and many different drugs. Nothing had made very much difference. There were doubts as to whether she was legitimately described as 'depressed'. A variety of other labels were suggested. In the week before Janet was readmitted to hospital she had come to see me as an outpatient. She presented herself as desperate. She wanted to get back into hospital. She told me that she had intense urges to mutilate herself. In the previous week she had, for the first time, actually succumbed to this desire by taking a pair of scissors and cutting herself slightly, so that she bled.

At this point I was the only person who was still outside her web of suspicion of the intentions of others. She told me this in a way that implied to me that I'd better behave myself appropriately or I'd be enmeshed in it too, and would then leave her with no one she could trust.

Communicating

One of the striking things about Janet, throughout the period of my initial contact with her, was that she was often very uncommunicative through the medium of ordinary conversation. She was an imaginative person who could express her concerns in images and pictures more easily than in ordinary terms. One day, soon after she came back into hospital she said she was feeling 'lost'.

Sometimes with her, as with some other clients, it seems to me important to try to get a more finely elaborated sense of what a single significant word or phrase may imply. The first direct words are then a beginning, but not enough. I asked her (just as I asked you at the beginning) if she could pay attention to this feeling of being 'lost'. Could she let go of the word and say something more about the feeling. I knew that she had the potential for a different kind of language to help us talk together and try to understand.

On this occasion I said to her, 'You're feeling lost ... can you just try to notice how you are feeling and see if you can convey a sense of that to me in some other way.... It feels as if ... See if any other way of expressing it floats to mind ... maybe some kind of picture of how it feels.'

A sequence of images

(a) the bull-ring

Janet says almost immediately that she has an image. She can see a figure standing in the middle of an arena, like a bull-ring (try to imagine it yourself) ... a small figure standing in the middle of an arena, like a bull-ring with walled-in arches all around her. She can hear people behind the arches, but they're all bricked up, walled in. She can't see anybody, can't reach them. In the arena only one archway is open, and it's empty.

Throughout all this she is aware there is a way out, but it is in darkness. The figure in the middle feels terrified of going through that archway because she feels that if she does, it will seal over behind her and she will never be able to get back to where she is now. Even if she goes through that archway, for a time, she'll be left in the dark. She doesn't know and is frightened of what might be out there, beyond the darkness.

The little figure in the middle has no hands. Janet feels that this figure in the middle of the arena will eventually decide to go through the door, but is not able to contemplate that at the moment.

Janet is someone who doesn't usually say very much, yet this kind of communication is fluent, fluid. We may have difficulty in picking out what it 'means' perhaps, but she is just describing a picture, shaped by how she has been feeling. There is no problem for her about it, and nothing to impede her in communicating how it is.

The figure in the middle is fairly young, a female, about Janet's age, with blond hair (Janet has dark hair). There is a feeling of danger. There's nothing at all to be said in favour of her remaining where she is, but she's afraid to move.

I'm not going to suggest meanings for different aspects of this or subsequent images. That is sometimes useful in therapy, but I more often use imagery as a mode of conversation, to get a clearer impression of how and where a person feels themselves, centrally, to be. Whatever the person may appear to be doing on the outside, this manner of using imagery can give a very different depth of perspective, though this kind of assertion would be difficult to prove in an external way. Its sensed validity rests on having access to shared feeling.

This was the first time she had mentioned the arena. Other things were also going on for her at this time but we'll attend only to the images that were evoked in subsequent weeks.

Janet continued to feel low and lost. After a few more days she is feeling a bit better. In the course of discussing other things I ask her what is happening now in the arena.

The girl is in the bull-ring. She still seems to be in the same position as before. She feels that at any time spears may come hurtling down and harm her. It feels very dangerous to be there. The girl is still standing in the middle wearing a white robe. Janet says that the white robe covers everything, and sometimes it changes to black. The girl has long blond hair. There is a lot of noise. Janet says *she* can see people in the boxes around the arena. They had been walled up, but now are somehow less so, though from the point of view of the girl in the arena, these figures are invisible. The people in the boxes don't seem to be communicating between themselves or with the girl.

I ask her if she could say something about the people in the boxes. She says that the only ones standing out are in one group. They look like Roman soldiers. They seem to be laughing, drunk, like men coming off the oil rigs, out to enjoy themselves.

Now Janet is quite engrossed in what she is saying. I ask her what kind of enjoyment these people are out for. There is a long silence. One of her classic silences wherein you know you are asking something important by the fact that she will almost disappear beyond the range of your feeling for her. I ask her again, what sort of enjoyment?

Janet says slowly that she's feeling very sad and unhappy. It is most unusual for her to say anything as direct as this about her feelings. She goes on to say that the soldiers rape every woman in sight. She is clearly upset as she says this. She feels very confused. She says that sometimes she feels that the only thing women are wanted for is their bodies. I ask if this is what she has felt. She is again silent for a long time, then acknowledges that this does apply to her.

She feels worse than ever. She says that she has the sense that she is not wanted by anyone except for her body. She sits concentrated on what she's experiencing in relation to these soldiers, and says that the only way to solve this problem (of not being wanted for anything but your body) is, of course, to harm yourself so that people will *have to* want her then for herself, because her body will be useless.

This was the first time any sort of explanation or understanding of her wanting to harm herself had been expressed by her to me. For the first time, she herself was hinting that harming herself *physically* was about struggling to preserve herself *personally*. The only way she could see of preserving herself as a person was to destroy the physical forms that were entailed in her having a female body.

She says that for her there seems to be no compromise. She can't have the essential features of a female body and be an acceptable person, because then people seem to pay no attention to the person she may be. Having put this idea into words, Janet is clearly taken aback. She begins to shake uncontrollably. She indicates that she feels very frightened because she has now uttered more clearly than ever before a further reason why she must harm herself. If she is to make anything of herself, the knife must be used. Hearing herself say the words has somehow confirmed even more strongly that this is the necessary course to follow.

I ask her again to go back to the image. What is happening now?

The girl is in the centre, crouching down now. She feels extremely frightened, hopeless, completely unable to decide what to do. Something of this fear licks around me too as I watch and listen.

In the days that followed, Janet was thinking a great deal about knives. She kept a knife under her pillow. She felt better with the knife there, knowing that she could use it at any time if she had to do that. This seemed to take a bit of the pressure off her. Her brother was very present to her at this time. His birthday was approaching and she was thinking actively about what to get him as a present (though he was, of course, dead). She had the sense that he was about to materialize and sit on the chair in her hospital room. Quite often she felt compelled to leave the room because of the terror that he might suddenly be there. Sometimes she sat in the chair with the thought that if she did this then he couldn't sit there too.

(b) the circus ring

It is now a day or two later. What's happening in the arena? This time, instantly, she says that through the doorway (remember there is one arch open, in darkness) there is another arena. In fact, she says, there are two

53

doors that she can now see. One door at the side is unmarked, and she knows that leads to suicide. The other leads into a circus arena. In that next arena, people are all around and visible. There is a crowd around the circus arena. They are shouting and throwing down words like 'hate' and 'guilt'. She describes these as 'solid words' being hurled down by the crowd at the girl crouching in the middle with hands over her eyes. The girl is dressed in white. It seems, Janet says, as if the crowd is like the crowd before Pontius Pilate, shouting 'crucify her!'

The girl in the middle is trying to protect herself from hearing what the crowd is shouting. She still has the choice about the door to suicide, and presumably, says Janet, there is some other way out as well, but nothing is visible at the moment. The door to the first arena, the bull-ring, is now sealed over. In the circus arena the people are throwing down these words. The girl is crouched in the middle. The other arena is sealed off. She has moved.

As she talked this time, Janet looked miserable and said she was feeling very sad. She said also that she didn't feel able to speak about that at present.

In the next day or so we didn't talk much about the arena, but did talk about other things, about her brother and the fact that she had been crying a lot.

At our next meeting Janet again looks lost, wandering, frightened. She says that the girl in the arena is now standing up, trying to get the crowd to listen to her. She feels desolate that they won't listen. The crowd keep throwing down these words. They feel that the girl is less than perfect as a woman, that she doesn't want the normal things women should want — to have children, have a home, look after an old parent. She wants to have a life of her own and not have people depending on her. Janet goes on to say that she, herself, doesn't want any of these ordinary things, not yet, anyway. She might want them at some point in the future.

(c) the circular wall

At this point she said she was feeling 'low and desolate'. I had the sense that there might be something more in this. I asked her if she could attend to the feelings and conjure up a picture, perhaps, of how she felt.

She says it is as if she is hiding and being held behind a circular stone wall.

So, it seemed, we had jumped into a new image. She has the feeling that an explosion is about to happen. Her hands are clawing at the wall. She has the sense of, perhaps, having raised the wall to hide behind it.

I am struck by her account of the hands clawing at the wall and ask if she can try to imagine what it feels like to be those hands.

She says she gets a sense that the body of the person in there is all hands, nothing but hands, made up of hands. The hands have long finger-nails. They are clawing at the wall. The wall is herself and the hands claw off chunks of flesh so that blood runs down. She is engrossed in what she is saying. They wipe the flesh off their fingers and make scars across the flesh of the wall. They seem to be doing this just for the pleasure of it.

At this point she said she felt even sadder. I suggested another brief meeting in the afternoon since she was in such a shaky state. In the afternoon she had a sense of something being nearer the surface, but she didn't feel she could go into it then. I had an impression then, as often before, that she had some view of things coming. Often before it had taken some time for her to dare to say them, perhaps because she knew that she would experience them more fully then and have to take greater responsibility for whatever was involved.

Again in the following session I asked her what was happening in the arena now.

Everything is as it was before. The girl is standing up and the people are still not listening, they are still hurling down words.

I asked if she had any impression of the wall.

As she begins to think of this, her face changes. She says she is feeling very sad. I ask if she can go further into this feeling and speak of it.

She says again that it seems that she is inside a circular stone wall. It feels as if there is to be an explosion and that her body has changed into hands, scratching, clawing, gouging at the wall. As she speaks it suddenly seems that she is all over the wall and the hands are clawing at her and gouging out bits of flesh, then wiping their bloody selves on her, the wall, and leaving long scratches. The hands seem to be doing this because they enjoy it.

The wall, she says, feels strong and confident. It no longer needs the person who built it, or so it thinks, says Janet. It has become stronger than the person inside.

I ask her if she can *be* the person inside. Can she use her imagination to allow herself to be that person. She tries to do this. She feels very trapped, with no strength to carry on. She's not able to summon up any will to do anything. She's frightened. There's no way out. She can only die there.

I ask her if *the wall* feels anything at all. She tries to imagine what the wall might feel, to see if it feels anything about the outside world. Janet says she has the sense that the wall doesn't know of its existence, or of mine.

What of the *person* inside the wall, is she aware of anyone outside? I am becoming concerned and want some contact with this frightened, clawing person on the inside. Janet replies that there is just too much noise, too much panic, for that creature to be able to know anything.

I ask Janet again if she can imagine herself as that desperate clawing figure, and if she is able then to hear me if I speak to *her*. Again she says there is too much noise inside the wall.

I encourage her to try again. I want that creature to know that I am there and want to help and to offer whatever support or strength I can. I want her to know that she isn't quite alone. Janet looks as if she has changed a little on hearing this and mutters something that seems to imply some recognition from within the wall. She also indicates that this desperate figure recognizes that she wants help, that she is prepared to make some contact with somebody.

Just as Janet speaks obliquely of these things, she says sharply, 'The wall is beginning to fill up with water!' The person inside is terrified of being drowned. 'It's filling up!'

Since Janet was an inpatient at this time, I was seeing her three times per week. The next day she was very quiet and looked haunted, frightened, with a 'mad' look in her eyes. She was terrified that she had said too much on the previous day, in acknowledging that the trapped creature needed help. Janet sat shaking with feeling. She had gone too far. She had given voice to her awareness that something in her, some part of her, recognized a desperate need for help from somebody outside the wall. Trembling and pale, Janet said that she had to find some way to help herself. She must not rely on other people.

I ask her again what the situation is now within the wall. The water is still there, she says, but even as we speak she says, 'The water is rising up again. It's going up and up!' The figure within is holding onto the sides of the wall to keep her head above the water. As it rises to the top, it becomes possible for the person to reach up, hold onto the top of the wall and pull herself out. She sits (this undefined figure) on top of the wall now ... and from there she can see the circus arena. The scene there is much as it was before with people all around throwing down words of condemnation.

After a few days I ask Janet again what is happening with the wall.

She is back inside the wall, but there is no water now. This time she's feeling very edgy. She becomes aware that the wall is closing in and is going to suffocate her. The walls are closing in, nearer and nearer. Narrowing until it becomes possible for the figure in there to climb up. She begins to climb because the wall has become like a funnel and she can press against the sides.

(d) the silent arena

She reaches the top of the wall again and finds that the circus arena outside it is still there, but silent and empty. There's no one there. An exit is visible now. She sits at the top of the wall, frightened to come down because she's aware that if she does come down the wall will disappear and she'll have no protection. She has decided, however, after all that has happened, that maybe it's not such wonderful protection after all. She decides to come down. She feels frightened. She fears that she will, almost certainly, have to go out through the exit if she does come down. She's frightened that all will then become again as it was for her before she came into hospital.

A couple of days later. The girl is still standing in the arena, as before. Now Janet is aware that there is another person there, though the girl in the arena hasn't noticed him. She could see him if she turned round. The girl is aware that she could walk over to the exit, but she is too frightened to do that. She's frightened to go out in case all the people are waiting to turn on her. She feels they will recognize her and will punish or kill her.

I ask Janet if the girl in the arena could turn towards the other person who is there. She indicates that she can, and then does this. I ask what she thinks or feels about this other person. She says he must be all right because he isn't shouting or throwing things.

I ask her what *he* feels will happen outside (she has produced him in her imagination, so she should be able to put herself into what he might think or feel). She says that he thinks her main problem is herself and that she panics so readily. He doesn't think anything will happen outside. He's aware that it is a market place outside with people wandering about.

(e) the market place

Janet says that the girl doesn't have the courage to go out alone, but she could go out if she went with him. I ask them if they will go out and tell me what they find.

Outside, it's bright and sunny. It's an open market with stalls. There are lots of people around. To her surprise she seems to blend in and isn't at all noticeable. She is still dressed as she was in her long white robe. There are other people dressed just like that. She's still afraid that she'll be recognized and wants to get away from the people as quickly as possible.

I ask if she can just walk around amongst the people instead of trying to get away. She slows down and manages to do this. To her surprise, it doesn't feel as bad as she had expected. No one pays any attention. She's trying to find out where she is. It seems to be somewhere like Israel or Egypt. All around are people who seem to have come straight out of the Bible.

She sees an airport nearby! What she wants is to board an aeroplane and get away fast. She has the feeling that she was meant to die in the arenas, and somehow she has cheated these people. She is frightened that they will want to carry on where they left off. She wants to get away on a plane, but also feels that would be running away rather than facing up to things. She has the sense that it's not time, after all, for her to die. Perhaps she could stay around rather than go.

I ask her what the male figure in the image thinks about all that is happening. She says that he thinks the people have had their fun and are not interested any longer. She feels a bit more relaxed. She is pleased that she has taken the step out into the market place. She's aware that she is dependent on him still, but ... We'll leave them there.

The continuing story

Janet stayed in hospital for a further few months. She experienced some powerful recollections and guilt in relation to her brother who had been obsessively on her mind for more than a year. Since then, all of this has faded into normality. She can now think and talk about him with only ordinary unhappiness.

Within a few weeks of the point where we left the story she became able to talk about and explore an issue that seemed close to the heart of the matter in much of her suffering. She managed to acknowledge that she felt her life to be controlled by evil. She said that, since childhood, she's had the sense that she was completely in the power of some evil power. Her friend dying and then the death of her brother were final proof that all her struggles had been hopeless. She was then convinced that evil had finally won out. At all costs, she decided, she must stay away from people. She knew, with total conviction, that she would bring nothing but disaster to anybody who came close to her or for whom she had any feelings of affection. This evil would also be passed on to any child she might have. This horrifying possibility had to be prevented at any cost. All this was the central, painful, enduring truth around which her life was structured. Much that had seemed 'mad' in what she had experienced and done could begin to make some more cohering sense.

Since leaving hospital Janet has managed to cope with life. She took the risk of accepting a teaching post abroad. She married. She has done better than survive.

Through her most troubled times she spoke with a poetic intensity I have seldom known. She touched and shaped my life and understanding as her own life was being changed.

Chapter six

Towards a poetics of experience

People struggling to make sense of their lives, whether in psychotherapy or elsewhere, often show us, as Janet does, the power of poetic speech. Here I want to turn again to speak *from* my experience in psychotherapy rather than about it.

The *manner* of my presentation will be a little different from the usual in psychology. In *form*, it is like a sandwich with a longer reflective section in the middle wedged between more personal statements at the beginning and end.

Try again, if you will, to feel yourself into these more personal sections as you read. They are not being presented for intellectual analysis, but to conjure up two moments in my own life which bear on the sections in between.

Sunday, 10 September 1978

It is Sunday evening. I've been living and working in Dumfries now for three years. I came here from London.

My life is at a time of turmoil.

For many years I've been struggling with profound dissatisfactions with the scientific approach in psychology. This is something that I don't just pay attention to casually. It seems to have me in its grip. It really gets at me. Gnaws at me.

I find myself writing, scribbling a lot of the time, trying to work out what on earth I'm so bugged about!

I'm sitting at my desk at home, thinking, writing again. Strained.

I despair, really.
What, if anything, am I wrestling with in this darkness!?
What kind of dissatisfaction am I really trying to meet and change?

I can't get hold of it, can't see it.
Can I even *feel* it?

Try!
Try to listen to how it *feels*.
Just try and *listen* to how it feels.
How it silently tugs and strains at you.

Don't interrupt.
Don't butt in.
Listen
(I say to myself)
Try just to *say* it. Say the feelings without question.

And I try (as often before) simply to *be* with this concern and to write it.
I try to let the words come without comment.
(And this is what follows without break)

I wish to speak us our world
I wish to speak the myness of our world
I wish to speak the world

I wish to speak the world between us

I wish to speak into living form
the reality of the invisible world
between us

I want to speak
as a painter paints
and a dancer dances
and as a poet sings

I want to find ways of
saying the world
Saying the saying
of the world

It means knowing
all the pain and sorrow
cowardice
cruelty
fear
frailty and hardness
of the world

It means being able
and somehow willing
to bear all things
believe
hope
endure
all things
It means
learning to love
and through and beyond that
coming to sense
whatever it might mean to say
that love is all there is

Knowing does not precede speaking
It is created and lives in speaking
But speaking from a possibility of knowing

I want to speak *to* the world
and not just speak it or from it
I want to let the world speak with me

Where there is conversation
there is a possibility of speaking
the world together
The world can come alive
expand and blossom
in meeting

You cannot speak the world
unless you can bear the world
It takes courage

You cannot speak the world
unless you can talk with the world
It takes care

You cannot speak the world
unless you listen to and hear the world
It takes silence

You cannot speak the world
unless you get close to the world
It takes patience

> You cannot speak the world
> unless you are heard
> It takes trust

I sit back.
Was that me? Who said that?
That wasn't the 'me' of a few moments ago. He didn't say it.
It feels strange. Exciting. Foreign. Familiar.
I can't say 'Yes' to it. I can't say 'No'.
I certainly can't say 'No'.

I'm embarrassed.
Such grandiosity.
How could you bear such aspirations, obviously far too lofty for me.
How embarrassing if anyone should actually know what I've just written.

I forget it, put it away, pay no more attention.

And now it is some years later.

I'm here again, still with the same issue, in a slightly different place. For the
   first time in a public way, I can actually bear to *say* what I wrote then.
But there is an embarrassment.
Such vulnerability is involved in speaking what you didn't know you were
   going to speak.

I had talked myself into being, in some form.
I had talked myself in a way that surprised me.
It was laid aside. I moved on, but am still there in a different way.

A poetics of experience

Psychologists, and many others who seek to develop further understanding,
are surely engaged on a tremendous undertaking if they are really trying to
make some feelingful sense of the complex world of our experiencing of
ourselves and our relationships with others. But how can we penetrate
more deeply into it? How can we move ourselves from where we were to
somewhere deeper in, more understandingly?

I want to make a few points which arise out of my own concerns to
understand something of myself and the patients I've worked with over the
years. I won't speak directly of psychotherapy but will draw from it, as
from other experiences. I'd hope that everything said here can be related by
you to psychotherapy or your own experience from elsewhere.

I'll mention only a few elements, moving towards a pattern that suggests
a different way, from that of measurement and conventional science, of

going about the business of reaching understanding in relation to each other. These few things seem to me to matter. They are, I think, points to which, quite generally, we should pay some more attention.

For myself, what I'm doing here is trying to move, to feel towards, that hidden 'project' that I've been trying to disentangle for so long. As it partially emerges, I find myself, of course, in the company of many others who have moved in this same direction at different times.

A poetic concern

Following on from much that has gone before, it seems to me that we need a poetic concern with our experiencing, our awareness of ourselves and the world, and not just a prosaic concern with experiencing. I'm not referring here to poetry, in a formal sense. Rather do I want to suggest the importance of a poetic understanding of our experiencing, of our world: poetic rather than prosaic.

As people, and as professionals, we are often bogged down in the prosaic, the mundane banalities of our lives, and have often forgotten how to sing when it is necessary and appropriate to sing — psychologically to sing.

Psychology, for me, is largely a discipline of prosaic solemnity. Yet we cannot hope to catch and care for the sparkle of moments of beauty, of reverence, of joy, or personal pain in lumbering and prosaic form. These times, the essentials of our deeper lives, are only to be reached and shared in a poetic expression. A poetics of experience, perhaps.

A poetics requires that you are deeply attentive to yourself and others, so that you become the meeting place of messages spoken and unspoken, the place of transformation of what is moving between and amongst you. So much of what we are involved within cannot be separated out or pinned down in objective form. The unknown has to remain in active relationship with the known, and the knower has to reside in both the unknown and what he knows.

You have to listen to the lilt and rhythm, to the use of words and phrases, the telling metaphor, the silence, and the moving spaces in between.

So much, almost everything, in psychotherapy (that deeper meeting between us) is in this poetic realm (I think).

Prosaic attention, prosaic consciousness, acts essentially to insist on a narrowing of options, so that the mundane rules and laws can be found and followed. Life there is simple, and the 'caring' professionals are likely to be more successful if they can call the tune as to what is and is not legitimate experiencing.

A poetics has no conventional security. We are cast into the midst of flux and motion, not stability and permanence.

In and amongst

We need to pay attention also, I believe, to the fact that we *live in and amongst* what we seek to know, though we are encouraged to stay separate and apart in the objective approach to the gathering of knowledge. 'The act of living in and amongst' is one of the definitions of the word 'conversation', and it is towards *conversation* that I will move here.

A poetics is especially relevant to what goes on amongst and between us. We are born into an ongoing and infinitely complex world, moving and changing in place and time, culture and substance. We are formed by the ongoing, criss-cross, multiple, and many voiced conversation of our times. Its speaking goes on through and around us, over and under us. Its words in silence make our silent assumptions. Its manner and style make the mould of *how* we live. We are spoken into existence by the language of our family, and more important still, of our culture, country, times, and place. Words weave the texture of our lives. We are made into awareness and into connected human beings by the already co-mingled warp and woof of words, shared, lived, and traded for all sorts of love and care.

All the time we live in and amongst, in the conversation of our lives. We never have the chance to stand back and see clearly where we have come from and where we are going to, as separate blobs of being. We are never clear of the surface of our planet earth. The gravity of our lives holds us close into itself. We are, at all times, deeply and endlessly compromised by our world. It speaks us far more than we ever achieve the distinction of speaking a fresh word to it. Others are intimately involved, from the very beginning, in whoever it is we take ourselves to be. I and you are many, and most of who I am remains unknown to me. I am, in a sense, a king of an unruly kingdom, whose people 'I' have inherited, from whom 'I' have been born, and over whom, in this curious realm of my being, 'I' exercise an uncertain sway.

Those of us who are concerned with understanding something of ourselves, personally or professionally, find that we are mired deep in that which we seek to understand. We cannot step out and see it from elsewhere. We are created within the invisible valuings and assumptions of our place and time. We have, somehow, to understand ourselves (something of ourselves), by attending *from* what we are invisibly and unknowingly embedded within, *towards* some more visible and tangible aspects of what we know and do. But, and this is part of the essential problem, we attend *from* the web of our world, which grounds and shapes us, *towards* what it allows us to see and know. We cannot easily know that *from which*, through which, by means of which, all our knowing is known.

In such a situation as this we cannot hope to learn much of what we are engaged within through the familiar procedures of experimental design.

Between

Next, I'm concerned with 'the between', as opposed to external juxta-position or statistical conjunction.

The between. The realm of the between. That reality which we feel, and which is going on, between us. Between you and me. Between this part of me and that part of me. The between.

All betweens are also amongst. There are always silent listeners looking over the shoulder in any relationship between. We should not forget that whatever is going on is under the eyes and ears of a certain kind of public. In everything I say, for instance, my mother or someone is looking over my shoulder.

This realm of the between seems to me to be of such powerful import-ance in therapy. And it is such a curious realm. It is intangible, invisible, moving, disappearing, expanding, softening, hardening, opening, welcom-ing, freezing over, clamming shut — you will know the feeling as the relationship between you and someone else changes. Somehow the atmosphere allows things at one moment that it doesn't allow at all the next. It's as if something had trapped shut.

The realm of the between is in motion. Meaning in motion is the nature of the between. Moving patterns of intention. It is very different from statistical association, which is how we deal with the between in almost all of our formal science of psychology. It concerns entering *inside* relationships, inside whatever is going on, and is sensed as going on, between us.

Imaginative participation

Here I am concerned with imaginative participation rather than manipu-lative control — though the latter is important in its place.

The ethos of scientific psychology still generally insists that the inquirer stay separate as an uninvolved observer. But much cannot be known by the disengaged, distant observer. You have to feel and sense it from within, from a position of deep involvement.

This is outside the conventions of what I'd call *the project of self-denying Puritanism* within which empirical science finds its place. This *project* seems to involve a Puritanical concern to make things plain, straight, simple, hard, workmanlike, external. It suggests that things will be done in a certain, right, way which denies or rejects self. Self must not be attended to, must be moved away from, ignored. Our psychological science has joined with others in feeding too readily from this implicit cultural injunc-tion.

In spite of this there are those, here and there, who speak of the import-ance of 'dwelling in' and 'breaking out' of our experiencing. Of understanding. Of really standing under that which you seek to know so that you are drenched and moved by it.

If we are deeply embedded within the web of the world, we must surely lower ourselves further in. Feel and sense and imaginatively recreate something of what we know, perhaps, but do not yet know we know. What you are involved in here is, in a sense, giving *the other* power to speak to you, to say that which, otherwise, you would not attend to or allow to be heard.

Imaginative participation seems, therefore, to be fundamentally important for psychotherapy and any other personal knowing. It involves really entering into the feel and sense of the body, the person, beside you. Entering into, and finding a way of bodying forth the experience of what is happening between you. Finding ways of opening up and realizing, through imagery or metaphor, that which is going on invisibly between you.

Speaking

Finally, I'm concerned here with the importance of speaking as opposed to counting or relegating words to a level of superficial chatter, which is largely what empirical science does to words.

Speaking is important for an understanding of ourselves and others. Speaking can be merely the use of words as noises or counters for barter and trade. But words can also be *emanations* of ourselves.

They speak us into being. These are living words, when someone really enters into what they are saying and may surprise themselves with the freshness of what, there and then, they are inhabiting in these words. Green words. Words in which there is the freshness of new life. Green words. Putting words together with freshness towards some new freedom, some new personal sense of being.

By speaking such words we own and know and find and create something of who we are. We are not already composed and there. Speaking the new words we grow and change. We become ourselves in a new place and in a new way in these crucially important moments of speaking the full word.

A conversational psychology

So what does all this lead me towards? If these things are important, what kind of discipline would allow them space?

It would have to be some sort of psychology of the between, speaking between us, of conversation. Such a discipline would not rule out, but would stand in contradistinction to, a formal experimental psychology of static relationships.

What might this discipline of intimate concern with speaking the between attend to? What *aims* would it have?

The basic question would, I think, be something like: 'What are you up to? What am I up to? What are we up to at this moment in meeting?'

More generally it would ask 'What is going on?' It would not be concerned with measuring movements or isolated behaviour, but rather with what is going on in the invisible, moving, world between us.

At a different level, the question might be: 'What is involved for us in coming to know what is going on?' What pains might we have to suffer, what passions endure, what patience develop? What ways of conjuring into being what is invisible might we require?

This is a very different *project* from that which empirical science pursues. It would not replace such a science, but might merit a place of its own, to cast its influence around psychological science as we know it. This alternative project would not give primary attention to the familiar issues of prediction and control, nor hope especially to uncover 'laws of nature'.

A conversational psychology of this kind might be somewhat equivalent to conversational French, as distinct from a formal study of the French language. As many people who studied French at school know, it is possible to be taught the subject and still be almost unable to utter a word in a real life situation. It may be that many people who study psychology are in something of the same predicament as regards understanding people. A conversational psychology would be active and on the move, there and then concerned with what we can make of the living relationship between us now ... and now ... and now ... or whenever it mattered. It would be a meeting place of many disciplines where we would try to find ways of giving voice to the many moments in which a particular passionate concern for what's there now may be found to speak a remarkably general theme, not by reaching for generality, but by reaching for precise particularity, again and again.

It would have to do with *meaning* and *intention*, with conduct, with what is going on between us. It would not be focally concerned with facts and explanations. It would deal in a world of fictions, with making up some way of speaking or expressing what is going on now. Such fictions would be more basic than 'made up' facts. A conversational psychology would recognize that fictions, in the realm of the human, are profoundly more important than facts. Fictions shape and ground all our searching for facts, and mostly we fail to attend to the fictional structure.

What else might this conversational psychology, this psychology of the between, be about? It would be essentially concerned with the issue of *good faith* and *bad faith*, and the many colours of faith in between. It asks the disconcerting question: 'What are you up to?' Are you up to what you claim to be up to, or are you in various, subtle forms of bad faith claiming to be up to something and doing something quite different? We are here in the province of the secret and furtive. It is a dangerous place, difficult to approach, fiercely to be resisted. To seek to live or work here is not a recipe for popularity or the easy life.

The realm of the poetic, I'm therefore suggesting, is crucial for any beginning understanding of human experiencing. Unless a psychology of psychotherapy attends to imagination and imaginative participation, we will endlessly miss the point and belittle what we are trying to pin down. The poetic imagination creates our world and does not just describe it. If it is stunted, we are too. I believe, and want to assert, that psychotherapy, and a psychology of psychotherapy, can survive and even flourish without any of the paraphernalia of current empirical science, whereas, without an imaginative concern for a poetics of experiencing it would be impossible or worthless! A properly sensitive psychology of psychotherapy has been stunted in its tentative development by our massive emphasis on scientific method. It has, I think, been crushed by method, and an insistence on the prosaic and external.

Thursday 25 June 1981

I will end this introduction to the idea of a poetics of experience within a conversational psychology by recalling another moment, a few years ago. I am sitting on a plane at Heathrow Airport, waiting for take off.

It has been a time of particular sadness, but I'm going to America to lecture for three weeks.

Forty hours of lectures lie ahead in a course that will have the same group of very bright, postgraduate students in the class throughout. I have not been able to prepare well — just haven't been able to 'get into' it at all.

It takes seven hours to fly to Pittsburgh. I hope that will be enough!

I am hard and frightened. Outside it. A long way off.

I have to reach somewhere different, 'further in' perhaps.

And once again I try to feel my way towards a starting place, somewhere different from the cold, hard place I've so far struggled in.

Without interruption, speaking from somewhere, words of a different kind begin to flow

You must go there
with tenderness
With the shape and texture
of there
Not with the hard certainties
of here
Almost always
I struggle to reach
the lush green pastures
while sticking to the dry
beaten roads
of the familiar desert

Alone
Isolated
You cannot go there
Somehow within yourself
you have to be met

Tenderness
is the womb
of new being

Tenderness
is like mist
rising from the river
everywhere
rising from the water
and the land
so that all familiar things
are sustained in newness

Tenderness
is diffused
all around
not sharply focussed
hardened for the kill

Chapter seven

Preaching what we practise

We are able to do much more than we can explain and in every action we undertake we are likely to be engaged in ways we do not easily recognize. It is because of this pervasive and many-layered entanglement in our ongoing circumstances that we need poetic imagination. Through a poetic approach to our experience we can conjure up telling images to give us richer clues concerning who and where we are.

In any situation of personal threat it is so very easy to retreat from the tentative, growing edges of what you want to try to put into words. We often fear that we will make fools of ourselves, that we will expose our own hidden sensitivities, that we will be laughed at or misunderstood. It is so much easier to take refuge in clearer, harder, more familiar, conventional, and well formulated assertions. These may not really say what we sense but will be safer. They will make us more invisible and more easily acceptable.

Any psychological approach which seriously tries to speak into recognizable form something more of what we are engaged in doing (more than the local social conventions allow) will have to attend carefully to this problem of how we can speak more fully of what we know but do not know we know. It is this issue that I want now to take further, having spoken of many relevant issues arising in psychotherapeutic practice.

The problematic nature of saying what we do

This title indicates in different terms what I'm concerned with here. It is a topic which seems simple but is, I think, deceptively difficult.

In a sense, there is no problem at all. Every day, and on many occasions, we say something of what we or someone else is doing, what we or they are up to, what we are involved in. We quite readily give accounts to each other of what we are on about.

This, however, is mostly held firmly within conventions of politeness and appropriateness so that we are not expected to put any special effort into giving a 'good account'. Rather are we expected to say something that is relatively inconspicuous and we may get quite upset about people who insist on really trying to *tell* us, when we ask them how they are. We expect the answer 'Fine!' or something equally conventional.

In some circumstances, though, it becomes much more important to try to go beyond the conventions of polite blindness (e.g. when we are confused and need to straighten things out for ourselves, or in psychotherapy). It is at this point that we often run into difficulties.

Clinical psychologists, I think, have generally tried to solve this problem by side-stepping it. As stressed in the first chapter, they have adopted the policy of announcing to themselves and others that theirs is an *applied science*, concerned with carrying across theories, procedures, and conclusions from general and experimental psychology to *apply* in the clinical situation. They thus claim that their essential focus is on the theories, methods, and results which have been tested by the procedures that are warranted by science. The clinician's contribution is then to find ways of fitting or 'selling' these pre-packed products in appropriate contexts. The focus of attention is on the already prepared methods and findings, and the clinician's duty is to use products of scientifically proven worth.

This has in many respects been an imaginative and socially successful undertaking and it will probably continue to develop as such. I want to argue that it is still not good enough!

The approach of focussing on application is, I think, essentially limiting, blinding, distorting, self-deceiving, belittling to our subject matter, damaging to ourselves (to our own resources, skills, competences, sensibilities), and bad science. It encourages us to avoid crucial issues, and allows an arrogant myopia, a professionally sanctioned tunnel vision, in that we attend primarily to pre-packed procedures and solutions, and little (if at all) to the immediate subject matter, the person in the clinical situation with us.

I want to encourage exploration of an alternative view in which the psychologist's primary responsibility is to give attention to *the person in the context of their life situation and the clinician's involvement with them.*

Unless we attend with all our capacities to the whole situation in which the 'problem' has its existence in the life of particular people (being explored in relation to other particular people, the clinicians involved), we are failing to allow ourselves to be seriously attentive to the proper subject matter of our discipline, people's active relations with their circumstances, including ourselves.

Over the years, I've tried to give primary attention to what my clients have been trying to tell me of what they are involved in doing or failing to do. In telling some of the things they have taught me, I don't suppose that others would have drawn the same conclusions, but I do claim the particular relevance of these matters in at least my experience.

Within the psychotherapeutic situation, people so often have to struggle with problems of saying what they are involved in, what they are up to.

Very often the first statements are in conventional forms that are allowed to them by the culture which sustains and deprives them, and which sustains and deprives the professionals to whom they come. To move beyond these initial forms brings difficulties if we undertake the professional responsibility of attending as fully and sensitively as we can, rather than the lesser obligation of attending only to what we ourselves are prepared beforehand to recognize as answers and as acceptable forms of questioning.

In the approach I try to adopt, clinicians are at the cutting edge of *inquiry*, not the blunt afterthought of *application*.

Lessons from helping people to say what they are involved in doing

In the psychotherapeutic situation, people often have to struggle to give adequate accounts of what they are involved within in their lives as they painfully and confusingly experience them. Learning even a little from these struggles is not done by sitting blankly and observing. It has to be an active relationship of to and fro in which you bring your own experience (your ways of experiencing and not experiencing), created from your own life in general, and as it has been involved with many clients. What follows are some ways of seeing and saying that have clinically stood the test of repeated use for me.

A different person with different sensibilities and blindness, courage and cowardice, concerns they need to probe and concerns they need to avoid, would create something different and would give a different account. I hope only that something of what I say will strike chords of recognition with some others who have the experience to judge and know, and not everyone may be in that position.

In some important sense 'man is the measure of all things'. All that we know of the world is only possible through the capacities of human understanding, and so all our explanations of every conceivable thing speak of our human capacities, of something of us, as well as of whatever else.

In earlier chapters I've already given some impressions of my psychotherapeutic approach. In trying to attend to people as openly and complexly as I can, it has been necessary to become more fluent in *the use of metaphor*. Metaphor seems to be a way of groping towards new understanding. It is a human act of feeling towards and giving shape and understandability to that which is sensed but not yet known in this particular form.

If you are to be attentive to the many meanings in what a person may be seeking to say, or express in their actions, you need to have many potential nets in which to catch the darting fishes of intention, the lurking predators of threat, the feeding shoals of untapped possibility. If you are to be as fully and variably attentive as you can, you need to allow a person access to a diversity of momentary models, rather than lean back on the meagre measures left by Occam's Razor. We need to be generous and multiple rather than meagre and minimal in the metaphors we use and offer.

So much that we are is unformed or only partially formed. So many patients come inarticulate and untutored in the possibilities of giving shape to their cramped feelings. In helping people to find a voice, it seems necessary to *encourage them to play*, to entertain possibilities, to allow themselves the luxury of foolishness in relation to the reality they may always have felt they had no option but to endure.

It seems so often necessary to help people to detach themselves a little from the grim insistence of the cultural imperatives they live amongst (which they have had to take as real, the way things are, the enduring reality they know), and encourage them to pretend, *to act as if* — perhaps it feels as if you are being crushed by a heavy weight — or as if you could break like a delicate glass — At last a way of make-believe can allow someone to say how it really feels, however foolish it would seem at home to be so fanciful.

It can become possible to begin seriously and lightly to attend a little to what a person *feels*, to what they are being touched or troubled by, terrified or excited by in the invisible darkness of their particular life. Previously it may only have been possible for them to speak crudely in physical-sounding terms like 'upset stomach', 'pains in the chest', or 'funny feelings in the head'.

With access to metaphor and play, and permission to value what may otherwise be crushed into a banal rejection of meaning, a person can begin to find a voice to give shape and colour, pattern and coherence to what they feel but have never before been able to say.

As people find some way through which something of what they are engaged in can be given particular form, they find that only the rough can be approached roughly, only the loud can be spoken in a loud way. You cannot have access to what is timid and still frail by seeking to approach it in the garb and style of the braggart or the hard-edged bully. If you would know what is soft in you, you must go there softly. If you would touch and sense some spot of tenderness, you must take on yourself the shape and manner of tenderness. *Everything that is different needs its own style.* No common style will do.

Even more, it is only when you take the unusual step of *dwelling right within* the shape and texture of a sensed possibility that you can speak within the real experience rather than speak about the outside of things. Only in this way are you there and then changed in the very act of speaking rather than, as usual, using words as signs and signals of what is not yet really understood. I am speaking here, as in previous and later chapters, of indwelling and passion rather than observation and externality.

One of the most striking things about people (for me) is that they/we *speak with many voices,* many selves. We are not units, single, coherent, all of a piece. As I hope will be illustrated in the *personal story* of Part 2, we are multiple and often contradictory. When a person speaks I have to listen, to begin to sense which of many voices this is. They move in and out with such rapidity sometimes to create the impression of a single self. One of the most clarifying experiences for a person can be when they are able to undertake some means of access to the many different parts they play, the community of selves that they jostlingly live through. To begin to be able to discriminate, sense, see, touch, and minutely describe many of the different selves whose voices speak under their common name, can be especially liberating.

Finally here, part of what makes it so very difficult to say what we are doing, what we are involved within, is the fact that we are all nourished by *the local culture of our family and the wider culture of our society, time, and place.* Where do *we* begin and where does *it* end? What is me and what is mother, family, nation? What should I be responsible for and what need I scarcely feel? (More will be said of this in the final chapter of Part 3.)

Mostly the questions are not so clear and we are spoken by, shaped by, limited and constrained by, our surrounding world. It breathes shape into our lives and gives us the tools with which to speak. It blinds us too to what it does not allow, does not encourage, does not admire.

Questioning our questions

So it seems that people often need a great deal of help to work out ways of saying and knowing what they are involved in. Their culture has not provided them with these means, and our professional culture is equally unhelpful, positively restrictive.

Let us now look more carefully at the questions raised in Chapter 6 when a poetic and conversational approach to psychological understanding was being introduced. 'What are we up to?' 'What are we involved in doing?' 'What am I up to?' There is some suspicion here that I'm 'up to' something other than I'm apparently doing. There is the suggestion that my right hand may not know what my left hand is doing. Or it may be that I've lost sight of, or have never had clear sight of, what I'm doing any of my particular activities for.

What would count as more or less adequate answers to questions like these?

They would, I think, be statements that undeceived me to some extent, or which clarified my goals or my tactics, routes or strategy. I would be illuminated to some degree, enlightened (if we use the usual metaphors of light and sight). They would have to be answers that carried some conviction for me, or for others involved with me. We are here in the realm of rhetoric, of culpability, responsibility, moral or other kinds of scrutiny, being 'shown up', 'flushed out in the open' — but also being helped out of some trapping confusion, led to see some purpose in what had seemed meaningless, or towards some different end. It would not just be conviction, but some level of 'ah ha' experience, whereby I 'saw through' or 'beyond' my previously blinkered awareness. It is this kind of experience with which psychology in an 'intermediary' mode (Chapter 4) is concerned.

A satisfactory answer could, however, come in many forms and at many different levels. There is no necessity for there to be a single correct answer. It may also be that someone else will recognize some truth in an answer to the question which I am not yet able to accept.

Since illumination at many different levels and from many different angles is possible, some are likely to be more within the range of my acceptance and recognition than others, at this point in time. So it is possible for me to be unable to recognize the penetrating nature of some answer till I have moved on and come back to it at some later point when it might then make sense to me.

A good answer to the question, 'What am I up to?' would have to add up. That is to say, it would have to incorporate a number of activities or happenings that previously had not made sense to me, or had been diminished in significance, seen as exceptions or otherwise relegated to little or no importance. It is in this way that the answer is likely to be similar in its claims to adequacy to other scientific answers. It will have greater coherence, make a more satisfying and complete use of the evidence or events, have greater explanatory power, lead to new possibilities of understanding and action that are sensed as relevant and peculiarly apposite in relation to the person in question. There surely has to be a certain sense of 'rightness'. Some sense of being landed with something that is 'obvious' now that it has been spoken or thought. All this may also be accompanied by excitement or uneasiness, perhaps even massive guilt (a loss of the self you have known).

There is more. The answer has to speak to the person involved. He or she has to be touched and moved, changed. It is not enough that the person be intellectually willing to say a superficial 'Yes'. The acknowledgement has to be a response of being, of scales falling from eyes, a turning around even.

And what will it demand of us if we seek to come to know and say what is going on, what we or someone else is doing, what we or they are up to or involved within?

We will need to be able to stand back and yet be intimately involved. What we are seeking to know may be, but cannot wholly be, spoken directly to us. And however well we may be able to 'tell it like it is', there will always be other views, other ways to stack up the evidence.

We will have to be able to listen to what is being said directly and what is being hinted at more or less clearly in manner, action, 'feel', outcomes. It is like interpreting an obscure text, except that it is considerably more difficult in that there is no initial agreement as to what constitutes the text.

We have to invent ways by which others may themselves come to speak something of and from the world of their intentions, even when these are partly hidden from their ordinary awareness and presentation. We will have to be scrupulously and imaginatively attentive to the essence of the situation, rather than primarily concerned with those aspects that are the focus of ordinary attention. We will have to be dedicated to, given over to, passionately available to, whatever is going on, but in some ways that allow the possibility of 'speaking the full word' in whatever form of accurately moving expression is needed.

In asking what we are up to or are involved in, we are therefore asking a radically different kind of question from that which is most publicly valued at present in clinical psychology and many other related disciplines. A radically different question implies a *new world*. It requires new eyes and new ears, tuned to different frequencies and different triggers, different patterns of movement and shade.

A question already assumes so much. It assumes a topic, something worth focussing on, a way of turning towards this focus, a type of approach coming from some prior judgement as to the kind of realm this is that allows this sort of approach rather than another. Our questions speak of our worlds. Our worlds already enclose us before we can ask questions or seek answers within them. All the questions we ask are embedded in worlds, though we often throw up questions and cannot answer them within the worlds of answering that we so far know or value. Questions are celebrations of particular worlds.

Our present scientific, psychological world is to do with impersonal explanations of causes and effects, things, divisions, comparisons. Its essential features are to do with measurement, probability, causality. In this world we ask typical questions to do with effectiveness and comparison. How many? How often? How big? How much more or less than?

In the alternative realm that I'm outlining here, it seems that we assume a world of ongoing, moving, multiple activity, striving for ends, hidden, enmeshed, within which we are composed, nourished, confused, tied. Its natural questions, speaking of this world, are What is going on? What are we up to? What sorts of projects are we involved within? It requires that we attend, not so much to counting and comparison, number, measurement, or analytic distinctions, but to motion, conjuring up or evoking creative descriptions of sensed patterns of intention.

What we are seeking is clearer vision or seeing through appearances, a different level of understanding or a different kind of common sense, clarification of possible intentions which are often hidden intentions.

Questioning our answers

When we ask seriously for some account of what we are doing, what we are engaged within, we are not just raising a different kind of question from those that are customary in psychology, and especially in applied psychology. We may also go on to question the kinds of answers we commonly accept or that are commonly allowed within the dominating constraints of our scientific culture.

What are we up to in what and how we ask, in what and how we answer? What are we involved within that shapes our common questions and dominates the answers that are taken to be of value.

Clinical psychology (and psychology generally) has mostly been blind to the cultural web which shapes our questions and constrains what answers we are allowed to give. We are still largely prisoners (often by inheritance rather than by individual choice) of the cultural web within which our values and aspirations are given their shape. We are used by the metaphors of our culture more often than we see something of what we are engaged within as individuals, scientists, professional practitioners, or clients.

A concern with asking what we are up to and what we are involved within could lead us to question the personal and professional answers we often give. A conversational psychology would certainly take steps towards locating itself in our historical and cultural context. We might thereby begin to sense and spell out something of what shapes us when we thought we were free, and dominates not only the questions we ask and the answers we accept, but the manner and style through which we ask and answer. As it is we exclude the possibility of other kinds of questioning, other kinds of answering that require different forms of gentleness and rigour.

We inhabit a world that makes powerful demands on everything we do and think and feel (and do not do or think or feel). Unless we identify and know something of this world we will not understand enough of what we are up to, trapped by, shaped and guided by. It is so easy to get a new idea and destroy it by the old methods of approach that change and bend it.

If we have strong cultural rules against delicate saying, or against certain possibilities of trying to say, or against the worth of certain sorts of speaking, then we shut off these areas from many who might speak a different word. They may then have no way of saying what they are doing or what they are involved within. We need to work at finding ways of allowing people possibilities for accounting for themselves or we shrink and distort our subject matter and our science.

Thus I am led to saying that a psychology which tells of what we are engaged in doing is and should be a *cultural discipline* and not just a neighbour of the biological and social sciences. Whatever else it seeks to be, it should also be an adventure in the personal and cultural life of our times. It should be radically questioning, offering new eyes. All our psychology is necessarily steeped in our culture and it is part of our task to find ways to question it and say something of all our involvement therein.

It is not, however, a deceiving undercover psychology that I seek, but a psychology of personal quest within the living context of our place and times. Therein we may enrich our practice through listening with compassionate attention and speak with vibrancy of what we find through our imaginative participation in what we share. It is not an applied science that I seek but a psychology of practical caring, of informed compassion. An informed and compassionate participation in a venture that we share with those who seek our help.

Part two

A personal story

Between thee and me

Jane Blackburn
In Remembrance of Thee

Setting the scene

This is a slice of a particular life. These 'short lines' were not written initially for anyone to read, but were scribbled in my own struggle to know and care. There are pieces of different kinds here which I would not wish to be too easily classified. These are not polished productions but more immediate attempts to speak from within the world of my own concerns.

This is a small piece of personal history from nine years of ordinary change. It moves from an ending and a beginning in 1972, through many others, to another more painful ending and beginning in 1981.

The first was on returning to London after a liberating year in Holland. Going back to work there felt like re-entering a prison.

The last was on returning to Scotland (where I had gone to live in 1975), after a month in America, to face a life without Jane, to whom this Part is dedicated.

In this snippet of history many dates are given. An important one is not. On 28 March 1981 Jane died, tragically (because she was so young and touched so many lives with painful joy) and mercifully (because through all the warm abundance that she lived and shared she suffered many years of illness, too much hurt to bear). So much of what is written here breathes and whispers and speaks of her, the moments of meeting between she and me.

The whole period has been a time of searching, struggle, happiness, and pain. It has been a time of reaching for renewed hope. Moving from London to Scotland. A marriage broken. The often cruel, and sometimes creative, testing of family ties. Moments of joy, turnings to the sun. The beginning struggle to find another way alone.

This is a tiny part of a human story, a searching to say something of what is so often not said. Mostly we put on public faces shaped to our particular profession, place, and time. Even to ourselves we often speak but a public tongue, rather than more personally, between thee and me.

So often too, we speak and insist on hearing only a prosaic style. Seldom do we suppose we could lift the stones which gravel over the familiar back yard of our ordinary lives to hear the songs within. In this way we make ourselves smaller than we are and share a more barren world.

All but an early few of the bits of writing collected here were produced at particular times, all of a piece, just as they are, almost without a pause. They were not intended as 'poems' but as more spontaneous reachings towards some hints of personal meaning. It was almost by chance that I found that a few of these forgotten moments could be plucked out to form a broken mosaic pattern, some struggles in time, struggles of mine, which may speak to some of struggles in you.

This is a piece of human experience, the substance of psychology. What is written here may be embarrassingly irrelevant to those who define psychology as the science of behaviour. But then, much of psychology is distant from the intimacies of human experience, the secret world between. Psychologists are mostly taught to stay well away, on the outer track, inland, far from the ambiguous sea.

So much that people yearn for cannot be spoken of in the respectable public rooms of modern, scientific psychology. So much of who we are must be left outside, far from home.

By birth and upbringing I am a Scot, steeped in a theology of ultimate concern that is almost always stunted by immediate respectability. Mostly none of this can be spoken of in the psychological world without apology or shame.

Both the theology that I grew up in and the science that I came to live seemed to share one simple thing. Both are afraid of who you are. Both lead you quickly from whoever you may begin to find you are to the way things have to be, the often unbending will of God or the often equally brutal strictures of the scientific creed. In spite of this the aspirations of the religious life and the scientific way are both important to me, not as they often are, but how it may yet be.

Whatever this is or is not, it seeks at least to be the sound of a human voice in the midst of complexity and competing ways to see. What is written here may prove difficult to classify as fish or fowl. Confession, autobiography, story-telling, psychology, philosophy even, all might bear some thought. None of these names will matter much.

I hope only that something of what is said is heard as a whisper, as a song, between me and thee.

How many?

How many
would you say
unleash their lives
and let them play
How many lead
their lives in chains
Circus tigers
manly maimed

How few unstop
the holes of fright
to let the fountains
splash delight
Or tumbling in
the arms of fear
caress each
circumstance
explore
each tear

I am the many
not the few
I of old
forever new
Clutch
the pale borders
of my day
while the globe
of my life
spins
down and away

30.12.72

Flecks of life

Flecks
of life
scuttle
from the darkness
of my room

Birds
of poise
wheel black
against
my winter sky

Sparks
of despair
consume
the labour
of my spidery hopes

Flowers
of hate
enrich
my stony soil

20.1.73

My life

My life it lives
in a shack by a stream
far from the passing road
it lives alone
it could scream and scream
and no one would find its abode

The crowds pass by
they meet and smile
their confidence combines
to calm their journeys
mile by mile
though their movement still confines

Yesterday I joined their throng
I became a traveller too
my voice repaid them
song for song
hoping that I could be you

The crowds pass on
they turn and bend
and I alone with you
whisper a hope to a friend
a friend whom I know to be untrue

We live together
but love apart
we cling to the end of our fears
but what a way to start
to start
and continue down the years

Someday I may
return to my life
and sit alone in the sun
that will not be the end of strife
but my life and death
will be one

20.2.73

My garden

My garden looks resigned
to waiting
outside
cross-legged
impassive

Digging in
brewing up
bringing out again
its troubador show
of death defying
delicacy
repeated every year

I remain indoors
safe
privileged you might say
to watch from the prison
of my city suit
the growth which is a part of me
turn tinker, vagabond, mystic
free

17.3.73

Why should I shuffle?

Why should I shuffle, crawl and sidle up to life
When anyone can dance, dance, dance, yes dance and sing
Can slip the noose and skip, leap, run and scamper on the hill
Roll, tumble, frolic, grin from ear to ear

So I am alone, deserted even by myself!
What then? Am I to crumble, pine, sulk, sink upon the ground?
Am I to grovel, hide my face in shame, slink homewards sad beneath the
    wall?
Or stand resplendent, glorying in the winter air?

Surely it must be life. It must, must, must be love and praise
As flowers which splash their glories in the air
And blossom even in the darkest days are lavish with a joy that cannot, will
    not, be contained
And so it should be, must be, will be now for me ..... Please God it can be
    so!
                                                                    9.3.75

Tears come

Tears come
Well over me
Are cut off at the source
Die
Again tears
Silent unreached anguish and relief
Eliminated

A scream
Muffled
Muttered only
As if from the depths
Trickles and stops
As if I stood thunderstruck with awe
Awful awareness before and within
Part of the enormity of all
Someone still unclothed
Horribly open
Vulnerable to a terrible and pathetic degree

92

Open and terrified of the world
Muffled and protected
by layers of avoidance and fear of pain
Respectability
Cloak upon cloak of pretence

But in me
is a screaming awestruck fragment
Aware
Open
Wild
Screaming *with* it all
(Not against but amongst and with and through and in)

This fragment of clear pain
pure light
is all that my life is for
It is (I am) inarticulate
Uncivilized
Unsociable
Alone and yet with everything
It has no voice but any I can offer
No hands but mine

There are many fragments about
Others have more obvious fragments
More powerful
More terrible
Many are lost and ignored almost completely
Some crush all happiness
Kill all joy
Overwhelm
Destroy!

It is when I lose touch with this fragment
This spark
This centre of life
When it becomes impossible to believe in
When the blankets and cloak
do cover it over
that I am nothing but fear and despair
Empty and lost
Cold and alone
But there is depth
in this fragment
this scream in the endless void

To give voice to this fragment in pain
To speak from this intensity of smothered awfulness
This is clearly a hopeless task
Who can understand
Who can sympathise
All else is hollow

There are no words there
Only pain
Though not the pain of being hurt
but of living
which is intensity unmitigated by pretence

Perhaps everyone
has a fragment of pure fire
The bush that burns
Screams
but is not consumed
The eternal flame   24.10.76

Meeting

It is without compulsion and easy
to walk in the light
There is no resistance
and spring
life in the air
Nothing needs explaining
in the form of
justifying
Meaning flows between us
only lightly clad in words
summer dresses
and see-through blouses
easily slipped on
and easy to discard
showing the
lithesome body
of our being together
sensuous and light
alive and moving
ready to dance   15.8.77

Gentleness

Gentleness
Delicacy
Lightness
Air
Sensuous frolic
Without achievements or purpose
other than beauty in being

Gentleness cannot push itself forward
Cannot insist on its rights
Cannot assert itself against attack and harshness
Cannot live in the midst of anger or strife

For gentleness to inhabit the world
there needs to be space free from menace
The making of space for living seems vital
If there is no space between people
there cannot be gentleness
It is so easily crushed and chased away

Gentleness will not walk in the open
unless it is possible to survive
Gentleness moves where there are no
fiercely opposing forces
Where there is conflict it disappears

Without safety or daring or trust
it is not possible for me to go into the open
unless the boundaries of my space are well guarded
and the wanderer well loved
Even the leopard and the panther are easily frightened
and become vicious
But they also play and frolic and run and kill
with grace and terror   8.10.77

A silent ache

A silent ache
at the doorway of whatever being
I am and have
Uttering no sound
Without form
pervasive
It becomes the ground of my life
invisible
unheard
Is it an awful fear unfaced
A persistent failure
Or is it more basic still
The awful screaming centre
where all is clamorously silent

I must stand alone in my own space
No one can join me there
That empty space is the gift of my life
I can scrabble round the borders
clinging to the edges in terror
turning my back on the ground
which is my being
my gift
my privilege and responsibility in the world
Or I can accept my place
and strive to move more freely within it
knowing and owning and feeling and receiving it as mine
A gift of emptiness from which all fullness flows   8.10.77

Search

I don't think lives should be searches
but mine seems to be so
Is so
My searching is wordless
My search is not even mine
I am inhabited by searching
Life is searching for itself in me
Life —

the heart of whatever is to be —
is searching in me for herself
I may give myself over
to making it possible for her
to become something more through me
I am God in the making
We are on a journey
and live in a painfully
growing and decaying multiplicity of living
We will not find God
or arrive
Our time of glory is now
where we may join in becoming
what may yet in the furthest reaches
and in the depths of each very moment
be what life and death may yet be

I am gifted with a longing
for what is to be
Already in me is a sense
wordless
buried
hidden
distant
shadow of a sense
of what is in the final day
to be
When time becomes space
Where the endless becomes
the ever present

I have a whisper
of the final solution
and a fragment in me which longs
for what is to come
Reaching into what is to be
Standing and walking in the fire
in the light
For stretching, even now, towards
the heart of what is and is yet to be
The future is already
The past is waiting to be made

The separation of God and man
is not to be
The sense of separateness is as when
something in us we fear is divided off
to frighten us as from somewhere else
What we fear is God
What we long for is already what we are
but fear in our quivering beginnings of awareness

So we exclude the larger part
and call it God
Lord
Master
when all the time we are one
indivisible
We are each
through and through
being in the making
We are becoming
what God may yet be

The search for the source
the river of time which flows towards us
from the ultimate day
carries with it scents and seeds
of what awaits us
and these
even now
can grow
to create a hint
of what we move towards   30.10.77

Between

Between us
we create
our own heavens
and our own hells
Between us
we allow
the air to dance
and the space to move

Between us
we stifle each other
with the pressures
and demands
of our own fears
Between us
we allow
some things to be
and others not to be
We give freedoms
and take them away
Even asserting
they never were
could ever be

10.12.77

Whatever anyone thinks

Whatever anyone else thinks
my life is my experiment
my journey
my encounter with eternity
Will I dare to live now
in the eye of eternity
or only sidle along in the eye
of past and present expectations of others
who know or care nothing of who I am

There isn't anyone
to support
or give significance
to what I choose to do
If I do nothing
it won't ripple any ponds
If I work my guts out
so also in that
no leaf will stir

So I am free to be
who I sense and feel
to suffer the breaking of my seeds
and bear the agonies of my growth
All of which will be thanked
only by withering and dying

All to cast my seeds
into the winds of time
In me
the seeds of my kind
Not to take over the earth
but to ensure the continuance
of a certain strain of being

There is no one
to thank me
No one
for me to please
No debts
to be paid
No threats
to be obeyed   11.12.77

To be available

To be available
to all and sundry
To suffer the coming
and being of things
is so painful
leaving exposed
unprotected
the soft underbelly
of my life
It is being hurtable
so easily destroyed
to scream inwardly in pain
and yet to be!
It is to learn to be with pain
as a familiar companion
a fierce companion
ruthless
determined
beyond argument
Pain is a master
in relation to us as pupils
A master to us
as seekers for truth
and yet we are
both master and pupil

Who is pain to me?
I am afraid of pain
Pain is both
male and female
strong and hurtful
subtle and deceptive
Pain is anguish
as well as beauty
Pain is the reality of the world
Pain is the inner scream of the universe
All is pain
growth is pain
dying is pain

Or is it pain
only if you resist it
if you fight it
if you try to separate yourself from it
so that it is something which attacks
and threatens your very existence

Pain is the coinage of the world
Through pain we are made aware
of our existence
Everything is blunted and sharpened
overwhelmed and
burnt to the core

I fear pain and run from it
at all costs
I will suffer persistent
self-created pains
rather than meet naked
the pains of being
there now
in touch with an
unknown pain
pain beyond my control

Pain in my control
is infinitely preferred
though always belittling
It creates a false world
Creates an illusion of seriousness
an air of tragedy
which is shallow and deceitful

Pain hurts
I am so easily destroyed
I cringe and crawl and hide
without much dignity
I try to joke
Pain is awful
Pain tests you
with unfair tests
There is nothing fair
about so many pains
Pain is!
and is not up for discussion
Grow or die!
Break or make!

Pain is the servant of courage
of big-heartedness
sent out to prepare us
for the coming of his master
so that those who are met
can begin to fit themselves
for courage
who will come to them
if they welcome her

Courage is the mother of love
and love is the sister of pain
Love suffers long and is kind
Courage is the mother of love
So often I fail to love
through cowardice
and fear of pain
Courage is the mother of love
Courage undertakes acts of pain
to allow love to be
and become
Without courage
the courage to meet pain
and be with it
love so often dies
is killed
pushed out
Courage is the mother of love

19.12.77

Does the universe?

Does the universe struggle
to meet itself in me
as in everyone
in different ways
When the universe 'peoples'
it seems to be meeting and conversing

Each of us is both in the conversation
of the universe
of the gods
and each of us is a conversation
or a phrase in the multiple conversations
of how things are in relation to each other
To settle for the known talking with the known
or even with the not known
seems irrelevant
hopeless

I am a fragment of reality
struggling to know itself
A talking partner fiercely thrown
into the world to answer back
and listen
and act into some form
the longing of what is in
the possibility of being   24.12.77

I am on a journey

I am on a journey
am a go-between
I shuttle back and forth
between this ordinary place
and that other country
which is this world
seen through another world
already in this world

The other world is already here
It is not somewhere else
In this other world
men and women, boys and girls
will learn to stand
so that they can
flow and move and change
Not change because it is demanded
but flow into
and out of
and around
without fear
to be with
those they meet —
To change is to be present to

I am an old man
weary from travelling
Without status
or claims of any kind
in any world
Yet I am a citizen
of that other country
He is what he is
poor
thin
brown
strange to the ways
of this world

I am a fanatic
fierce
passionate
beyond reason
prostrate with love
burning
committed
strong beyond my own strength

I am a child and a prophet
Not from merit
but by grace

I am a citizen
of that other country
that other world
which is this world transformed
reached into
abandoned

What I know
I know by being a citizen
not by thought or explanation
I know because I live
in and from that other country
where there is no force
but power lives in us
Where each has a space
Where all men are free

My whole task is to show people
to lead them to
that other country
which is already here
and yet is far from here
To go there is difficult
for any who insist on bringing
possessions
roles
escape routes
insurance policies
You cannot go there
with your belongings
Only *you* can go
It is a place of nakedness
where we are again
as little children
perhaps

The other country
is always with us
We are already here
but can neither see
nor hear
nor smell
nor taste
nor touch it

That other country
is the place of
our deepest desires
We can go there
as we find our way into
that in ourselves
which roots itself
In the furthest reaches
of our personal being in the world

Into our very
rootedness
our roots
in the darkness of the earth
without light and warmth
So that we may live
in our branches and flowers and leaves

We have wandered off
from that homeland
to other places
and suffer
and die there
And in desperation
try to find our way home
The joy of the prodigal returning
was surely that
against all odds
he could still find
his way home   20.2.78

In the main channel

It is somehow as if you could stand
in the main channel through which
the water of your being in life
flowed
Or you could stand somewhere else
somewhere distant and controlled
where you could turn a tap on and off
at will

and get a little trickle of life
Or somewhere even where you live
almost by hearsay
a long way from water
well inland

I have only been able to stand
in the main channel of my being
a few times
and yet when I do
I experience life most fully
frighteningly and deeply
But it is feelingful
and I am easily swept off
scamper off
scramble off
elsewhere
and then hide
and find it difficult
to find myself
to encourage myself
to go back

All my life is an escape
an avoidance of standing
in the main channel
You feel too much there
both pleasure and pain
The extent of the feeling
is more distressing than
which of these it be.
It is fear of feeling
fear of being touched
fear of being held
and gripped and tugged
and interfered with by
strange hands in the dark
Fear of being at the
meeting point of
self and world
fear of being moved   26.2.78

My place

My place is in the midst
of my fears
in the gossamer fragility
of my feelings of living
the awful sensitivity
to pain and joy

My place is where I am
most afraid to go and be
My place is where only love
can dissolve that fear

My place is in the awful
vulnerability
of actually daring
brazenly daring
to body forth —
and so tempt damage
destruction and
defacement —
a most individual
fragile beauty
which is not mine
as an individual
achievement
Rather it is what
is given into
my care

Do I shield it
round
or do I find
a way to bring it
to the eyes of others

It is not that I have
access through me
to how things really are
But rather that I am
how things really are
I am reality
I am what is possible
in life
what life is
just as you are

The beauty and ugliness
we touch and
body forth is
in itself the
beauty and ugliness
of life
To be what you are
is to be life
to be what is
It is not to show
something behind
what appears

My place is in
the very depths
of my fears
In the awful
fragile beauty
of the way things are
for me   5.3.78

Between thee and me

Between thee and me
it frightens me to acknowledge it
there is a pact till death
I'd rather run
or hide
and certainly
pretend it were not so
And yet it is
A bond given not taken
only gently held
in open hands   13.3.78

109

I have a dream

I have a dream
that each man
and each woman
come to inhabit
their deepest fears
and most dreaded pains
and through meeting the reflection
of those fears and that pain
in the love of another
come courageously
and with beauty
to know more fully
what it is
to be human
and alive
now
in the context of
these times
and this
place

My dream
is to take up
the fallen baton
of an age of faith
and carry it on
in new ways
into an age of doubt

My dream is to run
from the past
into the future
carrying with me
tightly wrapped
the tattered garments
of what was
so that they
can be woven
into what
may yet be

22.3.78

A go-between

I am not a forerunner
but a go-between
a link-man
a carrier across
from one period to another

This means I am
both radical and
conservative
A carrier of the religious
into the secular life
A carrier of ultimate concerns
into the area of immediate concerns
A carrier of good news
into a community where only bad news
is newsworthy

My task is not to carry across
one old bit of culture
to weave through
some new bit
both somehow separate from me
but by inhabiting
both worlds in myself
to speak from where I am
to where I am

24.3.78

No academic solution

No academic solution
is satisfactory
It has to be
a lived posture

That's why
I can't get away
with saying one thing
and doing another
or with preaching
and not practising

Everything has somehow
to exemplify
and be itself

27.3.78

In the centre

I ache silently towards something I cannot touch
Clothed in a city suit of suburban calm
My hidden thong of life strains unbearably towards the night
Fingers reach out in silent pain towards both dark and light

Is this agony of any worth
Or but an unresolved reflection of my childish times
Carrying into an unruffled world of day
The screaming anguish of a night of pain

How can I trust this trembling strain
Or know its anguish as my own
How settle into kind accepting death
Or struggle on towards a life I do not know

In the centre there is rabid faith — prophetic power —
the covenanters' cruel zeal —
Is this why I have sought to Anglicize myself and
long for gentleness to ease my hurts — why I have
spun a web of smoothness over all to hide the awful edges of this
raw blade of unremitting death?

The centre is power — it cries out in pain —
it is red and fierce and devoid of fear — crazed in
the eye of day — a burglar of the night

There is an Old Testament prophet locked in there —
displaced from his time to these — he has to learn to laugh
and bend the knee to the whimpering prattle of our daily noise

But he has not bent — he does not bow —
we force him down and cover him around —
and yet he stands
and in the middle of our days
demands with ferocious rigidity of mind
that we learn to live with high regard
even now towards an ultimate in man

is it possible to get into this central 'prophet'?

He wants to announce all sorts of things with a certainty
I don't believe at all — they arise from a sense of drama in
Bible stories and the sense of proclaiming to others — (to hell with
whether it is true as long as you can proclaim something and make the
    bastards take notice and feel guilty if possible)

(But this is me commenting on this narrow minded tub-thumper!)
(the moralistic, self-opinionated swine)

Is it possible to get into this person?

I suffer and die for you — I am torn so that you
can be whole — I reach out so that you may possess —
I love with passionate pain so that
you can bear flowers and fruit —
I wail in the loneliness of night so that you can
turn your face to the sun
I am beyond the beginning of time and after its ending
I love you beyond pain — I stand with you
as sharpened steel — I lie beside you in voluptuous
abandon — I am beyond what you know in order that
you will know what you do not know

That didn't feel very convincing — though a bit surprising —
I don't really care for this Old Testament type, Victorian
melodrama —
Actually, the terrible thing is
that this is what I *do* care for — this is my fatal
weakness of taste — this is what cowboy films are about —
what music hall and melodrama, pop songs and conventional
sentimentality are about —

But still he didn't sound quite like that either —
Is it conventional to say 'I love you beyond pain' —
'I stand with you as sharpened steel' — 'I lie with you in voluptuous aban-
    don'?

Something like this 'prophet' is who I have all the time
to bite back — I am so easily tempted
into narrow moralizing and rigid tub-thumping!

But perhaps that is a different person who mocks
the 'prophet' — A small-minded, frightened, clutching
bully who wants to control and diminish everyone else
(that doesn't sound like the prophet)

Who is this 'tight bully'?

I hate everyone and everything — I am ugly and
misshapen — my fears have made me ashamed —
I hide this face of shame in brutality and
shouting — dismissing and undermining, cutting and
distorting — putting down what is carefully made and
hating with fearful loathing anything which shows me up
as the frightened, greedy, little person I am

The small ugly narrow frightened person
is almost the opposite perhaps of the 'prophet' —
I don't know

The 'prophet' is old — he is the first sense of 'love' I've
found in myself — and his is a demanding love —
not that he demands from me but that love, as it leads,
demands of him and he gives and follows —
which is what I don't and fear to do

I've never really paid any direct attention to him before —
always confused him with narrowness and clichés

I'd like to hear from him and have him, if he will,
talk of love —

Love is neither a fine feeling nor a kindness shown to others
In its heart it is the searing of truth — it burns
like a laser beam — with terrible power into and
through the very hardest material thing —

Love is power — love is frightening power —
Love is in the terrible explosions of space and
the devastating explosions of volcanoes
Love is the gentlest, most slender rose — love
is lightning and instant death —

Love burns and hurts and scalds and consumes
and tortures and destroys —
Love is no mild mannered plaything — love is power

Love neither quavers nor fails — though we
often fail
Love is not qualified or contained
Love is power in all its forms and the endless
movement of time
Love does not demand as a demanding person
but love demands
Love demands in the very nature of things — love
demands all — everything — love is
ultimate and complete — love consumes

Love suffers — love is pain — pain is love turned
inside out — stretched across the barrel of time
Love is not a pretty sight — love is
beauty and the intensity of simple honour
Love is all there is — love is power
Love is ultimate demand — dare we even
enter the portals of love — we scarcely
yet know what it is to love —
Love gives everything there is — love is power

Love is no easy option — love demands of you
all you are —
Love is no cottage with roses round the door —
Love is pain — love is the ultimate giving —
the receiving of ultimate giving —

And for us love sustains — and fear of love
dominates our lives — fear of the power
of others creates terror and torture —

We cannot yet love more than a little and
we avoid love assiduously   27.3.78

What I am about

What I am about
is not to be followed
within the security
and the shame of churches
My place is in the
ordinary world

The death of God
is necessary
for the life of man
We are God
All is God
God is all there is
and all there isn't yet
So what!

It is about belonging
We belong
We are not so much
accepted
as here of right
This is our place to be
for explorations into
the possibilities of being personal

Being personal means
reaching into the heart of life
towards a way of being in relation
which may penetrate and challenge
and overturn being nice
or kind or obviously good

Being personal is awful
It is about consuming love
Not as an autocratic demand
but a powerful force
reaching to the core
to the centre
It means standing
at the centre
even in a hurricane
of power

28.3.78

I don't believe

I don't believe in a god
or some father in the sky
a larger than life being
Nor do I believe in something
called 'being itself'
But I think
hesitatingly
and out of the persistence
of its presence in me
I do believe
in the frail sensibilities
I have been born with
The messages born in me
and bred in me
mingle
combine
to hint at possibilities of being
which are
ridiculously unclear
yet seem to be
the only line of life in me

There is some kind of personal destiny
I am called to
and it is hard to keep
from becoming resentful and cynical
in being led in pursuit
through such darkness   30.3.78

I am not speaking

I am not speaking
from my beliefs
things acquired
and scrutinized
and accepted as true
but from my being

Not to claim rights
over others
but to give forth
whatever sweetness
or pollen or seeds
are mine to give   1.4.78

This life is special

This life is special
This is all we are
and all we have
We are patterned being
of beauty in movement
Extraordinary
We have powers and opportunities
to sing and glory

So much of beauty
is squashed
degraded
dismissed
and despised   1.4.78

Be personal

Be personal!
Being personal costs you dearly
Being distant, detached and separate
costs you too
but it is a postponed payment

Being personal means paying now
as well as later
Being personal means being ready
to die now
again and again
Being personal means
giving yourself now
again and again

Being personal requires
trust and faith and strength
again and again
Being personal means
suffering now
again and again
Being personal means
being honest now
again and again
Being personal means
loving more than life
again and again and again
It is the price that has to be paid
which is so frightening

All our security
is in postponement
in protection
in negotiated distrust
in survival at any cost
in keeping yourself to yourself
in requiring proof and guarantees
in avoiding pain
Being personal costs
so very much
I couldn't contemplate it unless
I was pretty desperate
and then only for as long
as I think I have to

To be personal is not
to be open indiscriminately
To be personal is not
to be extraverted or introverted
To be personal is not
to communicate every thought and feeling
you have when you have them
To be personal is not
to trust yourself to everyone
indiscriminately
To be personal is not
to give yourself away indiscriminately

To be personal in depth
you need to be met by another
who directly knows in his own
implicit experience
what it is you are about
You complete or are shaped to
each other's implicit forms

To be personal is to be lonely
to stand alone
no one else can inhabit your space
you are the world
To be personal is really
to put yourself at risk
again and again   2.4.78

Being serious

Most people strive
not to be serious

To be serious is
to live honestly
at the base of life

Our lives are given to us
We don't ask
and yet we receive
Some of us do not
want the gift
resent it
throw it back
turn from it
as much as we can

To live seriously
is to exult in life

To live seriously
is to be profoundly
reverent
Not bowing and scraping
but silently
open to the truth   3.4.78

The deep adventure

The deep adventure
Giving oneself away
Entering into loving surrender

You can't do any of this
from the top
It has to be some
basic giving
letting go

Letting go
stop holding on
Letting go
Trusting yourself to
the flow of life and death
That is some central
letting go
Not just giving up
peripherals

Letting go
dying
allowing to flow
away or stay
Letting go
doesn't mean
giving up
It means not
hanging onto
Not grasping
Clinging
Leaning
Depending

Almost everything we do
is based on holding on
Getting hold of
Taking a grip
Digging in
Grasping
Tying up
Nailing down
Fencing in
Building up

We hold onto failure
as well as success
rather than holding it
in open hands

I am nothing
and no one
Everything is a gift —
as if a gift —
given
and not given
into my possession

What about love
and faithfulness
and consistency
and duty?

To let go of everything
is surely not to let go
of love
since love is not
to be held
but is what lives us
What we have to let go of
is our insistence
on how things are to be
Our fears of how
it will be otherwise

I let go of life
I let go my fear of failure
I let go my terror of difficulty
I let go my endless self-flattery
let it fly from open hands
I let go of false emotions
grief and joy are gifts

Does letting go mean
you become shallow or deep?
Do I let go of everything
Hold only to Christ or
let go everything
Hold to nothing

Holding on tight and
clutching possessions
and concepts and knowledge
and prejudices and fixed ways of thinking
and habits and fears and weaknesses and pains
and joys and memories and hopes
and all such
is how we live
Cluttered down and over
and through and through
with possessions
possessions!

We need to empty ourselves
open ourselves
Bare ourselves
Trust not blindly but openly
for joy or sorrow
pain or strain

Let go
Cease striving
Do not cling
Let go of expectations
and guilts
taboos and
wrinkled brows

My life is a hesitant journey
but a journey into God
A longing
however faint and fearful
for God
For the centre of all centres
The profound and the utterly obvious

Do I care for such a journey
Do I care about this quest
this questioning of God?

Of course not
not yet
but perhaps I will dare
to give up daring
and live in the love
(so they say)
of how things are

18.5.78

I am not concerned to preach

I am not concerned
to preach at
or convert to
What I somehow want to do
is to be with people
in such a way that they can begin
to dare to be where they are
So that they can stand
when they were crouching
So that they can love
when they were afraid
So that they can be a part of
'the stupendous adventure of the universe'
if only for a little while

I believe that we can be as gods
not in the power of fear
but in the terrible power of love

If you are not to preach at
or manipulate
you need to speak
from where you live
and speak of
that which you know
so that in telling it
like it is
you talk in truth
not advocating something
others should do
to relieve some of your
or their guilts

I have a feeling at times
that I do know something
of living somewhere
different from here
Somehow all my journeying
is to inhabit that place again
To live there still
rather than in exile

Perhaps most people don't feel
that kind of thing
and every now and then
some do
and rekindle the lamp
of mythology

Why can I not
live in the Garden?
I don't believe it is
because I've been expelled
by an angry God
But rather that we are
offered
so many other choices
other experiences
other things to cope with
and lose our way
can't find our way
back to the Garden
Catch a whiff of the scent
every now and again
but can't leave where
we are entangled

It is also I suspect
that living in the Garden
is about something
so different
and in a different form
from living in
the everyday world
No matter how hard we try
by the methods we use
in the everyday world of affairs
these are just not in the form
that allows us to
experience the Garden

I don't think we have been
expelled from the Garden
but rather that we are given
the world
and have only faint memories
of the Garden

We are allowed to choose
to search
to make our way
to make a Garden of the world
perhaps

There is no God
to reach down and save us
We are a part of whatever God may be
God is everything in each of us
and we are all in God
God is all in all
We are God struggling to live
God's suffering is our suffering
Our suffering is
there and then
the suffering of God
We are alone and together
defenceless and all powerful

To live from the Garden
is to live in a different way
I suspect it is too painful
too acute
too silly
to entertain seriously
so we can struggle and strain
and try to get nowhere at all
and be assured we won't!

Knowledge of God
To live from the Garden
has always been reckoned
a madness
a folly
a kind of foolishness
We keep our structure
our defences
well in place
to ensure that we do not
lose ourselves in
the Garden of the beloved

We hold on tight to
the shape we possess
Don't let go
Cling to what you know
or you will lose everything you have
And yet it is said
you must lose everything
give everything away
holding to nothing
God will provide!

Let go
Trust yourself to
the shape of living
in the Garden
That means sensing the Garden
the place of living in your experience
and letting its form be yours

I am too sawn-off
Harsh
Linear
Jagged
The Garden is flowing
Moving
Formless
Nothing
You have to become
no-thing
You need to flow and move
on the face of the water

To live like that
is to be vulnerable
to the harshness of the world
so that tragedy is
almost inevitable   29.5.78

We are afraid

We are afraid
afraid to trust ourselves
afraid of others
afraid of feeling
afraid of responsibility
afraid of being found out
afraid of being inappropriate
afraid of being weak
afraid of needing people
afraid of failing
afraid of succeeding
afraid
afraid
afraid
fear
fear
fear

Fear so easily
turns to anger
to resentment
to cynicism
to blaming
and criticizing others
to being double dealing
to hiding
and pretending what is not so

But if fear
is the opposite of love
If love is infused with fear
love turned inside out
is terror and dread
awfulness
The insight that
God is to be feared is
but a step to the insight
that God is love

Fear is closeness to
the awfulness of love
when you stand outside
rather than lay down your being

to the power of love
Fear is clutching
holding on
It is avoiding and scurrying

The depth and pervasiveness
of my fear is the depth
and pervasiveness of
the possibility of love
Fear is a measure of
the possibility of love
and he who loves
thereby casts out fear
Yet you can be without fear
through blindness too

Fear of saying what you think
fear of invasion by others
fear of being hurt
fear of being misunderstood
fear of being understood
fear of trusting
fear of what will happen
to you in the future
fear of the fear of others

Fear of being taken advantage of
fear of losing a grip
fear of being changed
fear of what will happen if ...
fear of responsibility
fear of stepping outside
the expectations of others
fear of life and death
change and uncertainty

Fear is the other side of love
Fear is the dread of love
Fear is the dread of losing
what we have and are
of letting go in order to
become what will be
We are afraid of love
Love demands all we are

It leaves us naked
and without possessions
We do not possess love
We inhabit love
We are in love
or out of it
To be on the outside of love
is to be safe
To be in danger of entering love
is to fear
To be in love is to be
destroyed and composed

The idea that knowledge
will banish fear
is widespread
If we know more
we will be able to
combat our fears
and so it often is
but
because we fear
we seek not to know
in the hope that
we will thus keep ourselves
from pain
from destruction by knowing

Because we fear
we cannot know
We can only know fear
and the edges of
what fear allows us to touch

Because we fear
we distance ourselves
and collect outside knowledge
by which to manipulate and control
the world we fear

Is much of our objective
pursuit of knowledge
to do with fear and control
and prediction

beating the world to the punch
as Kelly says?

But what if we aim
to live into our fears
What then is knowledge
to be about?

What is it to enter
our fears
live into them
to find the empty seed of life
in the midst of the pain
Pain is the shell
which protects life
Seeds of life
are surrounded with pain
We fear pain and so
do not disturb many
of the seeds of life
Only when we learn to live
into our pain
have we a chance to
enter the seeds of life
Merely to live with pain
or tolerate it
go along with it
may not be enough
We have somehow to live
in the eye
the living centre
of emptiness in pain

We must come to inhabit
our terrors
so that we come to know them
their nooks and shades
angles and patterns
Till we see the beauty
we were terrified to behold
Beauty is shrouded in fearfulness
Perhaps much ugliness is
beauty strangled by fear

What is fear?
fear is staying on the outside
fear is holding to some notion
of yourself in the face of some
task or event
fear is drawing back
fear is a presentiment of pain
fear is placing some notion of
yourself in and between you
and the truth
fear is bad science
fear is when what you hold to
as yourself is more important to you
than the way things are

What is love?
Love is getting inside
love is giving yourself over to
a task or event
Love is staying with
living with
Love is the refinement of pain
Love is embracing the truth
so that it changes you to its form
Love is when you surrender any notion
of yourself in a longing to know
things as they are   12.6.78

Personal vision

To live in the world of personal vision
rather than conventional vision
is perhaps to live in a desert
or in a world of dwarfs
demons, pygmies and elves
A place of fear with flashes and sparks
of love and beauty

Certainly to live
in a world of personal vision
is to live in a very different world
from the world of conventional appearances
or the world of economic struggle
or of psychiatric disease

The personal vision encompasses
the struggle of all humanity
The personal vision concerns
how each of us stands
in relation to our life
and life itself
The personal vision concerns
how we separately and communally
dance our dance
weep our weeping
sing our singing

We do not generally know
the depths of our being
the whispering glades
of our lives between
We are places of meeting
Each of us is a conjunction
Each of us is in meeting
is a meeting place   21.6.78

A private world

There is a private world
which is a place of
infinitely precious peace
A place of gentleness
and love
where time hurries not
and claims are left
at the door

But so very readily
without sign or signal
we can be
in a different place
where all is
strain
pretence
and frozen smiles   30.6.78

For itself

For itself
and because I want to
I scribble and note
and attend to myself
and care about making
some kind of sensing
of the world

In various ways
and at some points
I want to share that
with some others

From time to time
I want to write and speak
and weave patterns
in the air
and through the very hearts
of those who listen

17.7.78

I think we should part

I think we should part
and try to live our separate lives in the round
rather than as cardboard cutouts who look real
only when seen from a distance and
approached from the right direction

I think we should part
though it may be I love you still
We may never find each other unless we
wander in the world exposed to our own needs
and reach towards our own levels of longing

I believe we should part
and fear everything involved in believing such a thing
the pain, suffering, failure, disruption and disgrace of so many
and especially you and me and our beloved three

I believe we should part
if honesty is to mean anything between us
and am almost able to think I could believe
that in all the misery this would cause
it might just possibly be better for the children
it might just possibly make it possible for us each
as person and parent to come to know them
and make it possible for each of them
to come to know each of us
as people as well as parents

And yet I dare not say any of this
and risk that awful slide over the edge of the road
towards the sickening, slithering, desperate
panic filled, mindless crash into the
wreckage of the valley so far below

21.7.78

Words

Words are my medium it seems
the medium for forming and touching
and holding and conveying
and handing over lightly held
the possibility of life
to another

Words are so limited
dried meanings
ingredients
ground and mixed
waiting to be blended
and chosen for cakes and curries

Words are so limited
funny things words
Arms length things
formal restrained things
Blunt instruments too

Why bother with the
restraint of words?

Words are growths

Words are so often
husks
empty

Full words
Marrowful words
Words which pulse
with your living spirit
are what matter
So very rare
And even then
only to be picked up
for a fading time by
selected geiger-counter minds   26.7.78

Living words

Words are strange things
to focus a life around
They are so thin in some ways
Especially as they are used
in strict logical forms
Also self indulgent and mere
expressive jabs in the air
when used individualistically
They are then perhaps
a relief
giving some pleasure
which fades into loneliness

It is when words are the living
delicate, vibrant, texturing
forms of the between
really the between you and me
when they touch and caress and hold
and shape and finger and tickle
the very being between us
the you and me especially
that they are such living forms
and even then they are alive
because we bodily sustain them

But words last
They can live on
Can carry the soul
They contain the spirit of man
to hold it in being
cold storage even
till another you meets
this very me within me
which is between us

Perhaps the living word
is living because it joins
my life to your life
It is constituent of meeting

The living word is between
It is not merely expressive
but is both expressive and
deeply communicative
it touches the life within your life
It is not surfaces and appearances
but life within life

When my words contain and are
inhabited by my life
spoken into the open darkness
the welcoming darkness
of your life
then between us
the word is living word

My word can only be full
and inhabited by my life
when it is cohabited somehow
by your life
I cannot live into nothing
I need to be met
Somehow to speak within our world

It is when our lives commingle
live together in my words
that there is living word
In the beginning was the word
the closeness of being together
at one

The development of language
may be the means by which
we reach for atonement
It is not that language by itself
in some abstracted sense
can achieve this but that
through the word which is spoken
when it becomes from time to time
the living word
The word which vibrates with
the recesses of your life
as well as mine
and mine is met and recreated by
the ripples of yours in mine
then the work of atonement
is underway

This makes learning to speak
to each in other
a vital task for us
taking centuries
involving a loving concern
for language and the developing
declining uses of language
in word and picture
and all else between us

It is important to notice
that speaking personally
is not just bursting forth
ejaculating your pent up
feelings for the world
but a betweening
It is in already living
in your life
already being alive in
the centre of my living
beyond even where I know
and hold my life
that your word becomes living
personal word
Expression is not enough
Communication is not enough

You have to travel right into
and inhabit my world
and live into your word
already rooted and living
its vibrancy
all unknown till the flower bursts
and the seeds in time
fall and scatter

The receiver of the word is already
the mother of the word
The audience is relevant to the communication
He or she who hears the word
is already alive in the word

You cannot I think
speak personally and merely
unburden yourself of your secret fears and hopes
Much intimacy is little more than
mutual masturbation
not that that may not be intimate
but it may be a doing to
and a relieving of
rather than interinanimation
Speaking personally is when you somehow
whether by design, struggle or nature
speak within the living space of others

I am not interested in speaking
just to be sociable
I am interested in speaking the full word
the word which shares worlds
the word already rooted in the darkness
of your life as well as mine
In speaking it I am not speaking
from knowledge to ignorance
but from a moving nothingness
into a knowing from which
light returns by the very act
from the movement of roots and leaves
and even flowers which enrich my garden
fertilize my darkness

28.7.78

The life within the life

I will speak only to the poor
and the oppressed
the fearful
and the bright eyed children
the life within the life
I will listen only to the voices
within the voice
the cries and laughter
within the garden

I will speak to you within you
I will not trespass on your privacy
but will accompany your pain
I will come to know the world
within the world
the hidden bestiary which shields
the secret garden
the life within the life we live
I will try to be me to you within you
but that is not something that is
but what will be when you are you to me
and I am me to you and you

We create singing in the midst of despair
terror in the midst of suburban calm

Some already live themselves
in the world
but often harden and bend themselves
by meeting the me who is not me
and the you who is not you
To continue to be themselves
in such a world is an
alternative prison

I have wedded myself to a star
which is not near and comfortable
but out there and beckoning
not to reach it
but to remember
I become so very afraid
when I live only and only
in my place and time

When I do not remember my star
My star lives and dies
for other places and other times
as well as my place and my time   28.7.78

Questions on the frontier

Big questions
life questions
have to be lived fully
with your whole life
Not just mentally
on the back of an envelope

Big questions
have to be lived
Not just asked
with the head

Big quests
have to be lived
Not just thought about

If questions really matter
they need to bear the full weight
of your life   29.7.78

This world of business and affairs

What is it about this world
of business and affairs
which just does not make sense
for me?

It is too small
We have fenced off too small
a space for living
We have made arrangements
pathologized and tortured
so many of our living experiences
of fear and beauty

It is too external
We attend from ourselves
to the bits and pieces of things
including ourselves
We do not receive the world
and flow from the nowhere land

It is too brutal
Too inconsiderate
unaware of delicate strength
Too rushed to do and make and change
and impose upon
Harsh and cowardly
but buttressed by the power
of armaments
so that weakness
can be hidden
behind the fearful strength
of things

It is too crudely claimed
Too inarticulate
too unformed
too blatantly stated
asserted
rather than said
with careful strength

It is too concerned
with getting by
rather than with
living and dying

It is too afraid of fear
Rather than coming to know fear
so that love can endure and grow
We hit out at fear
protect ourselves in rules
and defences of all kinds
Narrow down
substitute go-getting achievement
for the shaping of personal courage

29.7.78

We are the world

We are the world
Speech for us is our way
of inhabiting the world
bodying it forth
We have come to talk
about the world
and separate ourselves off
We have forgotten how
to talk the world
to speak the world
to ourselves itself
We have turned
to speak about
and must not
from there
retreat
It is impossible
but move further on
to speak again
so that our very being
in the world is tinged
with spokenness

This does not mean
we do not reach
towards further shores
in speaking
We are always on the verge
of the possibility of touching
further up the beach
But always so much more remains
beyond the ken of seas
except in the rain
which rises and falls
and returns with its
unspeakable knowing
to the parent who remains

Speaking the world
is the human condition
a seeding of the spirit
The evolution of spirit
is in and through
speaking the world

We speak in our actions

Speaking is a participation
in community
All words are our avowing
community
But we have lost track
of our being together
in the arrangement of being
apart and separate

All speaking is already between us
We are already together in our words
If it were not so
they would not be words
Our apartness is already commingled
in the words we share
In our ways of putting words together
we build the very texture of our lives

6.8.78

Buried deep

My life is somehow buried deep
and is struggling to be freed
to be given a voice
to sing its deep song
to stumble its grunts
and first words even
to inhabit a shared world
a word of cohabitation

My life is deeper than I am
it is buried
it is in the being I cannot become
till I allow myself to sing
unchecked by analysis

All the time
always and always
I want to talk about
how things are
but I know that what matters
is to speak the world

to sing and dance the world
to tell it like it is
and that is so different
from describing or analysing it
standing apart
and appraising how it seems

Because I am starved
barren
shut away
half dead
the life I live
is a form of death to me
Somehow what is central
hidden in me
is just not there
not involved
passed by
excluded
not taken account of

There is another world
I belong to
which I can't
won't reach into
or which has to be
created
through the belongingness
that yearns for home
in what is not yet

Speaking the full word
personally
between ourselves
beyond the barriers
and bounds of particulars
and preventatives
is rich and deep
Is restoring
like water to roots
Is creative and allowing
Is confusing

Is frightening when
you step out of it
into the ordinary world
and look back
Is magical
Is invisible very quickly
Is hard to believe
Impossible to catch   12.8.78

The price of knowledge

The price of knowledge
eternal banishment
from security
labour
sweat
and pain
Endlessly giving birth
to good and evil
Good being
killed
by evil
The eternal
struggle
uncertain
This is a
desolate view
of knowing

An alternative

We are born
from the depths of knowing
We come from knowing
Our lives are as outcasts
but we are cast into
that which we have
the possibility of knowing
We are cast into that
from which we come
to bring light
We are in the process
of reclaiming
our birthright

(rather than selling it
for a mess of potage —
though that might not be
such a bad exchange
at times)

We pay for knowledge
with our lives
But we pay
the same price
in the end
for ignorance 4.9.78

Knowing and being known

I am not prepared to be known
at levels that will deny
the depths I feel

To be known too obviously
and too easily
is to lose the possibility
of deeper knowing
the further reaches
because if you once reach them
you can come back
to transform
even the most ordinary knowing
It doesn't happen the other way
I don't think 10.9.78

The deep language of pain

You cannot listen
sensitively
delicately
to a language
you do not know
You must know
in your very bones
the language

147

the deep language
of human longing
and pain
and joyfulness
Otherwise
when a voice
whispers
in the distant
darkness
through the rumble
of traffic and crowds
you will not hear
cannot hope to hear
cannot begin to jump
the gaps of silence
to enter the stream of life
flowing still
beneath the city streets

You must come to know
as a lived
and living
flame
the language of
risk and fear
courage and compromise
longing and hiding
But to know a language
is still not
to have something to say
It is still not
to have the courage to speak
It is still not
to suffer the shapes
of living beauty
packed in death
which are the seeds
of generations of love

13.10.78

It's not a question

It's not just a question
of how much of me is involved
but whether parts of me have depth
enough to allow me to live
below the normal surface
to tunnel and filter up
through the normal earth
transforming it with
some different life

Everyone encourages me
to be superficial
to somehow live
at the top
rather
than in the depths

Everything lifts you
to the surface.....
To inhabit a tiny bubble
at depth
is to grow and grow
and explode eventually
on the surface
How is it possible
to indwell
live inside the deeper places
and stay there long enough
to know the world anew?

It is so hard
struggling to get down
to any depth
What is needed is to
catch yourself in some way
in fragments of being
below the normal layers

Instead of reaching higher
and running faster than the others
I have to go lower
and walk back
Not run forward
to any shining goal

4.11.78

A pursuit of ignorance

Do we work hard
not to know each other?

Do we make ourselves unaware
of the means by which we make ourselves unaware?

Do we limit our concerns strictly
within the ambit of our seriousness
deciding how much we will get involved
how much put ourselves out
and then create a reality that
smoothes over as many of the rough edges as possible?

Do we ignore those aspects of ourselves
we cannot be bothered coming to know
which don't fit the web of reality
we decide to rest on

In deciding what is real
what matters in our lives
do we thereby relegate to flimsy
voicelessness what otherwise
would constitute the basis of
a different reality?

Do we listen to
too few themes
the content of words
not the sound
flow
syntactical arrangement
pattern of expression?

We encase our lives
our awareness
our understanding
with sameness
Sealed over with the obvious
so that what we see as reality
or what we act from as reality
is all but beyond question
all but unnoticed

8.11.78

The desert wanderer

It feels like an awful puzzle
he's been landed with
Somehow dropped in the middle
of nowhere
and having to find a way

Or rather, others
out there in the city
have somehow to find
and guide
and meet
and know this character
dumped from the beginning
in the desert

No one has ever met him
Goodness knows where he is
or how you speak with
such a strange person
Even if you found him
How to learn to speak with him
and listen
and let him speak his way of speaking

For city folk to find
and learn to listen to
and speak with a desert wanderer
would mean a depth of concern
quite outwith their normal range
Why go to all that bother?
Is it worth it?

Somehow the answer must be 'yes'
because this desert wanderer is myself
He is what the city
fears to be about
He is incapable of city life
so very threatening
when most will live in cities

He doesn't make sense to people
He is impossible to understand
So easily dismissed
There is no benefit
no kudos
attached to spending time with him
Except
in trying to capture and bottle
his essence
to make you famous and rich
in the markets
of big cities

But unless you approach him
with purity
in innocence
you will not learn
will not be met by him
He sees what others do not see
He is not a fool
Only a fool within the wisdom of cities
He is proud
in a different way
Held carelessly in his body
not in himself

I cannot reach him
he is too deep
he breaks the bottom
of my mind
It is a woven cradle
well above where he begins   8.11.78

'You must return to the beginning' says Rilke

The beginning is me
That whatever I say
is not so
but a serious
superficial
attempt
at what is so

in one small corner
for me
now
at this point
in place
and time
Seriousness
must begin
by no frivolous
exaggeration

The problem
is to speak
ourselves
into a
knowingness
of things
To see
along the shutters
of our ignorance
a kind of disrespect
neglectful vision

8.11.78

The messenger, the fugitive

I am on a journey and cannot stop for you, or you
Behind every pretended task, I cheat and scratch my way

I don't want to know what others know —
I don't care about knowledge of this and that —

My only longing is to be free, and if need be, to suffer
the messenger to survive and reach his secret goal

If needs must have it so — if it must be so —
the messenger will live

If it must be so — he will be given
food and shelter from the rain

If it must be — we may come to care
that he carries our future we will never know

Go he must into the night, yet again
into the awful uncertainty of pain, the trickling
terror of a hunted escaper's death

There is no glory — he is under orders of another
power — of a secret army without arms, without uniforms
or stars — he wears ordinary
clothes, tired eyed, wild

He is not glorious or grand — a messenger only —
of another army — no one will mourn if he
dies — not long anyway — he is all but
dead — most likely to die — many
are sent, only a very few take the message to its goal
as salmon in a stream
It is life to reach upwards itself — we are fingers

All else is secondary — the messenger must live

He is a person of no pretensions — no special virtue —
no special powers — no claims to fame

All he is is in what he does —
he cares enough to risk and give his life for what he loves

He is hunted and in danger at all times — when
we abandon him and fear to have him in our
midst in case we get into trouble or have to pay —
his life becomes a living hell

We are his only chance — even then he is likely to
die for something he and we scarcely understand
(neither he nor we *really* understand — we scarcely
begin to understand)

If we can support his furtive life so that he survives —
we will not understand any more —
but will have learned some kind of courage —
some kind of human response other than cowardice and
treachery! I am a traitor to the messenger —
the fugitive — the soldier behind enemy lines!

All the images of war are as it is

What of the messenger?

I have chosen and cannot do otherwise —
I have been chosen — not because of specialness — but
because there is no one else — because I am
recognized by someone greater than me — who I admire —
I somehow sense I am, in my fear, to carry a
message, about another world — another way to be
together — *another country beyond the frontier of fear —*
another country beyond silent betrayal in the night,
another country, a different world — a rich world of
poignant gentleness — loving care sustaining itself on the knowing brink of
    destruction

We inhabit a world of fugitives — hiding and scurrying —
frightened, starving, maimed, horribly tortured —
the playthings of dreadful complacency and ignorant fear

We live our comfortable lives with fugitives in our midst —

There are fugitives in our midst — dirty, wide
eyed, broken, fearful, outside our settled ways

Our future rests with them — or rather between
us and them

                                            10.11.78

Low rather than high

    Care for the messenger
    the fugitive
    the wanderer
    the down and out
    in our midst

    To live in
    the place of fear
    living in fear
    may be how we bring
    the desert to bloom
    at a price

To live low
rather than high
to stand under
to talk and feel
from below
rather than always
rising above
going up
getting on top of things
being a jump ahead

Life is a moral venture
It is about living
from and in
your lowest places
and having your highest
care for and with them

Repentance not repression
is the theme   12.11.78

To grasp and penetrate

To grasp and penetrate
is to ignore
is to assert your impatience and pride
to trick and seduce into opening and receiving
is to steal and debase
and lose yourself

To know is to bear the pain
of staying close
The frustration of wordlessness
The searching to say

There is a longing in me
to know beyond the ordinary
knowing of the world
A longing to know the world
from the inside rather than the outside
A longing to know it whole
rather than bit by bit

Is this really so?
Or is it only if the cost is low?   31.12.78

Understanding

Understanding requires
putting yourself in a position
to be taught by
to learn from
to experience
to be affected and changed
to be humble
to stand under

Not to be aloof
different
superior
separate
high up
out of reach
remote
professionally untouchable

To understand
is to be drenched
and washed and
flowed over by
It is to take the form
of the other
to give your form away
and in yourself to assume
the form of the other
so that you can be
informed thereby

It is to become
a pupil
It is to care enough
to give the other
power   13.1.79

Much of me is afraid

Much of me is afraid
and runs from love

When I love it is
an invisible
bodyless stream
not to be touched or held
but moved in
It is to enter through rock
into a cavern
which opens and opens
its promise of space

Love is not going anywhere
other than to itself
It is not an end to be reached for
but a place to live

What is it to live in love?
Love and pain are
intimately related

Love has an inside
and an outside
Sometimes the outside is
soft and warm
while the inside is
hard and sure
Sometimes the outside is
sharp and fierce
while the inside is
flowing contentment

Love and pain live together
Love destroys just as it makes
To live in love is
to live with pain

Why would anybody do it?
Why go in
for all that pain?

14.1.79

The world has an inside

The world has an inside
as well as an outside
Perhaps it is
that the world — all —
is deeply personal
though we scarcely begin
to know what it is
in the depths
to be personal
This is our little
bubble of understanding
which is to be lived
till it bursts
into nothingness

To know personally
at the centre
from the centre
is only possible
in giving
your whole life
The whole weight
of your being
your hopes
savings
possessions
and wealth
of whatever kind
is to be laid
on the ice
of your trust
your faith

To know personally
is to give your life
not as one standing apart
hands over a gift
to another
but as one is oneself
the gift
There is to be no giver
remaining to see
how the giving is taken

To know personally
from and to the centre
is to be subject
and not experimenter
Yes, experimenter
in the sense of he
who utterly experiments
tries and experiences
with his life
No, not experimenter
as he who controls
and directs others
to risk what he would know
without danger

Dying is what living is about
In everything you must be prepared
to die
You must actually die
Possessions of all kinds
things, knowledge,
characteristics, friends
are all ways of staving off
dying
They are means by which
we claim to be something
to amount to something

To be entirely worthless
empty is
yet to tingle
in the reality of all
To live between
emptiness and fullness
is to live with death
to live dying

22.1.79

What do I want to know?

What do I want to learn
or come to know
in the psychotherapeutic situation?

How to heal
How to encourage
How to kindle hope
How to grow trust
How to dare to love
How to touch and trace the spirit
with care
How to reach the person at the centre
How to comfort
How to mourn
How to say goodbye
How to rejoice in everything
pain faith hope death love fear anger

I want to come to know
in the living of my life
in the texture of who I am
what it is to reach for
the spirit of man
I want to know
what it is to care   3.4.79

Up and wandering

Up and wandering
in each room
beauty of sun
and buttercups
and flowering clover
and long overgrown grass
in the field at the back

When the sun shines
there seems often
no reason to think
or achieve
or struggle for meaning
It feels present
just in itself   18.6.79

To love you

To love you is to care for who you are
behind all guises and disguises
some of which I may even fear and hate

To love you is to learn to trust you
in the depths
to trust who you are
and are yet to be

To love you is to trust myself to you
even to risk great pain

To love you is to undertake to care
through thick and thin

To love you is to somehow commit myself
to a struggle to become more of myself
with you and for you —
to be who I am
though who that is
may be unwanted by you
I suppose

24.7.79

Making and sustaining our worlds

We actively go about
at all times
composing and sustaining
the kinds of worlds
we seek to inhabit

We are at all times engaged
in making and in sustaining
the worlds we seek to inhabit

Not necessarily the worlds we claim
we want to inhabit
but those we feel we dare to share

We actively and at all times
compose and sustain our worlds

We actively connive and collude
in composing and sustaining
limited worlds between us
so that much of who we are
capable of being remains
private and hidden
and beyond sharing

We actively and at all times
compose and persistently sustain
what is supposedly between us
and obscure the real hidden world
of to and from
that lies beyond the shop window
or diplomatic appearance of things

Our problem is that we come from
partly rise out of
but always remain deeply embedded in
what we do not know at all
the web of social being
of the nature of how things are
Like little waves we rise
momentarily above a huge sea
gain some little perspective
think ourselves something
and then fall back into the sea
from which in other forms
having forgotten who we were
and were and were
we rise high or low again
a different being
in another transitory place

This struggle to rise and turn
upon ourselves and the mystery
of what we are embedded in
and always return to
is vital to understand a little
We do not start
out there
somewhere separate
We are thoroughly drenched
in belongingness

12.11.79

Death as the necessitation of love

We have to love
because of death
To be able to
accompany another
and be with them
you need to love
so that you dare to go
and be with them —
to be together rather —
to the very place of change
the point of death

Love casts out fear
so love conquers death
Where there is no love
there is death

I must love you
recklessly
in spite of
and because of death
so that we can
come together
and walk
hand in hand
into and through
the valley of death

Somehow
you need my love
to be with you
and I obviously
need your love
to begin to make me
whole
to bring me to life
in the doorway of death
Death is change
Death is a place of
change in life

10.12.79

I need your need

I need your need
otherwise I will never sense and find
anything of what my hidden longing
longs towards
You are the gate
and the life itself

My need is at least as deep as your need
perhaps even more lost and removed than yours
since I need the honesty of your cries
to touch and find at least some of the cries
I cannot find

My need is as needy as yours
so I cannot stand before you as a helper
to one in need of help
My need for you
and the generosity of your offered need
is what I have to give
If I am able
helped by you
to receive your need
into the aching arms of my own
forgotten longings
and let myself be held
by the strong arms
of your offered weakness
I will be blessed by your love
more surely than you by mine

All my life I have struggled
to appear strong, stronger than I am
composed, when I have been
ragged and in disarray
self sufficient, when I have been
so lacking that I dared not show
even the tiniest edge of my emptiness
superior, when I have always sensed
that I am nothing in comparison
with so many I have and do despise
I'm trying to say to you that my bitter need
my lack, my failure, is my only gift to you
whatever strength and honesty
courage and love I have

It is easy to talk of need and feel quite comfortable
with that neat, well packaged, little word
scarcely a hair out of place
clean and surprisingly composed
I can even be very proud of recognizing
that I have needs like these
They are like extra possessions
the riches of the appearing humble

But need is in so many unwanted and unlovely shapes
and textures and colours and smells
It is where you fear and despise and reject and are ashamed
where you are dirty and unlovely
quite beyond what you would wish to appear to be
It is easy to offer well packaged
and fashionable needs
But enduring needs are baggy and old, smelly and torn
not dressed as those you might wish to come to the party
but really the beggars and buggers
the outcasts and the half-castes
the desperately proud and the utterly rejecting

Is there anything more awful than
the pride of the nouveau needy?
The coinage of need is so quickly debased   16.12.79

To stand close

To come to stand close to someone
to be able to speak and listen to them
even sometimes to be able to hold them
and let them go
to let them hate and despise
kick and destroy you
is to create
the possibility of loving growth
the very foundation of life —
to give birth to a dictator or saint
torturer or gardener!
Your extremity
only creates a possibility!   18.12.79

In conversation

To be in conversation is surely to live in the open
To be yourself even when with others
Be what is central to you
To be in and amongst others and not be frightened into invisibility

To be in conversation is to think and feel 'on your feet' and not
to speak only from prepared positions

To be in conversation is to be in who you aren't as well as who you are
It is to live in what is not yet — in the other
and what they are leading you to —
as well as in whatever position you hold or place you know

To be in conversation is to be forever incomplete, forever in question —
nothing fixed or final
(and yet we long for stability and fixity and final resting and fixed
boundaries and firm structures)
Always to be beginning
For it always to be early is — it seems — hard for a tight, rigid person
to bear

To be in conversation is to be in uncertainty

To be in conversation is to entrust what you are sharing in others
To value what is growing and potential between you

Everything between us is in motion — flow — movement
Personal meeting and conversing is when our rigid boundaries break
and some of whatever we are flows between and amongst us

My centre is not where I thought it was
and I may live from more than one centre
so that all I can often be and give is conditional
It is when centres meet that the world is changed

The serious conversation of my life
will take everything I am
It will cost us everything

Everything must be given (but how?)
and everything must be received (how, how?)
In this you become nothing, less and less,
to allow the possibility of more and more

How is it that our lives seem to be about what we particularly cannot bear
That we somehow grow in an awful conversation with the boundaries
of our incapacity
our fear and weakness
our lack
— Why else does the person in deepest
anguish of pain
live in and create pain?
— Why does the person tied in to himself in separation and fear reach
out to be wounded by love?
— Why does the person who cannot bear to speak
reach into the pulpit or orator's stand?
Is this just compensating for lack
Or is it that our need is the most powerful friend
if we live therewith in conversation?

Our desperate needs
Our limitations and failings
are the main, perhaps the only thing,
we have to give
in the serious conversation of our lives
Our strengths are the servants of our desperate needs and we generally
confuse ourselves into thinking
that we are what lives in our strengths
when they are but the servants of our desperate needs —
where we are nothing — aching — shameful — crying — empty
Our emptiness is where there is fullness
Our crying where there is joy
Our shame where there is beauty
Our nothingness where there is life abundant

We stay mostly on the outside of who we are
living in a far country
and only sometimes in our desperate longing return home
If only we any longer know how and where home is

The prodigal son was lucky in this respect
that he still knew where home
the centre of his very living
was to be found
We are outsiders even to, or mainly to, ourselves
We avow this and not that

Or hang like leeches to the underbelly of whatever fashion
passes in our youth
promising to take us away from wherever we are
afraid and lonely and lost

Only if we are able and willing — deeply willing somehow
to join again
to join and become members one of another
accepting ourselves on the same level as everyone else
the lowest and the highest
can we seriously converse
It is the beggar in us as well as the prince
that we most fear
Those who give everything and have nothing

To live in serious conversation is to live with the converse
to live with and in contradiction
with opposites
with the other than we are
To be a place of meeting
not a place of judgment

We can become so close that we lose
whatever surprise and mystery there is
and need to 'go to Manchester'
to find again who we are
The prodigal may have been wiser than he seems
because he went
and came to know
more painfully, deeply, fully than any at home
that his need was greater than his pride
and that in responding to and acting on that need
both to go and to return
he made it possible for his father to have joy
and his brothers to have themselves confronted
with what they did not know
Distance can make the heart grow fonder —
but out of sight can also mean out of mind —
It is need which speaks through both
Distance is inseparable from closeness —
Closeness can kill just as distance can —
In contradiction, the conversation of opposites,
is the dance of life

No one ever
almost never
speaks seriously to me
Perhaps that is so with you also
We keep our centres well apart
Perhaps it is only certain kinds of people
people with certain kinds of needs
who need to be spoken to seriously
to live in serious conversation with their lives
I don't even begin to take the people I take most seriously, seriously

My life and death will be one
My living *is* in conversation
in serious conversation
with my dying
Only in this conversation does my life
accept and receive nourishment from
the deep contradiction
we are born into
(to die is to be born, to be born is to die)
This is not the deepest contradiction
only that which spans whatever our dying, or living,
is immediately about
Deeper is the contradiction of
suffering and salvation
ugliness and light
pain and promise
What is it for this to be so
in the conversation of my life/death
How am I to listen
other than by stepping aside
from the small self who grabs and fears
and lie in the arms of that larger self
who embraces us in the conversation of our living
who becomes the container
wherein we flow together
the bed wherein intercourse becomes falteringly possible

Conversation is not about words and ideas and things
given and handed back and forth
Conversation is about melting
'To melt and be like a running brook
that sings its melody to the night'
It is about flowing together
the interinanimation of lives

We have created
solid walls
solid things
solid boundaries
solid lives
We think it of value if it *matters*
Matter is where we put our trust
not *motion*
or the spirit of life
We live with things
We become harder and harder
Walled in
We build places of security in hardness
Softness is weakness
We value what is cut and dry
But conversation is the river of life
not the pebbles thrown into the water
or the fishes that swim and die therein

Mostly nothing flows between us
Everything is hard and bounded
and solid and upright
and fixed
We take fixed positions
Why is there so little flowing
in and amongst and between us
Why are we hard and separate and fixed?

To flow,
we need to be released by love and into love
melted down
softened
somehow accepted
and to accept that acceptance
to know that we are loved —
To know deeply that we are loved
is, I think, what it is to be 'converted'
Your life would be changed
But whether this needs to be
religious
or ordinary
I don't know

To love is very, very hard
But to accept and receive love into yourself
To know and rest in a love you do not deserve
that seems harder still
How, after all, have I earned it?
It is almost belittling,
insulting
to be loved and not to have earned it
and so not to have achieved that place
by merit
Loving is not part of the meritocracy
It is grace
The ocean lets you know for a moment
that you swim in it and are sustained therein
when you had thought you were doing it yourself
and being incredibly clever

Conversation flows
Lovers melt into each other's arms
The hard man softens
with the touch of a child's care
Ideas pour out of the person in creation
The desperate burst into tears
The happy man bubbles with mirth

The sights and sounds which speak most deeply to us
move us
move us
where we thought we were sealed over
and solid
Perhaps Christ was saying something paradoxical
when he said of Peter
'On this rock will I build my church'
Someone who is moved and fails and is not there when needed
but who cares and suffers and loves
this is 'solid'
A solidity in motion

Conversation is to do with self and other
The possibility of otherness being redeemed by self
and self
blessed and fulfilled by otherness

To be in conversation is to live in at-one-ment
as the sea in which all our differences swim
in which all else
which is other and strange and separate
belongs

Communication is the ground of our being
the very water of life
the spring from which all being flows

To be in conversation is to enter into what flows
in and amongst and between you
To be present in conversation is to speak of and speak to
the world
now

For conversation to be the water which sustains and supports our life
for it to be loving intercourse
the juices have to flow
there is moisture and velvet
liquid smoothness and intimate stickiness
The flowing between and amongst
renders the act of meeting easy and welcome
rather than painful and forced

To flow between ourselves
each to the other
we must be melted down
so that the juices of want and need and longing
become the vehicle for life to pass between us
We can melt only in being and becoming real
which may be like cracks in the earth from earthquakes
or the breaking of ice into massive floes
The thaw comes
and brings rushing water
death, danger
hope and life

To live in conversation — as opposed to unity —
or complete-in-selfness or separateness —
is to live in change
in difference
in incompleteness
in a place of beginning
as a beginner who continues, in uncertainty,
without any fixed or final place of resting
You rest in motion

To live in conversation is to suffer and love
what is being created now
not to care only for conclusions
and the exchange or trading of decided responses
To live in conversation is to live in sin
always where the unknown is recreated in the light of new knowing
on the frontier
where the most radical trust must be in the nature of life
To live in what is being created now
means actually caring more for some other viewpoint
than your little own
It means entering into what matters
to someone else
and so having to abandon your own narrowest concerns
for a time
perhaps never to return

If you don't want to know
and don't want to be known
you cannot and will not
enter into conversation   3/6.1.80

Through other lives than mine

My life is one of self effacement
of trying to shine
through the sparkle of other lives
to rise and tower through
the precarious scaffolding
of their lives
and the renovations
they can afford to pay

The therapist
the psychologist
hides
becomes a no one
in his chosen self-importance
which never risks itself
upon the stage —

a secondary sheltered
omnipotence
protects his fears
from facing destiny
alone

I don't want to live
only through other lives
a scavenger
from the tables of the great
a beggar
paraded as a king
of a minor kind of place

I want to be where angels are
where dragons scurry on the plain
I want to give you this from me
and sign it with my name
and
I don't want to speak
in this kind of jingle

I've hidden behind
just about everything
and everyone
Partly to hide
partly to find some hint
of who on earth I am
or who in heaven

Percolating through the gaps
and spaces others leave
and make and give
is a beginning way to be
before the trickles
find themselves
a stream
before the river grows
before the smell of the sea
calls all back
to where it all began

Will I settle into age
or
trickles to a stream
become another spring
a butterfly on wing
a child, a boy
a mother to a son
or dare to really die
to shrink
to fall apart
and risk
the slightest possibility
of birth

10.1.80

Retreat

Without arms or legs
in a room
bright with unnatural light
I sit alone
wrapped in inch thick silence
over naked pain

Were there ever hopes
of an active life
of moving in and out
among the things of men?
Certainly a longing
once upon a time
to talk and be heard
above the babble
of the rain
the all absorbing strain

From time to time
someone comes
to take me out
Sherlock Holmes
in hat and cape
inquisitor of crimes
in battlefields
where screams of war
and gruesome mutilations

of the slain
counterpoint
with cups and cakes
and everything that's plain

But no one enters
that bright room
No one cares to call
What is there to say
to such a one
in such a place as this
where speech
disintegrates in vain
and silence enters all

And silence enters
all there is
and gnaws upon the bone
and scrapes its teeth
with silent fun
as legless sit
who cannot run

9.2.80

Words are weasels

Words are weasels
which bite and gnaw
at the cake of knowing
I can't bear to be without
their squirming lively forms
They take you over
swarm everywhere
till you are
a crawling mass
of words alone

And after a period
of scrabbling activity
ripping and pulling
they will abandon
an empty shape
a few well picked bones

You appear alive
but it is
the squirming mass
of little words
eating everything away

21.3.80

The passion of knowing

Almost everything is unspoken
and will never be spoken
If everyone were to speak for ever
almost everything would remain unspoken
And yet we attach ourselves so slavishly
to words
Words claim the reality of things
Words tend and civilize our fears
Words weave and shape the web
of everything that is for us
Words cover and protect our nakedness in pain
Words attack for us and defend us when we will
Words become the substance of our survival
the bread of life for us
the very air we breathe
And yet all but the very smallest part
remains and will always remain
beyond the reach of words —
where neither moth nor rust corrupt
and thieves do not break through to steal

Words are living forms
forms of life
informed in what we touch and know
Words abandoned become shells
which can still be inhabited
by other lives
Words in dying become all but things
coating every surface
with hard and thickening crust
sealing us from whatever life remains
Words lay on us a high claim to reality
since we give them birth
as they
before us
give us whatever we know about life

Words are fathers and mothers
teachers and trainers
We are their children
We live and see and think
and breathe amongst them
How can we not
all but worship them?

For some
to leave the cultivated plains of words
and seek the mountains
or the sea of knowing
is fearful beyond saying
and so
too fearful
even to entertain   21.3.80

After La Mancha

We have a dream
in the very heart of our lives
we have a dream
We grow from a dream
and lose ourselves
in wakefulness
We have a dream
We have to live that dream
together
We live from dreams
we so readily forget
We have a dream
in the very centre
of our lives
Our little lives
are the outward emblems
of that deep dream
which is the power
of beauty
utter majesty

Beauty at the very heart
of life
Beauty at the centre
at the core
where everything is more
much more than alive
Where everything is power
Where such beauty
strains the fullest limits
of bearing
to become the deepest
stillest vibrancy
of silence

We have a dream
which we must catch
glimpses of
Must not forget
Must remember
even in the bleakest
wakefulness
We
all together
have a dream
All our straining
for beauty
is in memory
of that dream
painting and song
poetry and love
Beauty is at the centre
of everything

2.4.80

The spirit of man

The spirit of man
is what psychotherapy
is about
To touch and hold
in open hands
the spirit

The spirit is one
we participate in spirit
amongst ourselves
and can destroy and fragment it
between us

There are many ways
of killing the spirit
breaking, bending
starving, ignoring
confusing, scattering in pieces

Many people walk in bodies
from which the spirit has been
expelled
quelled or banished or killed
the walking
living dead

Smiling
moving
doing
caring
but the living spirit
is dead
abandoned
sacrificed
given up

In institutions and families
and all relationships
the spirit is tortured and killed
so that the husks can serve
the limited structures
of power and control
in the system
So that obedience and control
can be effected

Breaking and parting
separating off from
into lonely fearfulness
in anger and difference
is part of the possibility of meeting

at a new level
and in new forms —
the prodigal son —
children growing and leaving

We participate so willingly
in the destruction of the spirit
Much of our knowing
grows in and through us
We are led to the world
by being led into ourselves
Yet we turn to what is out there
and seeable by others
To care for the spirit
is to suffer and die
It is so much easier to live
in deadness
or some other kind of excitement
which is of the spirit
but not *in* it

Some of us
are so terrified of the spirit
that we will not dare
cannot dare even to begin
to stand

Why suffer and celebrate
the passion of knowing?
What's so great about knowing?

Not the building of knowledge
or know-how
though these can be important
but the participation in
self
other
world
the depth and kind
and texture and shape
and feel and richness
of living in deepening conversation
into the possibilities of meeting
and even the celebration of communion
from time to time

18.9.80

The realm of the personal

It is a place of newness
frontier
space
desert
wilderness
battle
The realm of the personal
is the realm of
oldness and newness
It is often a getting back
to a place of youngness
where pain became
too much
When it is a place
of going forward
it is a place
of risk and loneliness

Going into who you are
is going into
who you are not
through the gate
of who you dare to be
You become who you are not
and yet will be
Going into and through
who you are
is to go out
to a world beyond
with trust
Giving away
who you are
by living it
rather than saving it
for a rainy day

To be who you are
is to become
what you are not
It is not a matter of
retreating
into individuality

but of going through
individuality
towards
a new and as yet
unknown
way
of being in the world   8.12.80

Rather than being at the edge

Rather than being at the edge of the world
We are involved in creating
and being held
in being

We can really come to know
ourselves
the world

Rather than standing hopelessly aside
Aware that we can know
nothing much that matters
We may come to know
that we can reach
into the heart of life
the centre of the world
And yet
All that we can know
are our interactions with events
There are not events in themselves
No separate existences

There are ways of knowing
and ways only to know from afar
But wherever we start from
we will arrive somewhere else
the opposite most likely
So those who go furthest away
will find themselves nearest to home
Those who stay in the way of the good
will end in the further reaches of evil   17.3.81

Let go

Let go of your guilt
Let go of your pain
Let go of your failure
Let go of your longing
Let go of your aching to love
Let go of hope
Let go of despair
Let go of future
Let go of emptiness
Let go of past
Let go of anger
Let go of meaning
Let go of joy
Let go of death
Let go of life
Let go of Jane
Let go of self
Let go of God
Let go
Let go of holding on

What a letting go
that would be
Could such be possible
Is pain too precious
Is hope too vain

What loneliness
What fear
What terror
What lack

Only by abandoning you
Letting you go
Letting go of my dreaded loss
of all you are
to me and
in me

Only by letting you go
may it be possible
to set you free of me

and set me free of you
So that we may be
in each other
without ownership
or awareness
to the end of time
beyond time

Have I
Do I begin
to have the courage
to let her go
To hold her in open hands
So that she may stay or go

Can I begin to dare
to let go my cruel failure
My lack of readiness to love
Can I begin to risk
so big a loss

She has died to me
Can I begin to choose
to let myself
die to her

Would I ever dare
to say so big a 'yes'
to let my lover go
to choose myself to die

Dare I
even for a moment
dare so large a dare
Offer up the dearest thing
in all my life
a sacrifice to God
as smoke upon the air

Not turn aside
to look elsewhere
And fill my mind
with emptiness
or other kinds
of hooks

25.5.81

With you

With you
there was
the glorious gift
of being flown
right into the heart
of love

Now
I'm back
at base
and any progress
will have to be
a hard slog
by foot
over rough ground
with no great likelihood
of reaching
where I briefly visited
from the air   21.6.81

We travel backwards

We travel backwards into night
While still in our small bubble
it is day

Tears and passion
beyond the limits that I know
How to speak the unspeakable?
There is no object
No focus of attention
It is the passion itself
that is all there is to share

It is not caring for
It is caring from
a place I do not know
and do not own
Only by
Somehow
being able and willing

to be a channel
a messenger
who will never know
what the message is
or who it is
to be delivered to —
Can I hope to
peddle out my time
with some kind of honesty —

But how, how, how
to live that passion
in the midst of nothing
towards no end I know

I am not an ordinary
simple man
I am a fool

30.7.81

No words

No words
deep enough
to pray

Too deep
to reach

Too deep
to ask

8.8.81

The answering depths

The answering depths
of your life
are necessary
to me

Without those deep places
beyond where you know you live
I cannot speak
an echo of the truth

Everywhere else
there is only superficial noise
conventional music

1.9.81

To speak with your life

To speak with your life
rather than in words only
To speak
minute by minute
the deep language
of pain and joy
To be consumed by life
To live daily
What is at issue for you
To live into being
the cascading abundance
of new life
uncontained
profligate
not to be summed up
but tumbling forward
in ever new
unevaluated
disrespectful
forms

Life tumbles and gurgles
multiplies and divides
towards whatever its
immediate and ultimate
destiny may be
We cannot hold it back
or stand in its way
As a river in flood
it will overcome
it will destroy
it will go where
all plans have sought
to prevent it going

As an army
it batters and tramples
mutilates and rapes
its way onwards
to whatever it will
Victories and defeats
combined and
endlessly confused

Against this rumbling
tumbling cascade
of new life
we build shelters
and protections
rules and restraints
of all kinds
Life in its onward rush
is a ravaging beast
breaking and savaging
frightening and surpassing
the weak and the small
Life has the force and savagery
of hell
and is the voice and countenance
of God

We turn
again and again
to the past
holding onto the mooring posts
of ancient Greece
or the glories
of Rome
We map out futures
which we assert
as true
We assert our determination
to control the future
through our projects
and prejudices
of today
Even if we can't contain
how it will be
at least we can infect it
with our pains

So that it is slowed down
in licking the wounds
ripped in its sides
by the poisoned arrows
of yesterday

Over and over again
I have tried to catch the river
in my hands
to hold it still enough
to know for a moment
where I stand with it
as it stands with me
But of course
it is no longer the river
when it is held
and the river in fact
simply flows round and away
quite without the slightest
suspicion of concern
as to whether I settle anything
for myself
or not
I hold back
Seek to order and arrange
domesticate and tame
handfuls of water
But the river flows on

What sort of thing is life
that we misjudge it so
What is life that we are
So unprepared for
its disregard
for what has been
and who we think we are
What images of life
do we set up to worship
as the golden cow
and hope that superstition
will sustain our fears
What is life to me
that I misjudge it so

or so wilfully
delude myself
that it will be tamed
by the assertive
will of man

The aim of science
seems to be
to tame life
in its every form
to make of it
a domestic affair
within the bounds
of our own powers
to control

The personal venture though
Can only for short periods of time
Stay within the known
the comfortingly controlled   29.9.81

Sombre detachment

Sombre detachment
the mystery of the between
when touch to touch
the world renews itself
Invited back within
that realm of darkness
in search of places
further in
where warmth and light
are grown

I am so far out
upon the wheel
and have to travel
very far from anyone
who may suppose
they are nearby
The wheels move secretly
out of sight
and we in close proximity

can scarcely know
that our faces will be turned
towards some different views
held at that distance
from the source
that we and it
conspire   30.11.81

A discipline of discourse

Part three

A discipline of discourse

Hints of a conversational psychology

Through all the chapters in this book I am aware of reaching repeatedly towards some further fragments of understanding of that 'dark embryo' which seems gradually to be taking more specifiable form. Little by little some scraps of new clarity come to me concerning this 'poetic' and 'conversational' approach to human understanding. In this final section I want to indicate a few important issues to do with the practice of this kind of psychological activity and some ways of thinking arising, for me, from that practice.

Any approach to psychological understanding has to develop its own ways of working and these will make their own demands on those who seek to undertake them. The approach I am concerned with is *narrative* rather than *computational*. It involves speaking together and telling of what we know. In this it is of importance that we try to speak the 'full word' from a position of imaginative participation, as well as speaking from more distant positions of reflective afterthought.

One example of speaking in this way has been given in the 'short lines' of the previous section. Another instance of a 'diary' method is illustrated in the present chapter. Here a number of fragments of my more recent struggles, week after week, are offered to show something of the gradual emergence of ideas, some of which have been developed further in other chapters, some of which may yet be helpful in spelling out more of what is still unclear.

Any 'recording' of live speaking has to be done at the time. It cannot be done at some more convenient later date since the lived moment will have passed. So also with thinking and writing, if the imaginative forms are to be caught fresh they have to be 'recorded' at the time. For me, this means that a conversational psychologist has to speak and write in a present and living way whenever he or she is wooing, pursuing, or fighting for some new understanding. This kind of 'present' writing has been necessary for me through this whole presentation, and especially in Parts 2 and 3. While the 'short lines' of the 'Personal Story' were given without comment, there is much more movement between speaking from 'within' and speaking 'about' in this chapter and the two which follow.

In a discipline which concerns speaking and listening it is necessary to be attentive, to wait and allow yourself some chance of silence in which to hear what needs to be said. This places very different demands on the inquirer from those of a more obviously active and manipulative kind which are familiar at the experiment-performing end of science. This passionate waiting is seldom noted in current psychological writing, though in other contexts (religious and artistic, for instance) it is recognized in different ways. Some of my own experiences of, and reflections on, this 'passion of knowing' are presented in Chapter 9.

But imaginative participation, speaking from 'within', passionate waiting, the use of imagery and poetic diction are not just ends in themselves. They are also means to the greater end of seeking to understand more fully what we are up to, what is going on, what we are immersed in and shaped by. In telling what we begin to sense we may give ourselves a little more chance of 'preaching' something of what we are engaged in 'practising', having mostly been blinded by more conventional stories. A conversational psychology should be more light-footed and questioning than the more established, formal methods of conventional science. New vistas for a psychological discipline, somewhere between the current encampments of psychology and psychotherapy, should begin to open for those who are willing to journey out into the barefoot world of personal inquiry.

A conversational approach to psychological understanding should make some differences to how we think and live. While many possibilities are beyond my own imagining, a few of the ways in which this approach may make a difference to our understanding of ourselves and the discipline of psychology are offered in Chapter 10.

Throughout all this final section, however, I am only able to offer 'hints' of what a conversational approach to psychological inquiry might be like. Much remains to be done.

Clues and fragments of thought

It was in 1969, after a number of years of struggle within the psychology that I was trained for, that a point of no return came for me. In 1959 I went from Aberdeen to London to do my clinical psychology training at the Institute of Psychiatry. Soon after arriving there I came upon George Kelly's writings through the recently completed PhD thesis by Don Bannister (1959), and was excited by what he said. In the following years I was lucky to get to know and become friendly with Don himself.

In 1968, the book which Don and I wrote in order to summarize Kelly's ideas and provide a convenient reference point for the growing amount of empirical work that was already showing signs of burgeoning had been published. With Don's support and involvement, I undertook to organize an international symposium concerned with Kelly's ideas, but seeking also to reach towards implied, but still unexplored themes. The symposium (which took place in August 1969) was entitled, 'The Person in Psychology and Psychotherapy' and among the contributors were leading figures in the personal construct world at that time. All the papers were published in the *British Journal of Medical Psychology* (1970).

In the months following the publication of *The Evaluation of Personal Constructs* (Bannister and Mair 1968) and before the symposium took place, I was scribbling my thoughts as I had become accustomed to do. I was straining towards some different understanding of psychology, some way of working that would *feel* better for me. The emergence of fragments of new understanding would be followed by weeks or months of getting nowhere. Reading and psychotherapeutic work implicitly helped me trace out some of the still muffled contours of the kinds of dissatisfactions that could not yet be said clearly.

Then one afternoon, it was the last Thursday in July 1969, I was sitting in my room in the Academic Department of Psychiatry at the Middlesex Hospital Medical School, London, where I was then a senior lecturer responsible for the behavioural sciences course for the medical students. I was reading an essay by Gordon Allport, from his excellent collection *The Person in Psychology* (Allport 1968), when I became aware of some quietly clear resolution of whatever I had for so long been struggling with. I read on, though it was not to this particular text that I was silently attending. I felt remarkably cool and yet aware that a handful of pennies had somehow dropped. A powerful 'image' hovered in the background of my mind. Foolishly I see now, I did not give immediate attention to trying to speak this image into a more permanent being. It was not something 'seen' or 'touched' or 'heard'. It was not graspable by any simple form of words and yet the patterning of its being was substantial and alive, vibrant with a new coherence. All that I could draw afterwards for myself was a crude 'figure of eight' type of pattern lying on its side, but representing something more substantial than this flat symbol seems to suggest. It was at least three dimensional and in motion, powerfully flowing out and through and back in. As I continued to let my eyes nibble at the words before me I 'knew for sure' that some fundamentally new patterning of understanding had become a part of me.

The quiet way in which this resolution of years of struggling had come upon me did not persist. Within a few minutes, I was up and pacing the passage outside my room. Excitement possessed me, still unformed but clear in its recognition that my ground had changed. I was no longer a traveller seeking to catch glimpses of a land I could not enter. I had been given an entry permit. As I paced up and down I repeatedly punched one fist into the other palm. 'I've got it! I've got it!' I all but hissed aloud. I knew that 'it' had become available to me, that 'I' had changed.

Whatever I had previously intended to talk about at the coming symposium was changed too. I had to take a risk and try to say something of what

I sensed. This felt necessary for me and dangerous. I could not see whether what I had to say would make any sense to anyone who might hear. I had to try to hear it for myself, to give myself a chance to see round the edges of what I felt but soon discovered I could not clearly say. This first attempt to catch for myself what I had begun to know was an outline of a 'new' approach to psychological inquiry. I had to choose a 'label' to describe it which seemed faithful to some of what I had so clearly and yet unclearly 'seen'. 'A conversational model for psychological inquiry' seemed appropriate, though I toyed for a little with 'A role relationship model', to recognize its kinship with Kelly's personal psychology.

Two papers, at that time, explored this first awareness of what I was reaching for ('Experimenting with Individuals', Mair 1970a, and 'Psychologists are Human Too', Mair 1970b). Even then I knew I had not quite understood, had not gone far enough, had perhaps chosen too familiar and tight a form to express what I was seeking still to sense.

For me, new ideas on analogy and metaphor in psychology and psychotherapy began to grow. New freedoms from the restrictions of mind and talk that I had been trained within came with these. I had the sense that there was so much more that I had still to find a way to say. After the first moment of feeling the new form in me, I was swept into a rapid, tumbling stream, rethinking much of what I knew or had read. I had to scribble everything as it came. I knew early on that if I let things go by I would never be able to remember or recreate them as they first appeared.

The river flowed rough and fast for days. I could hardly sleep. For a time I dared not go out for even a short walk in case more feeling-thoughts came tumbling through. I was inhabited by excitement of a kind. It was as if a film crew had suddenly appeared within a quiet village. Everything normal continued, but much was changed, charged with a new urgency, to be sensed and seen again. I longed for release, for quietness, to be set free of this passionate intensity. My feeble frame of ordinary understanding was not built for such a strain. Almost worse than the years of painful reaching towards some frustratingly uncertain goal were these times of rich provision when fruit, it seemed, fell freely from the bough. If only it would quieten and go! I must hold on and see it through!

While knowing only too well my very limited abilities for thought and writing, I expected that some clearer vision of what I was beginning to understand would dawn quickly and I would be able to spell it out in a relatively short time, and so move on to pastures new. For the academic year 1971-2 I was remarkably lucky in being offered a place as a Fellow at the Netherlands Institute for Advanced Study in the Humanities and Social Sciences in Wassenaar, Holland (founded that year by the Dutch government and universities). This wonderful institution provided (and provides) its Dutch and foreign Fellows with complete freedom to think and write, wander the countryside and the Atlantic shore. Here was the perfect opportunity to pin down whatever this line of thought was struggling again to become.

Not so! It seemed impossible then and ever since for me to go in straight lines. I read poetry and explored issues concerning metaphor. I undertook a lengthy written conversation with my various selves, sometimes finding them available companions, sometimes finding everyone turned cold and locked away. I sensed something of how variable I am, and how many ways I have for attending away from where I hide.

Beyond this I tried to write more coherently on the 'conversational' theme. Many possible sets of chapters were outlined, rough sketches tried.

Months and years of continuing struggle of a somewhat different, but no less demanding kind, followed on from there. This sense of having been intimate with some basically different patterning of the ground for some psychological understanding had confirmed my path, but not brought an identifiable goal much nearer, as far as I could see.

Intermittent trickles of clarity followed over years. The time in Holland had allowed the groundwork to be done on some issues concerning metaphor which seemed to be crucial to the kind of theme I sensed and sought. A paper on 'Metaphors for Living' was presented at the Nebraska Symposium on Motivation in 1975 and published later (Mair 1977a). One particularly fertile metaphor, that I have found continuingly helpful for understanding myself as well as clients in psychotherapy, is that of our selves as a 'community of selves'. A paper on this could also be written now that the more generic issue of metaphor had begun to find its proper place in my understanding of things (Mair 1977b).

Following this came 'The Personal Venture' (1979) in which the cost of personal inquiry was more fully recognized. Then came 'Feeling and Knowing' (Mair 1980) in which some form was given to the crucial importance I was increasingly recognizing in our 'acts of feeling' and to some of the issues that we may need to be sensitive to if we are to enter into personal conversation with others or ourselves. After a further long gap, as far as writing was concerned, came another piece of the fluid pattern. This expressed in its title and content the sense of time and ever renewing search that I and we are involved within. 'The Long Quest to Know' (1985) allowed me to say something of the wider perspective in which I was increasingly having to sense my own timid questioning.

All of these earlier papers are an integral part of the theme in this present book. The issues in these earlier papers are only alluded to in this present series, not because they are insignificant now, but because any more cohesive account will still have to wait till some further clarity becomes available to me. I do not want here to pretend that I have arrived at some seamless and fully woven world. All that is said here is part of a journey whose end is not in sight and whose eventual worth is still unclear.

Along with the papers already mentioned there have been many talks and teaching presentations of the emerging notions that still have a sense of hidden purpose. Repeatedly I have valued responses from others even where no elaborate statement was made. The notions that have gradually formed have been aired and sometimes polished a little more in the conversation of my repeated attempts to involve others in what is still trying to be said. This presentation is of a similar kind. It is a question, many questions, in the form of statement and surmise.

In what follows I have selected some pieces from my continuing, almost daily, scribbles. The segments given here are some of my attempts at beginning, yet again, not just to speak but speak *about* that speaking. A psychology surely has to be a discipline of reflection as well as other kinds of exploration of a world. Something of my psychological world has been shown in earlier sections. Now it is time to reflect a little and begin again to try to tease out a psychological theme.

I will pick up this irregular story of mine in the autumn of 1984. This point is chosen because it was then that I returned more explicitly to the conventional theme. It had never really gone, but I had been following leads that took me to particular places that did not require me to focus explicitly on the superordinate theme of 'A conversational model for psychological inquiry'. In October 1984 I was able, at last, to get a little more on paper in a formal way when versions of a couple of the early chapters in this book were done. Along with this unusual amount of formal writing for me, came a welcome growth of confidence (even if only for a little while).

Friday 26 October 1984 (afternoon)

I sense an easier run . . . barriers and tangles, blindnesses and distance are beginning to dissolve. Rather than having to find my way by air, to allow me to drop into this strange other land from there, I begin to sense a way to walk, to approach it over land. To move from where I am to where I have been flitting to, and then failing again to find, over all these years, may still be possible. Perhaps it will still prove to be a long way off but I sense a change . . . and some joinings . . . as well as a new thought (which turns out to be entailed in everything I've done).

I can now try to write more honestly, directly, telling it more just as it has been and is. I have been stabbing in the dark, struggling to sense where I am and am silently stumbling towards knowing. I've had to struggle so hard, not understanding or being able to 'see' the landscape that I've been involved within. This is partly why I've had to wait for the spirit to move, why I've had to speak in a heightened poetic way, to conjure up a living sense of whatever I am secretly engaged within, out of place and out of time, conjured in the air (the value of the poetic voice is here). I have only so far been able to speak from within it, not see what kind of thing I'm on about.

Saturday 27 October 1984 (evening)

Different themes are, I hope, still lurking and waiting their time. . . .

Approaching psychology from the direction of psychotherapy: I have been trying to do this in practice, but now I want to move towards doing it more clearly and intentionally. I want to attend in all seriousness to what I am involved with in psychotherapy, and really try to use that as a legitimate perspective from which to view some issues of psychological importance. I want to take the psychotherapeutic encounter more seriously as a 'basic bet', a worthwhile centre of activity of a special and yet generalizable kind. I want really to take up residence within the psychotherapeutic situation and the sensed knowing that it begins to allow me, and to attend to the psychological world from there.

Knowledge by analogy; in metaphor: This year's Reith Lecturer is Professor John Searle. In this week's *Radio Times* there is a highlighted quote, 'If one is completely honest, you're always doing philosophy to satisfy yourself. So with the Reith Lectures I'm in the business of talking to myself in front of a hell of a big crowd.' Perhaps it is always true of creative work. It is certainly true for me that I do my psychologizing first and foremost for myself.

There is something important in this. We take on, put on, try on, lay over ourselves, the creative undertakings of others. We enter into the pattern of them, and in doing so we live in and through them. We become someone different thereby. Somehow we create a *new meld* of 'who we were' and the 'borrowed clothing', the new (selfishly created) patterning of possibility.

There is something here about metaphor as the means by which we take on the new colouring of others. We thereby become new melds. There must be different ways in which this entering and living through the cobweb patterns that others strew across our path is done. We need to be self-absorbed, self-creating, reaching towards what is being created through us . . . then we become clothes, fancy dress, coloured paint, make-up . . . others always *walk through us* as if we were ghosts (or as if they were) and end up with our features and self-sought possibilities covering them in new traceries. They somehow, like the mingling of ghostly beings, take us to and through themselves.

We (or I?) tend to have supposed that people *take in* new knowledge as if swallowing pellets, or putting things in our pockets for future use. I've had a sense of us being more or less complete, and then taking in from others, bits and pieces, this and that, for future use. This kind of thing may, in the course of time, lead us to change as we make use of it, but essentially we remain intact. We merely take something on board, undertake to swallow and digest something from outside ourselves. Somehow this is importantly *not* so!

The passion (passivity) to know: This can now be spoken of in a different and more straightforward way. We have to be covered with the spider's web of another. We must wait and simply allow it to become part of who we are and become, as we move through it. It is we ourselves who are almost immediately changed by the presence and ideas, offerings, projections, of others. We can rush off and diffuse our awareness of what is happening. We can pretend to ourselves, because we are so active in running away, that we are thinking *about* and evaluating *from* afar, but we are already changed. Through the passion, the waiting, the being handed over to, we recognize and allow the change to be felt and realized, owned as such and drawn from, towards new life, new, changed vision and sensibility. The quest is to be understood (partly at least) as being given over and blindly struggling, without knowing what kind of struggle it is and what kind of web of being I am ensnared within. There is the awareness of already being changed, and being given over to years of struggle to know that change.

Conversation — We live in it: I am still almost entirely unable to make this leap. Conversation still seems to be like bullets going from one person and then back to the other — firing questions and shooting out answers. The sense I'm reaching for is when we are *in* conversation. And, of course, *we are in conversation all the time.* We mostly do not notice it!

This again is where the new melding of metaphoric knowing/changing comes in; and the business of passion, of being handed over to be available to the conversation within which we have whatever being we have. We are in the conversation of the universe! We seem to want to be mostly deaf to what is passing through us, constituting and composing whatever we are. We want to suppose we are in charge as origins, not intermediaries!

Sunday 28 October 1984 (morning)

We are *organs of sensing,* transmission units, boosters or suppressors, receiving, allowing to pass through into awareness or diminishing into continuing ignorance, the silence of obscurity. We are places of meeting and transmission. We are vehicles of culture, tuned to particular complexes of attentiveness and to phase out all sorts of other possibilities, transmissions from other 'stations'. We are places of transit, places of potential meeting.

We are spoken as letters, words, or phrases in the conversation of our times and places. Mostly the world speaks us. We are the words and phrases spoken by the world. Seldom do the words achieve a life of their own and in the startling juxtapositions of their sentences, refresh the world which uttered them. We are words in the syntax of history, in our place and time.

We are mostly spoken by the world, part of the arguments and assumptions of our time. Yet words can become living words.

The excitement that is too much to bear: I have to learn to take the long view rather than seek the quick and dirty kill. The excitement of new ideas, of a sense of a way forward, throws me into disarray. I start to grab and scurry. Jostling hordes of the greedy and the hungry press forward, everyone saying 'Me! Me! Pay attention to me!' There is perturbation in the square, no space to walk or look or see.

To be able to listen and find a way to say, it is necessary to be calm, to wait, to be available, to rest in wakeful readiness. It is necessary that you conjure space from time (this is the essential goal). This is the necessary passion, the struggle through distortion and demand towards the space and freedom of a god.

This greedy excitement tells you of the coming of a child, but also of false hopes and clamour, self-seeking greed, a longing to be freed from the burdens of place and time, to be released into magic air where there is no resistance, where everything is light and ease and without care.

This excitation has to be suffered and allowed to die. Till it does die, or at least retreat, there is no way to go. You have to become disinterested (not achieved through pretending not to care, but through entering the madness and bringing it to nothing from within), given over, centred somewhere other than in greedy insecurity. This is the place of prayer, of surrender of the self. Small and fearful self has to give way to that larger sense of reverence for what is bigger and wider and more enduring than our momentary phrase.

The value of coming to know ABOUT: I have so far had to diminish 'knowing about' in favour of 'knowing as living personal experiencing'. Yet in the last day or so, as I've sensed something of the way forward, there has been a relief in the possibility that I may be more able to talk *about* what I am involved in. To become able to talk about it means that you are beginning to move beyond the 'poetic' stage wherein it has to be felt for, inhabited, spoken from within. A poetics of experiencing is essential, surely, as a place of origin, or beginning to give voice and substance to what lives you still, still beyond what you grasp and know about. In coming to know about it a little, after the long struggle to body it forth (whatever *it* may turn out to be), there is relief in the possibility of talking *about.*

The next phase (though this one is far from over, and even when it is, it will always be necessary to live on the edge again) may allow some map making, some cultivation of the plain, the identifying and growing of some of the peculiar vegetation of whatever this place may be. It will become possible for tourists and settlers to find their way here and to enjoy or work the land. The day of the discoverers will be over, and the time of cultivation, of population growth, of increasing use and then abuse, will be there.

I will, perhaps, find a way across country, to begin to plan and build tracks and roads, to begin to see clearly what this place is good for, what it is about. I will begin to see something of the dimensions of 'the place', though I still cannot do this. I sense that it is coming, soon perhaps. I will begin to recognize the lie of the land, where it lies close to other known places, what other realms already have sympathies with where I then am.

Becoming almost able to talk *about* may be different in its opportunities and dangers for me and others who only come as day trippers, single visit holiday-makers, as get-rich-quick merchants, or whatever. For me there is relief in seeing the possibility of talking about, getting whatever *it* is 'out there' rather than tangled up 'in here' in whatever it is I am. It may then be possible and 'easy', worth doing, to labour in more practical fields for a time, to dig the soil, plant some trees, nurture the beginnings of a community of inquirers, located somewhat differently from those who have gone before.

I may then become able to see the point in doing many practical things (in research, for instance) that I have wanted to do but had no perspective on a suitable place to begin, no worthwhile realm to till.

For other people, there will be the continual danger of only knowing *about* 'conversational models', or whatever. They may only act on the surface, taking the easiest pickings, giving nothing to the land. They are the scavengers and the carpet-baggers of the psychological world, worldly wise, not centred in the soul, committed to the land.

What kind of thing is this alternative psychology about? This is the old question, and yet now it is differently posed and fresh for me. It feels as if the landscape of an answer may almost be in view. Is it about questioning the ground on which we stand? Is it a human geography of the between? Is it about the conversation of our lives? Is it about trying, through a poetics of experiencing, to tell it like it is? Is it about style and manner, conjuring up, bodying forth the passion of receiving? Is it on the edge, on the frontier, at the centre, the place of new creations, the magic of imagination? Is it about helping ourselves 'to see'; helping us to find where we are and what sorts of worlds we live? Is it 'to help the lame to walk and the blind to see'? To help us attend in a fiercely loving way to where and how we are arrayed? To help us undeceive ourselves? Is it to help us to begin to survive without the clutched support of external skeletons of objective fact and to live more within the moving patterns of the world?

Sunday 28 October 1984 (afternoon)

What is going on, what are we up to, in the invisible world between, in the conversation of our lives?

If this is something like the theme I'm after, what characteristics would such a discipline have? What would be its crucial concerns?

1 Creative description

It would have to depend for its 'secondary data' on various activities of creative description; finding ways to tell it like it is; conjuring out of our experiencing (out of the experiencing of those who are involved); casting in vivid, dramatic, genuinely feelingful forms, what is going on (what, possibly, is going on).

This would not necessarily or often lead to measurement. It is the drawing into sense-able form of complex and moving patterns of interaction, of not-sayings as well as sayings, of positive ignoring as well as more passive ignorance. Some kinds of measurement instruments could be of preliminary use, sometimes, in spelling out something of the life of things, but the primary 'instrument' would be ourselves as 'interpreters' or 'speakers' or 'intermediaries' or 'formulators' of whatever may be going on.

2   Conversational psychology

If it needs a name to provide it with the semblance of reality, to give it boundaries of a kind, this could be it. 'Conversational psychology' could then be one amongst many other psychological worlds. This could distinguish it from experimental, psychological, cognitive, Freudian psychologies. The name draws attention to various important features of this mode of undertaking the disciplines of knowing. It indicates that it is to do with the between, with speaking rather than more formal experiments, with meaning, with meeting, with movement.

The name also indicates that this sort of psychology will have a bearing on all those human situations which are to do with living exchanges. In psychotherapy, ordinary speakings together, or any other active 'betweening' we may need to question what is going on, in institutions, families, work, etc. The term 'conversational' is being used both literally (at times) and metaphorically (or figuratively). It draws attention to the pre-existing webs of culture and languaging (of whatever kind, not necessarily verbal) which are the preconditions for any kind of human culture, any meaningful exchange. It refers to the turnings-together, from which we each and every one are born and composed as cultural beings, words in search of syntax, sentences for life, seeking a place to live.

Its aims reach far beyond the bounds of psychotherapy, but it will be clear that the encounters of psychotherapy can play (lopsided but) important parts. Introspection and writing, and every kind of human activity in art and science, religion, sport, etc. are all relevant.

It can be a discipline that touches almost every part of life, a psychology 'on the move', living off the land, relevant to nations speaking to nation as well as person to person, self to self, world to world.

Like 'conversational French' it has to do with language, but language in its living form, as used and spoken, open to development and life.

3   What is being 'said' or 'understood'

It is concerned with drawing meaning and possible meaning (possibilities of intention) from the silent world beyond our ordinary attending. It is not concerned to be dogmatic and to claim that this or that is definitely so, but with seeking to tease out and offer in a more explicit and even personally understandable and undertakable form. It is therefore essentially about *meaning*, and not primarily about behaviour or doing as such. Since meaning is invisible and intangible, its essential concerns are therefore invisible and intangible, and yet crucial to our lives.

It is also concerned with the basic bet that we are more deeply engaged in intentional action together than we mostly recognize. What we tell ourselves we are doing is often at variance with what we can be seen as doing behind the appearances we create.

There is also, here, the basic assumption that we are repeatedly involved in bringing meaning from non-meaning, with making human sensing where there was only 'dumb' nature. We are also destroying meaning just as often.

4   Entering into and coming out from to talk about

To sense what is going on we need to feel our way into the situation, engage in it, immerse ourselves, give ourselves over to it. It is possible to say useful things without doing this sometimes, but not usually. When we enter in, indwell, we need to be able to feel our way around and become a sensitive receiver. We then need to be able to 'break out' and 'spell out' something of what we may have been engaged in, so that this can now be looked at and undertaken or modified or rejected by those involved (always recognizing that immediate rejection does not necessarily imply that the interpreter has been in error).

We need to develop senses for feeling our way in the dark, and this will be largely through the elaboration and spontaneous creation of metaphors of 'imagination', not just 'fancy'. We will also need to develop means of allowing expression to what is being sensed and felt, so that it can become available to be shared, or otherwise undertaken. All sorts of issues to do with secrets and their purposes, and the uses and abuses of spelling out are involved here.

5   A radically questioning, charitably sceptical attitude

To ask what is going on is to ask about the 'hidden agenda', the 'meta-conversation' or the 'submerged themes' of what is happening between us. This means we are concerned with opening our eyes, taking a penetrating look, not being hoodwinked by obvious reality, obvious conventions. It means that we can be in dangerous territory, behind or below or above the things we assume we are saying. We listen here with the third ear and look with the third eye (the eye of love, though a demanding love). The attitude of charitable scepticism is important, or else the whole project could become a witch hunt, a turfing of skeletons out of cupboards. But the point is that we are all in this together and we have to live together. The charitable nature of our listening and speaking is of crucial concern. It is the kind of charity that already informs any good psychotherapeutic practice.

6 Self-deception and good faith

Following from the posture of 'radical questioning', it becomes clearer that this whole project is focussed on the issues of self-deception and 'good' or 'bad' faith. This is what is *central*! It is centrally to do with the issue of what we (you and I or someone else) can *trust*.

The issues of self-deception are of considerable importance in Freudian and post-Freudian psychology and also in existentialism, for instance. But I suspect (I don't yet quite see) that I am likely to come from a different angle (e.g. indicating that this is the fundamental issue in all knowing; that science – and especially the science of psychology – is necessarily involved in this issue, but largely ignores it, and repeatedly falls into bad faith and self-deceptive hostility). I want to make this a central issue for science and everyday life, and to take it out of the somewhat rarified atmosphere of European philosophy or latter-day Vienna.

7 What can I trust?

The current approaches to science in psychology do not really address the question of what we can trust, or whether what I can trust is the same as what you can trust. This is one of the ways in which I want to take as a *question* what is so far treated by giving answers!

The issue of trust is still cloaked in obscurity. The 'scientific method' or at least the 'experimental method' solves the problem by outlining certain kinds of procedures which, if followed, will allow for tentative trust. But in most of life, in relation to most areas of human meaning, the experimental method in its formal sense is not applicable. So how do we go about establishing who and what we can and will trust for different things and to different degrees. Much of our lives is taken up in camouflaging distrust, in appearing to trust, but, in fact, withdrawing secretly from what we seem to be involved in, so as not to put ourselves at risk.

What are you placing the weight of your life upon, and in relation to what ends?

In psychotherapy we respond to a complex patterning of cues, clues, feelings, probings. Often in therapy, the basic issue is whether we (or the client) can trust *ourselves*!

8 It is essentially PERSONAL in that it is between persons AND to do with the GROUND OF THE PERSONAL

Persons are made possible in the context of 'persons in relation' and the language and culture which has shaped them. A conversational psychology has to pay as much attention to the wider context of our lives, the worlds we inhabit and which sustain us, as to the foreground figures who draw from and sometimes contribute to such worlds.

If we are in the conversation of the universe, as well as being participants in particular local conversations, it is necessary to attend somehow to worlds as well as persons. We cannot do this by separating these out into watertight categories, since it is only persons who can conceive and make something of worlds. We are in it up to and over our necks. We have to find ways, again, of entering into and questioning radically the implicitly assumed worlds built into our very sensing of and defending of ourselves. Selves and worlds (lived worlds) are intimately related and perhaps we cannot know 'world' unless it becomes 'lived world', so that we are at risk in any opening of selves and submitting to the possibility of world that might damage or destroy.

9 Other psychologies must earn their keep in relation to CONVERSATIONAL PSYCHOLOGY

So far I've been cheekily rebellious, but somehow feeling that the other, empirical, psychologies have some more obvious claim to *validity*. Now I hope it will become possible to begin to put the boot on the other foot to some degree. The unspeakable can be spoken. . . . It is clear that you do not need a scrap of general or experimental or physiological or animal psychology to be an adequate, or even a good, psychotherapist. We pussyfoot around in our conceptual sackcloth and ashes because, within psychotherapy, we do not have a psychology which can conceive of what we are doing and lay claim to a discipline of our own. Hopefully this can change towards a wider recognition that there is a legitimate claim being made here to a form of psychology that has been overlooked (except within different psychotherapeutic theories, which mostly have not risen to the level of being PSYCHOLOGIES).

I want to try to make conversational psychology into a PSYCHOLOGY, not just a THEORY!

It must become possible for us to say boldly to experimental psychology 'What have you got to offer us? You must make your case to us, not we to you!' Conversational psychology has to develop its own methods and values, ways of achieving validity and illustrating grounds for trust.

10 Serious and more frivolous conversation

It is mainly the serious conversation of our lives that I am concerned with; what we are more deeply involved within. I'm not primarily concerned (if at all) with the surface analysis of conversations in the ordinary sense. I want to attend *through the words and deeds* to what is going on in the dark, out of the illumination of attention, beyond our conscious recognition often. I'm also concerned with studying, and trying to conceive and spell out something of the worlds we take ourselves to be inhabiting. These worlds are mostly beyond our ordinary capacities to notice and question. They are so much built into the defences and strategies we use (our ways of experiencing more or less or otherwise) that we live from them and mostly cannot attend to them.

Monday 8 April 1985 (afternoon)

Is there a space to be cleared and made use of between the mainline disciplines of psychology and psychotherapy? A space wherein certain kinds of issues, certain ways of exploring issues, certain kinds of people who do not usually share the same space, can come to know themselves and each other.

There is something like the sort of thing I'm after within the psychoanalytic world, wherein literature, art, sociology, psychotherapy, philosophy, etc. can be related to each other. But that world is not my world and it is not the world/language of many who are thereby deprived of that kind of potential mix.

I want, somehow, to start from and repeatedly return to personal experiencing rather than start 'out there' in the midst of some objectified topic or generalized discipline. While I want to create a meeting-place for the riches of many disciplines, I do not want to start where they are, but to start from where I/we are in our understanding and daily living. Just as in psychotherapy we always have to create a new conversation within the wider conversation of our place and times, so here I want also to start from where someone actually is.

There is much that is invisible because it does not fit into or get shown up by the dominant conventions of our times. It therefore gets used, lived, and assumed, but is largely beyond question and outside our available understandings. I want to create a space within which some things that are taken for granted, are usually invisible, are often silently relied upon, can be given substance, form, and attention.

Different disciplines seem to struggle with many of the same issues, but with only minimal awareness that others have been there before or will come after. Disciplines keep discovering what others are discarding, and seeing in these discoveries new hopes for breaking through to new pastures. Could any way be found to get comment and help on particular issues from those who have already trodden these paths? Conversation between different scholars with different directions of intention, but temporarily sharing some approach or concepts, could be encouraged. Thus Biblical scholars, literary critics, and psychologists could share concerns about hermeneutics, deconstruction, parables and stories.

But this is again sliding away from the heart of the matter. I am concerned at two levels at least. *First,* I'm concerned at a substantive level and want to create space for a certain kind of psychological activity. *Second,* I'm concerned with generalizing a concern for conversation so as to allow for some kinds of sharing and struggling to understand what presently is hidden, occasional, and frequently non-existent.

There are powerful conventions at present which make some issues difficult to attend to with any degree of intensity and which make others almost totally unrecognizable or deprived of any significance. I need to be able to identify examples of what I mean here and highlight some alternative conventions, e.g. attending to 'moments' and not just to supposedly enduring features.

Friday 23 August 1985 (morning)

Everything has to be fought for. The ongoing conventions of the conversational 'soup' and the cultural 'web' reassert their power (like weeds taking over a garden that is left). Nothing ever stands still, everything is in motion at all times and if things are not growing they may be falling apart. Everything has to be fought for and everything has to be actively maintained.

The deadness of routine and repetition blunts and distances everything that was once new. Many (perhaps most) things that are done for the first time are not new, however. They are previously packaged and traded combinations. That makes it easy to use them without understanding or even knowing what they are composed from and what has gone into their making. To achieve freshness again and again is remarkably difficult (is probably impossible) and may be both unwise and unnecessary. Every occasional freshness is immediately denied the possibility of a repeat performance.

The fighting that has to be done is within ourselves. We have to work at taking nothing for granted (though most of us most of the time will want and need to take almost everything for granted and already given). Swimming upstream rather than letting ourselves be swept along with the enveloping current is required.

At all times, every minute of every day and almost everywhere, we are at war. Only a few themes can (so far) be given an official place. Almost everything has to be suppressed so that mostly it is unnoticed. Seeds that were not planted or were immediately deprived of the necessities of growth will not be noticed by their absence.

Are we necessarily at war, or is it that we are using and being used by this metaphor of struggle? The idea of fighting is woven so very deeply into every aspect of our lives. War, battle, life, and death, the ultimate tests of courage and rights, all of this is the basic stuff of our lives still. Even (and inevitably within this world metaphor) the maintenance of peace has to be fought for.

Peace movements are battlegrounds. War is present everywhere and there are casualties on every road.

We have to struggle again and again (always somewhere different and in different ways) for freshness. Almost all of us almost all of the time seem to want what is more routine and familiar. Freshness of vision is only sometimes wanted and only occasionally suffered for. Perhaps we want freshness without pain or the commitment of living a life on the edge. We want to be refreshed as well as cushioned tourists in strange lands, rather than undertake the enduring tasks of renewing our eyes in the contexts of our ordinary lives. It is this latter task that I am concerned to pursue, rather than the brightness of tourist trips to here and there and yonder.

Living with fresh eyes is surely what occasionally comes to lovers and mystics, worshippers and revolutionaries, artists and outsiders, parents and children.

To be always beginning, to have continually renewed refreshment, sounds highly unlikely. Maybe such a moving state is possible for the committed religious (in some undogmatic sense). For most of us, with more ordinary levels of courage and ability, something more occasional is much more likely. For us it may only be in exceptional moments that new eyes are fleetingly possible. Only in moments of transcendence of our ordinary rootedness can we hope to glimpse the world anew. And yet, these exceptions to the ordinary run of things may have the most profound influence on all our more familiar days.

Refreshment may be what a psychology of exceptional moments, of the edge, is about. This is such a different basis for a psychological undertaking from that of creating familiarity. So far we have generally supposed that 'psychology as a science' is to do with the discovery (the uncovering) of regularities, the recognition of repetition, the championing of the usual. Our main concerns have been with 'laws'. The idea of 'law' has been used in both senses, as having to do with hidden regularities in nature, and the conventions of societies that are enforced by social sanction. We have often supposed that we are in pursuit of 'laws of nature' when we have actually been delineating some of the entailments of unnoticed 'laws of the social or psychological world'. Gradually we have been recognizing our participation within the structuring of conventions, but we are still largely blind to our involvements in 'feeling for fresh vision'. We do not adequately conceive of 'refreshment' as a different basis for knowing.

There are ways of making this renewed vision something of an assault, an attack, a tearing away of familiar and conventional coverings, an act of war. There are also ways in which it may be more gentle, more shared. The brutality of new vision, being renewed through what is known and needed being stripped aside, is part of the ongoing war. There is threat in anything that will strip us of the habits and habitations that we know. We fear to be homeless, without familiar habitations.

Thursday 5 September 1985 (morning)

I want to have concepts that help us to work with more discrimination and sensitivity in the dark, on the move. Reality becomes available to us in metaphor. Our structuring of things and fantasies is through the metaphors offered silently in our culture or sought by ourselves. To understand our reality we must understand our grounding in the shaping metaphors of our place and time.

My concern, perhaps, is to 'make light our darkness'. If we don't do more of this we will continue to act in the light of our present understandings from the hidden ground of our unnoticed assumptions and postures, the postures we assume without being able to recognize what they are.

It is a *questioning* psychology that I'm after. A psychology of questioning. It asks where many assume we have answers. It probes into what most take for granted. It goes towards that from which we normally come.

We are so involved in getting answers (not surprisingly)! I don't know how, usefully, to ask about asking. A psychology which goes 'up stream' will attend to that from which we normally act, to assumptions and the silent struggles in the dark which are woven into all our acts in relationship. Such a psychology would have to be different from the psychology of answers that we presently pursue. Would it simply be something like 'philosophical psychology'? A discipline that is concerned with the concepts we use and the coherence of our claims? Would it be more like a 'philosophy of science for psychology' concerned with paradigms and modes of scientific change?

Sunday 8 September 1985 (morning)

I struggle repeatedly to find a place within which meaning grows, lives, moves. . . . It is not some superficial account that I'm after but feeling alive, living meaning that is not yet drawn out and woven into the garments of playfulness (and eventually the strait-jackets of convention).

It is not spoken of much in psychology, this ongoing struggle in the course of a single life. It is somehow assumed that you have quietly to get on with it and attend from whatever your struggle is about to tasks that can be attended to in public places. Psychology itself should be struggling with what it means in every generation. What does it mean to be a psychologist, a student of our living in time? We seem to assume that our meaning is officially given.

We, as psychologists, have to be traders in meaning. We are meaning-merchants who have to draw on the craftsmen and artists of meaning in our cultures. We have to be able to attend to what people mean and do not mean, what they want to mean but cannot, what confusions they have in not knowing what they mean or what meaning there may be in what they do. We are workers, also, in the abbatoir of meaning.

We kill and sell the remains of meanings for tasty snacks and cer-
emonial banquets.

Sunday 8 September 1985 (afternoon)

There are certain sorts of groupings and modes of expression in cultures
which consider the mysterious as worthy of attention. Those who write
within the mystery of their lives may often speak of and to the mysteries
of other lives. A world or culture without these further reachings would
be impoverished.

It is this sort of concern that I feel from afar. The very ordinary
experience of an ordinary life can be spoken of with attention to mystery,
rather than neatly swept out of reach by others who more readily go with
the moving herds of meaning as they graze on the most available cultural
pastures of our time.

It is faithfulness to the moving mystery that I want to write, the passion
of knowing. I do not want to attribute that knowing to some divine source.
It is not knowledge of a 'Someone', but of 'being in context', my being in
my context, which may articulate something of relevance to others with
similar concerns.

What if, following Don Cupitt (1985), and speaking of psychology rather
than theology (which was his concern), we see it not as a 'dogmatic system
or ideology, but an ethical project aimed at human emancipation'. Should
a personal and conversational psychology not be seen as an ethical project
and a spirituality, closely related to critical thinking, seeking freedom from
the tyranny of the world, the fetishism of objectivity, learning always to use
theory instrumentally rather than dogmatically, stressing self-examination
and seeking to clarify consciousness and enhance freedom by recognizing
and discarding inner blocks?

Similarly in psychology, should we not be more positively 'mystical' rather
than 'mythical' in our thinking. Mythical thinking, says Cupitt, 'projects
realities outwards, objectifies them and pictures in them an invisible world
of . . . forces and causes of events'. Mystical thinking on the other hand
'draws them back within the self. It internalizes and spiritualizes. Mystical
thinking carries out a kind of inner critique through which the self is purged,
purified, emancipated from bondage to dogmatic illusions, illuminated and
transformed into freedom and godlikeness!'

As Cupitt also says, 'The way we construct our world, and even the
way we constitute our own selves, depends on the set of values to which we
commit ourselves. Our preferences reveal what we are, and we are reflected
in the world we establish around ourselves. The outer world reflects the
inner, and the constitution of both is ultimately ethical.'

So much of this is of relevance to the kind of psychological activity I
seem to be reaching for. Perhaps a conversational psychology should remain

intentionally lightweight, able to move ground and methods, seeking always to take something like a Socratic posture within every developing context of culture. Its allegiance is towards truth in action, the hard task of being true to what we are and to what we seek. It stands always on the battleground of delusions and illusions by which we clothe our fears with solidities that deceive and assert powers we do not possess. Its aim is dis-illusionment!

Monday 9 September 1985 (morning)

Conversational Psychology. (That name still seems weak, insipid.) It should both draw from and contribute to ongoing psychotherapeutic activity. It should draw into the realm of psychotherapeutic work, and many other relationships (e.g. in committees, teaching, negotiation, etc.), ways of thinking and speaking that may help sharpen, deepen, or variously strengthen our understanding, helping to identify tangles, problems, assumptions, illusions. It should draw from psychotherapeutic practice (as from any and every other relationship in ordinary living that is participated attentively within and reflected upon) an enriching context of understanding, an open-ended and ongoing context of struggle wherein we necessarily move beyond what we can easily tell.

But *what kind of knowledge* will such a psychology be mainly concerned with?

It will be close-up knowledge, knowledge that affects the knower. It will be knowledge in practice (not applied to practice). It will have to do with how we live, how we relate, how we anticipate events, how we are arrayed in the moving seas of our circumstances. It will have to do with understanding (participating in and learning from what we can endure) rather than distanced knowledge about things in the world.

It will be a psychology of understanding rather than a psychology of information about (understanding and the struggle for differing understandings is likely to be central to any notion of conversation). It is therefore going to be more in the ball-park of wisdom than knowledge of things.

What is quite clear is that this psychology is *not in place of* a psychology of knowledge about, but is an important companion to such a psychology. We have been living with a grossly unbalanced approach to knowing, seeking knowledge-about while not taking any serious note of our profound involvement in and various relationships to our acts of knowing. We have mostly acted as if we could freely speak about 'the world' without serious attention to the speaker's involvement in what is said and claimed as knowledge. A psychology of understanding and misunderstanding is very much akin to I.A. Richards' claims for rhetoric (1936). It would be concerned with giving accounts (how else are we to try to understand?), telling our stories, and responding attentively to those of others.

All this makes it seem very much a matter of philosophy, criticism, moral training, and attentiveness. It is more than this. It is to do with passion, with the most personal and most mysterious aspects of our selves and our lives together. Literary criticism is relevant but not enough. It is not the heart of the matter. The heart of this kind of psychology will be in the depths of our relationships to ourselves, others, and our world.

It is here a psychology for explorers not for accountants and administrators. We have suffered too long under the ridiculous tyranny of those who claim that what is most personal and profound in our experience is irrelevant or outside our remit.

Monday 9 September 1985 (afternoon)

There are crucial changes in focus and attention that I have not yet grasped adequately. This kind of psychology has to start with and remain continually attentive to our being up to things and on about things in the midst of everything that we know and do not know. We are in business towards ends (many of which we have not chosen and do not recognize) in everything we do. Every question, claim, silence, and action is to be heard and read within the cultural projects that shape us and the personal projects that we are often coherently but implicitly pursuing.

Every statement is a statement of greed. It expresses our needs and our desires to have. All our claims are extravagantly biassed towards what we want and need. We are endlessly nimble-footed in obscuring what we were up to or what we want. Very often we are able to deceive ourselves as well as the publicly available selves of others. At all times we assert our worlds and insist on structurings that we know (even when they strangle us). Almost all the time we do what is required of us. Almost never do we act with freedom.

Fear of freedom is endemic. Freedom from the bonds of illusion is rare. It has been the highest quest of man for all recorded time. We have not progressed far. In each generation there are both new and enduring traps, ways in which we are traduced and blinded, led off to comfort and continuing bondage. Perhaps our ambition should be 'for freedom alone' and not for any particular purpose.

We are objectifying (object-creating) creatures. We insist on solid reality. We express our longing in the very texture of our language. Matter is what matters. Things provide us with our security. Firm ground is necessary for us to stand upon.

Our reality is woven make-believe. We mostly want to survive as easily as possible and swallow almost any kind of social lie if it is fed to us early and continuously enough. We have arranged methods of knowing which are precisely tuned to keep us in ignorance — and yet we always fail here because everything eventually becomes its opposite or some thing other than we planned.

I want to pay attention to knowing which still carries the smell of the marriage bed and the kitchen. We are so quick in hiding our secret involvements in knowing as droppings of our own bodies, our own sweating and characteristically incompetent constructions. We build deodorant into our favoured methods so that our tracks will be covered, so that no one can pin the guilt of ignorance and partiality on us. We would rather, by far, share in the common guilt of those who disown themselves and treat that prodigal part which goes forth and returns as someone else, not part of who we were or failed to be.

There is something shameful in being caught with your hand in the cookie-jar of knowing. Perhaps it is frightening to begin to suspect that we might have a say, rather than everything being safely supplied.

All this is going round in old circles. It is not increasing my understanding of what I'm after (what I'm already so deeply involved in).

There is *no method*, and yet it is also about our ways of going about our affairs. In contrast to the (relatively) do-it-yourself rule book of conventional 'scientific method' (which allows people of little ability to produce a great deal without much thought) this psychology will be occasional and individual in its public achievements. There can be no easy reaching for publication (as if every class essay were worthy of wide circulation). There can be no route to mindless production ('knowing' in this person-affecting sense cannot be mass production). We are here necessarily dealing with exceptional struggles, exceptional moments of clarity in the midst of ordinariness.

Does understanding matter? In what ways does understanding matter? What can it do for us, that someone has tried to understand?

If I am not understood (e.g. when in a foreign country – most of us are foreigners to most others!) I will be lonely, isolated, an outsider, a spectator, and not a participant. I am liable to begin to lose a sense of reality, feel frightened, become hungry for contact. To find someone who speaks your language can be an immense relief, even though in normal circumstances you would have little in common.

If no one understands your language (what you mean, what your meaning is or might be) then you are likely to have to shrink. You may only be able to stumble a few incoherent words. Any competence you might have had vanishes. You are reduced to a state of foolishness, childishness, idiocy.

Those who can speak the necessary public language, and seem to understand and be understood, have all the power. Only by outbreaks of action, signs, and movements, can you try to convey something of your concerns, make yourself noticeable, draw attention to your plight (even though that also may be misunderstood and simply confirm the rejection you already feel). To be noticed you may have to act extravagantly, violently, anti-socially, disruptively.

Being understood a little and by someone may remind you of yourself, may keep you sane or return you to some sense of belonging (however tenuous that may still be). If someone does seem to understand a little (even if only a 'professional translator') you are liable to become dependent on them, eager to ascribe them special status. You are liable, also, to land on them your frustrations and anger for the hurts you have endured and not been able to convey to those more appropriately involved.

The occasional chance to speak with someone who understands you a little may be enough to give you some sense of existence, of being a real person in spite of your lack of recognition or contact with those around. I suspect we are quite remarkably resilient and can survive on very little recognition, understanding, life-size recognition.

But this is not quite how it is. We live in worlds where no one quite understands everything we are. Perhaps for many, enough of who they are is understood in the language that we share. For many others, their 'words' are not heard, they have no meaning to others and so can have no meaning for themselves either. Those around do not credit the words and manner of saying that they may require if they are to conjure up the shape they know but do not yet know they know. If those around do not wish to learn the language that you need, what then? Are you to go elsewhere to find some ghetto or subculture where your voice can be heard (and so confirm your distance from those who did not want to know)?

We are almost endlessly variable creatures capable of almost endless forms of disguise, camouflage. We deceive and lose ourselves in our many changings and hidings. We are chameleons of remarkable diversity, twigs pretending to be stick insects.

This psychology of conversation will be especially difficult since it is incapable of the kind of rapid self-advertisement that has characterized the 'scientific method'. As anyone makes progress here, they are likely to say less not more. Only the 'saints' will be able occasionally to renounce their places of achievement in order to stay amongst those of us who have a long way to go.

This metaphor of a foreign language has been used very often. Rycroft (1985) was using something like it when talking of psychoanalysis being concerned primarily with 'meanings' and not with 'causes'. Such a metaphor, of course, fits well with a conversational psychology. That, surely, has to be about speaking together in a language that we can share and which is adequate for saying what we feel and seek to know. It puts new emphasis on the business of understanding a shared language which we can both or all speak. Understanding is what language is about.

Language creates and furthers both understanding and misunderstanding. Conversation is an ongoing necessity wherein we twist and turn towards misunderstanding and partial understanding. There is nothing fixed or final.

We cannot speak intimately and creatively in a language we are only beginning to try to use. To begin with we may only manage simple and personally distant things, out there in the world, not within the places of mystery where new meaning is created.

Tuesday 10 September 1985 (evening)

Being misunderstood is one thing (or many things). Not being understood at all is quite different. There are some who live lives of unbelievable horror, the extremities of loneliness, madness even, because what they sense and know within their own experience is not what they see around them. It is something very different. Some may find no obvious trace of their experiencing even in the private lives of others.

I am running out of steam for this 'understanding' theme at the moment. Maybe I have to go elsewhere and return from a different direction. Further threads are needed.

Sunday 15 September 1985 (morning)

What is the status of what I am trying to do?

Is it an attempt to (pretend to) replace the hard-headed experimentalist, fragmenting approach to our study of ourselves with something more cosy, soft-edged and warmed with the embers of longing for an all-fitting-together-in-one-family, rustic past? Is it a more serious attempt to bring back into focus something that has been improperly excluded, while recognizing the here-to-stay centrality of the experimentalist policy of divide and rule? Is it an attempt (however slight and uncertain) to reach towards a new vision of the whole enterprise?

Is it a form of rustic wistfulness (essentially conservative and timid) or an attempt at reaching a new vision of revolutionary passion (essentially transforming and reappraising all our foundations and aspirations)?

Is it a poor relative (or bastard child) of religion and science? Or is it an inheritor of both of these in that no adequate study of our human nature can exclude almost everything that is not measurable and still consider itself worthy of respect?

There are probably strands of all of these, some stronger than others — but where do I want to stand? At *least* I want to try to help *correct the balance* by making credible again attention to much that has been submerged in the continuing drive towards the experimental science model. At *most* I wonder about the possibility of shaking and renewing the foundations of the whole bag of tricks.

Redressing the balance. If this is all I can aspire to, or legitimately consider, what are the main requirements? I need to clarify what has been neglected or lost, giving illustrations and examples of how and why it continues to matter; offer renewed ways of considering and crediting these matters within our present world; try to delineate something of the kind of knowledge that is being attended to here and some grounds for recognizing its areas of relevance, ways of appearing, and modes of investigation; indicate also how attention to some or all of these may have implications for the questions, methods of inquiry, or answers derived within the experimentalist perspective.

Shaking and renewing the foundations. If this is a possibility, what then becomes of primary importance? The basic assumptions sustaining the whole currently familiar psychological enterprise have to be shown to be implausible or incoherent. (Almost certainly this will mean replacing the 'realist' aspirations of much of psychology with a recognition of 'fictions' and the diverse stories we therein tell and live — stories are habitations for communities of speakers and believers rather than sideshow entertainments only.) Alternative assumptions have to be posited and explored for their radical differences in implication and for the way they may also sustain old actions but cast them within a different kind of dramatic enterprise. It is usual to expect that a new perspective will bring to light new problems and will provide solutions to old and persisting problems (e.g. the dubious 'effectiveness' of psychotherapy and its growing availability in spite of this).

Friday 27 September 1985 (morning)

We are inheritors of a psychology that seeks to be a psychology of facts and a purveyor of truths. This psychology has determined certain classes of procedures by which reliable facts and truths can be claimed. The 'applied scientist' model that we teach ourselves in clinical psychology is largely related to this kind of parent discipline.

There is a different level of psychological work that we already undertake, but do not fully recognize or own as (perhaps) our greater responsibility. This is a psychology of imaginative and questioning honesty. This is a very different kettle of fish. Of course, it also seeks reliable knowledge, but it firstly seeks reliable understanding. It recognizes that relying on someone or something is a *human activity* and not something inhering in the thing or person. It recognizes also that imaginative and persistent questioning of all our beliefs and claims is, in the long term, especially important. It recognizes that facts come and go and that 'truth' lies wholly beyond our grasp. All that we have to go on is our human understanding and a struggle for honesty to ourselves, others, and our world. This is fallible and changing.

We are riddled with limitations and ways by which we deceive and entrap ourselves for safety or gain. This is a psychology of human activity, of imaginative probing, from every angle and on every front. It recognizes our complete involvement in culture and time, and seeks to struggle for vantage points from which to look and ask, and look again.

Within this kind of psychology, there is an important place for all kinds of formal and informal experimenting and assertion. These can contribute a lot, but much of that may be in showing up how inadequate what has been done has been. This becomes a psychology of imaginative, questioning discourse. Within this wider discipline there is a focal need for attending to the ways in which we fool ourselves and others by the manner in which we claim power for our particular versions of the truth.

We have to be versed in seeing through the blandishments of easy cover-stories and slanted accounts (and all accounts, including our own, are prejudiced and partial). We have to recognize that no story-telling is altogether frivolous. We are insecure beings and need to assert our worlds. They are not given to us, we have to insist on them and then have to go on buttressing their claims. To ask questions of this is to enter realms of quite profound insecurities. We may become outsiders and enemies even as we seek most to help.

Friday 27 September 1985 (lunchtime)

This discipline is concerned essentially with *understanding and misunderstanding* between people and peoples. It is as if we are dealing in learning, using, and speaking foreign languages. Only some of what others mean can be caught in our terms and we have to struggle to find new terms and new frames of reference within which their terms begin to be understood more fully by them and us. It is one of the especial difficulties for a native speaker to say what is meant by words that are often used in context but never looked at and talked about.

Understanding is a wider concern than explanation. Explanation is an impersonal ploy within the wider ambit of understanding. It is a valuable tactic which can both clarify and confuse. If we are used by our own tactics we can be as confused by our actions as if we are used by the metaphors that we unknowingly take to be truth itself.

Understanding and misunderstanding are also human activities, firmly rooted in someone, somewhere, at some time, within some context of constraint and concern. We do not eventually have the right to fly off into impersonality or pretend that what is being claimed is by immaculate conception. This is a discipline rooted in, starting from, and returning to, human action within the context of culture and language.

Such a discipline is essentially *a discipline of discourse* and not a discipline of 'pure' or 'applied' or 'experimental' science. In the human realm, it is more necessary to recognize that ours has to be a *conversational discipline*.

There must be many implications of this that have not yet been touched. One of the immediate ones is that such a discipline of discourse must attend to everything that can be understood and known of the nature of discourse, the many ways in which we shape and frame, construct and deconstruct, bias and straighten, colour and bleach our ways of understanding and misunderstanding what we are about. Its fundamental focus of concern will be to learn about human discourse and our many ways of clarifying and confusing ourselves and others. It is a discipline concerned with the secret and the devious, the straight and the hinted, the apparent and the hidden. It is rooted in our needs and limitations and as it develops we must too.

The psychology we currently claim as modal is concerned with establishing knowledge about the world, including the human world. It conceives of knowledge largely separate from any particular individual. The idea is to achieve the kind of routine control that can be taught and communicated to others, so that it is not intimately tied to the implicit characteristics of anyone in particular. This is in many ways a noble aspiration, and has resulted in a great deal of technical control in other spheres.

A discipline of discourse, being firmly rooted in culture, society, and persons-in-relation, involves a different relationship with knowledge and knowing. Knowing has to be kept on the scene and cannot be shrunk to knowledge about this or that. Knowing and being known are intimate human activities and to participate more fully in these is to be affected and changed. Only by becoming more aware can you become more aware, only by being willing to listen and wait can you learn what may thereby be learnt.

Put briefly a discipline of discourse involves different levels, but is fundamentally 'a way of living' which requires and necessarily involves the moral issues of courage, choice, and lived questions.

In the cycles of discourse, any 'end' or new 'beginning' is always a telling, a story, a way of putting something, an exchange in language, seeking to understand and be understood (and raising just enough uncertainty to suggest the next way of using what has been achieved, to reach for what may yet be). We are engaged here in changing and being changed, movement. Personal and social movement is what is sought. Writing, speaking together, creative expression that touches and moves, seem to be what we are reaching for here. This does not deny number and mathematics an important place. There are many languages for different purposes and people.

In all this, therefore, I am proposing a perspective on the venture of psychology that is wider and more demanding than our present mythology allows. It is a perspective that can be seen as growing out of, and making wider sense of, the psychotherapeutic venture as well as the experimental approach. *It relocates an experimental approach within a wider framework of ongoing discourse* and recognizes the importance, but not the focal importance, of such activities. It draws attention to many different things, but gives initial and continuing attention to the nature of discourse, conversation, and the ways whereby we struggle for and away from meaning. Meaning tortures and kills just as it gives hope and life. Meaning must not be raised up as some gloriously benign deity, but it is the whole realm within which human life breathes and grows, suffocates and withers.

Such a discipline should claim to be a distinctive breed. It is not just a biological or a social science. It is not just a science or an art. It is not just concerned with the manufacture of knowledge or the ongoing activities of knowing. It starts from the notion of 'the between and the amongst', discourse or conversation. It is an ongoing and complex activity of relationship, rooted in human experience and action and requiring that we develop or shrink, improve or deteriorate, as we risk undertaking the questions of our lives. There is absolutely no guarantee of 'upwards and onwards'. We can destroy ourselves just as easily as we can develop our potential. Our potential is for evil as well as good, and every kind of mixture in between.

In this scheme of things, everyone (from all the existing aspects of psychology) in a sense has been right, and everybody wins prizes. How could it be otherwise? If most people have been seriously struggling from their perspectives, then as part of the 'conversation of our times', they must be on about something that needs to be taken seriously if we are to try to understand more of the whole picture of psychological discourse.

Sunday 29 September 1985 (morning)

I seem to have the beginning strands of an answer, without knowing what it is an answer to or for! If psychology as a discursive or conversational discipline can be developed, what will it be for? What will it especially allow us to do or foster? Is it anything more than a general framework within which to carry on doing all the things we are doing now, and nothing much else?

In psychology as a discursive/conversational science/discipline what is the heart of the matter, the centre of the difference from what we have now? What are some of the important changes in basic assumptions around which it is to grow?

Monday 30 September 1985 (evening)

Reach tall and far!
Stay close, touch and feel!
Aim high and deep!
See your place in the sweep of time!

It is a calling and a passion.
It is a matter of ultimate concern.

Be wary and willing.
Be cynical and yet simple.
Try to speak always to the heart of the matter.
Reach beyond the conventions of politeness and superficial pretence.
Do not live in the lap of protectionism and petty professionalism.

Do not live mainly for immediate gain and self-flattery.

We are baffled creatures in time and know little of ourselves or our neighbours.

We are on a journey and have a long way to go.

Sunday 20 October 1985 (morning)

The notion of 'being in conversation' is a complex one that needs to have some of its different levels understood more clearly: (1) the idea of the ongoing, cultural, conversational brew out of which we all evolve; (2) the various local conversational values and conventions that highlight some aspects of what our wider cultures allow; (3) the current conversational ferment which has its implicit forms of constraint and exclusion (and which has a mostly hidden distribution of powers, rights, and privileges that most of us fail to reach); (4) the ongoing conversation of particular lives as they are argued for and asserted, questioned and blustered around in continuing reconstruction (like boats being repaired at sea); (5) the moment by moment, event by event conversations in which we participate with another or others; (6) the hidden conversational companions who play decisive parts while mostly remaining out of sight.

We have to learn to leave behind our sensing of ourselves as blobs in place, and become patterns of movement, meeting and parting, weaving together and falling apart, endlessly in conversation. We *are* conversation as well as being *in* conversation.

There are some moral challenges here that are too great for me yet (or ever) to undertake. My failures in conversation are so obvious and so defining of my ordinary life that I cannot easily undertake this metaphor without shame or a serious turning towards where I fail. I cannot bear to give ground, to give away the hard security of a protected place.

What is at risk in entering into conversation more openly? The security of a fixed position? A place of relative safety defined by solidity, fixedness? 'Here I stand, I can do no other!' There is a threat to your claim to power. If I give way on this I am surrendering the higher ground.

Issues of power are crucially important in conversation. Having power, being in a position of power, having power over others rather than being subject to the power of others. All these are important to me. I and we are frightened to be vulnerable, subject to the power of others, weak, wrong-footed, at a disadvantage, one down. In all conversation there is a hidden patterning of power.

Perhaps even within our grammatical structures there is a hierarchy of power. The 'subject' wields power through the activity of the 'verb' over the 'object'. Beyond this, all conversational circumstances are arranged so as to stack the cards in particular ways (in committees, social events, etc.).

Within a conversation there is the structuring of advantage and the fight to persuade, to come off best, or at least escape creditably.

To allow yourself to be vulnerable is to open the door to hurt and damage (though some become expert at vulnerability as an alternative route to safety and power). There is the fear of being destroyed, of having the ground cut from under your feet so that you will be proved worthless.

Friday 15 November 1985 (evening)

If psychology fails to be continually self-critical and encouraging reflexive awareness in those who use it, it becomes just another weapon in the hands of the powerful (who will use it to their own unavowed and unacknowledged ends). If psychology fails to maintain its moral base (in honesty, sensitivity, courageously and seriously recognizing its own human partialities in what it may be doing to others) then it will fail in its wider and higher aspirations to become a humane science, and will remain largely as an administrator's tool, a set of technical competences (inevitably more limited in the longer term trust and good will they foster), used by those with local or wider powers for their particular ends (their own moral rights and starting-from positions being ignored).

This is such a tall order, and so very far from being recognized widely or explored, that it is unlikely to be attended to.

Friday 6 December 1985 (evening)

> Touch the dream
> Don't let it die!
> Scream and scream
> Touch the dream
>
> Touch the dream
> Touch the dream
> Don't let it die!
> Help me to cry
>
> Touch the dream
> Please hear my cry
> Don't let it die!
> Touch the dream

This is a dead man's tale. Dead words fight over the legacy of sentences and lose their claims. Arguments of the dead suffocate the tree. Arguments of the dead are all that he can see.

These are strained strings of struggling words, forced into postures and the pretence of movement. This is a dead man's tale.

Speak from the dream. Speak from the dream, not from how it seems. Is it possible to speak from the dream? Speak for the dream!

It is young and green
when you touch the dream
Young and green
Young and green

It is young and green
when you touch the dream
Young and green
King and Queen

King and Queen
through eyes unseen
Touch the dream
Touch the dream

Whisper the dream
whispers the dream
Seen yet unseen
Whisper the dream

Wednesday 15 January 1986 (evening)

There are at least *two very different basic assumptions about* a psychology of human relations and action.

1. One set of assumptions rests on the notion that mostly we are ignorant of human affairs except for various crude, common-sense, starting-points. These crude notions are useful for getting us going in scientific investigation into the real state of affairs. Disappointingly, this approach often seems to end by confirming 'on a scientific basis' what has been assumed and commonly understood all along. Sometimes, though, our experimentation does provide us with some counter-intuitive claims which stoke the fires of our professional willingness to dismiss the common knowledge of everyday experience. Often, of course, such findings are later cast in doubt when more appropriately read into the wider context from which our investigations severed and removed them.

2. The other starting-place is to assume that, essentially, in our culture at large, we know everything that can be known at the present time, of human life and relations within that culture. Much else is possible within other cultures which can astonish us about our blindness and our unrecognized limitations of understanding and action. From this alternative starting-place, we have to rediscover what we already implicitly know and tell moving stories of what we find, renewed by each generation.

Not surprisingly, much of what is to be known is already available in particular forms in the art and literature of our people, though mostly that is little taught by those who would claim to be scientists of human behaviour. But even when such cultural knowledge is lying mute in the pages of some great story from the past, it often has to be brought to life again, seen afresh, for our needs, now. It has to be kindled with new words towards experiences we did not know we shared.

Though I do not believe we have to make a choice of one or the other of these approaches, my own preference as a place to start is with the second assumption. Those who take the other route will, anyway and thereby, help create new stories for our times (or more likely, tell fragments of old tales in terms and conventions that appeal to some who do not know or believe that the past has important tales to tell). It may also be that creative experimentalists will conjure up new tales, and may contribute new twists or even new themes in terms that will themselves become coated with the dust of soon to be outdated conventions. Again and again our stories have to be revived, reformed, told in a different voice, with a different set of characters, a different lexicon of terms.

These two different approaches to psychology should not be treated as if one were sensible and the other foolish. Both can be of value. Each will speak to some. Both are, as I see it, in the business of *story-telling*. They tell rather different stories perhaps, but stories nonetheless. One set of stories is concerned with 'causes' and the hidden particulars of circumstances and physical make-up which necessitate outcomes. The other kind is concerned more with 'meanings' and alternative interpretations, finding meanings that ring bells and allow the flush of new action.

I wish to pursue this idea of a psychological approach which assumes that we know more than we can ordinarily say. It is an approach which assumes that we have hidden depths (or heights or widths). These depths are reached by various means of dwelling in and feeling our way into the hidden sensings of our lives. But these places are parts of our culture that gives us life. They are not primarily parts of a private unconscious. We are each neck-deep in the sea of our culture and as we lower our awareness into the interstices of our normally unnoticed feeling, we can begin to sense and specify some of what normally we act from without attending to.

There is a sense in which a psychology from this perspective of 'total immersion' does not require any special training. We know it all (or a lot of it) already and have only to find ways of saying and sharing what we implicitly know. Everyone has access to wide and deep seas of normally ignored and unspecified particulars of vital importance to the normal running of our lives.

Yet it is also false to suggest that nothing but 'common sense' is involved. It is easy to speak of 'common sense' but it is not easy or common for this implicit knowing to be available to questioning and sharing. To 'tell it like it is' is a gift more readily available to some (e.g. poets, song writers, novelists, creative scientists, artists), but it can also be widened and deepened in the awareness of many.

The disciplines of compassionate attention, of waiting and acting in relation to the hints and clues along the way, are all needed and can be practised. The doors of greater understanding do not stand open, waiting for armies to march through with alacrity. The platelets of concealment and camouflage are everywhere. It takes need and caring, persistence and the patience of the birdwatcher and the hunter to sense the tiny movements in the grass that tell clear tales to those who know what they are involved in coming still to know.

Alone and out of reach, cold and at a conventionally low temperature, nothing but easy-growing weeds thrive. There has to be a *context of caring* wherein there is a glow of respect for what matters in particular lives. This has to be felt and not just manufactured for the moment. There also need also to be *nourishing concerns* in the midst of such a place. It is often not enough that people there are just given some general encouragement.

Saturday 18 January 1986 (afternoon)

What distant drummer are we following in the longer term?

There are no single or right answers. There are always going to be differences in what we consider to be answers, and gaps between what is said and what is done. So what are we reaching towards?

Perhaps something like trying to increase our understanding of ourselves and each other, and in the context of that, to seek to develop ways of predicting and controlling aspects of our lives so that we can be challenged repeatedly to 'get out of that one'. All our searching for understanding will be tested and tried by repeated attempts to set limits, assert finalities, in the wider knowledge that we have thereby also to expect and encourage novelty, the never before seen or sensed!

This perspective sets knowledge-about ourselves and others in the wider context of 'understanding, misunderstanding, and creative action'. It also sets our attempts to 'predict and control' within a wider context of dialogue and creative challenge. We could then respect those who pose particularly demanding 'traps' as especially valued instigators of inventive reconstruction. We could also see that we are at war with ourselves, seeking to control and set limits (by many instances of sleight of hand and cooking of the books, as well as honestly intended studies and claims), and seeking again to question and reframe the issues so that openness is again a possibility.

I believe that we leave out of focus and out of the reckoning the context of discourse. We thereby exclude any focal attempt to understand what goes on in discourse, whereby we understand, misunderstand, seek to achieve ends by various ploys and manners of doing things and seek to use power where understanding fails. I believe that we have to step back as a discipline to reckon with this wider context within which we seek to work towards understanding, rather than focus only or mainly on some of the tactics by means of which we challenge and entrap ourselves at particular times and in specific ways.

Understanding and misunderstanding are achieved through language and the use of language. Understanding more about our use of language (rhetoric, metaphor, conversational style, assumptions, cultural framing, etc.) would seem to be essential if we are to be actively and more sensitively informed and more ready to tackle the kinds of 'final answers' that are repeatedly claimed.

A psychology of experimentation, testing, and assertion needs to be set within a wider psychology of discourse, of probing and questioning of all claimed answers and all final solutions. There is no one to say what psychology should be for (nor any reason to suppose that it should be for anything in particular). It is up to each of us to struggle towards our own understanding within the discipline we inhabit and the society we share, and may wish to change.

What I am suggesting is that psychology, which has so often in this past century been notable for its claims of having limited human freedom, abolished it, redefined it, could be undertaken as a *venture in human freedom*. It would always be in question and under threat, but struggling to find another way. In this psychology of discourse, of conversation, we are reaching for new freedom, beyond the bounds of any particular claims to have finally explained, summed up, pinned down, the human venture. In this sort of conversational discipline, we are at war. We are threatened, we may be overwhelmed, we may have all liberty stripped from us by the organized power of some explanation or some force of arms or influence. But, in the concluding words of the Declaration of Arbroath (1320) 'It is in truth not for glory, nor riches, nor honours, that we are fighting, but for Freedom — for that alone, which no honest man gives up but with life itself.'

It is a political realm wherein we are all involved in the limitation of freedom. We keep asserting worlds, while mostly thinking we are being more neutral and dispassionate. There is a rhetoric of persuasion and hidden assertion, a sense of unquestionableness in much that we do and say. To seek freedom is also to get to know our limitedness. We are involved in the battle of freedom and being determined.

Faith is perhaps the willingness to turn experience into experiment. Beware the smothering of experiment by experience! Beware the smothering of experience by experiment!

There is something especially open-ended, tenuous, vulnerable about this kind of psychology. We are more in danger of crushing ourselves than others.

All life is vulnerable, and all environments are delicate balances which can be destroyed by carelessness as well as catastrophe. Increasingly we are recognizing the fragility of our wider world. Inside its thin protective envelope of an atmosphere it is constantly being bombarded from without and threatened from within. Increasingly we need an ecological consciousness in many of its constituent parts.

Psychology is a very fragile discipline. We have tended to take a tough, experimentally based and statistically buttressed stance towards the world, though many psychologists do not live that way or welcome some of what is thus being claimed in our names.

Wednesday 5 March 1986 (evening)

I do not offer a comfortable or rosy view. We are walking in sleep and cannot bear to waken. Yet that is what is necessary if we are to survive. We need to undergo a radical awakening. We are blind and seek to remain so.

Friday 14 March 1986 (morning)

Start again! I'm getting nowhere with this section. I keep trying to make it do what is logically necessary rather than attending to what wants to be said.

Is there anything I *want* to say? Anything that wants to be said?

Try to forget all the requirements, all the bits and pieces that I seem to want to shove into this section. Start again with absolutely no requirements!

Start somewhere that feels enjoyable!

I need to find the crest of a wave, and ride it towards the shore.

A poetics of experience cannot be written from a safe outside place. It means involvement and being at risk.

I am suffocated by the desire to have this done. There is no air to breathe.

I want to speak from within my world, and perhaps from within the world of others, let them speak.

My tendency is to speak about my world, not to speak myself within it (where I and world are intimately involved with each other).

I have to speak this world into being because it is invisible and intangible. I want to conjure a sense of crisis, of the edge.

Chapter nine

The passion of knowing

It has disappeared again! Gone! Vanished behind screens, evaporated into invisibility by the glare of ordinary understanding.

Again I have to wait, to poke around, try this door and that, bluster sometimes, pretend to go away. Eventually despair, sink down, try to pull myself free of this terrible servitude.

I *have* to live some other life. Nothing is to be gained here. Everything is being lost, polluted eventually by this sickly desperation, greed perhaps.

It is a relief to begin finally to despair. To know that it will not be. Nothing lives here. No seam of life remains open to me to share. I have to go. Let go! Do simple things. Touch the earth, see the sky, feel the wind, listen again to those nearby.

Only in real despair does real beginning come again. Pretending does not seem of service here. You must really go, actually move your place of being to begin some lowlier, more simple way.

But these times are the ending of phases, not how it always is.

Sometimes the waiting is rewarded. The active waiting, the reading and the listening, the juggling of possibilities to and fro, the scribbling of alternate themes. Returning to how *it* feels, to how *I* am feeling now, taking this as friend and guide, doorway and direction, always different, finding a way back in, a place of refreshment, cleansing, like going through the shower to the pool.

There are so many different ways and kinds of waiting, many ways of being lost, seeking still to find.

There is waiting when the air ripples with strands of possibility. There are times of waiting when the surge of the sea unsettles the ground and disturbs the night. There is waiting which is not really waiting since nothing is coming, everything has vanished and will not return. This is the overgrown bomb site. Gone for ever are the remnants of a past life that can hardly be remembered.

The ground shifts. The web of who you are within the shuffling texture of the world unravels. The old and mostly silent metaphors have dissolved away leaving the sightless troops to find whatever way they can.

Vision is required to find eyes. Everything is cast towards some undiscovered goal. It is necessary to draw back to look behind the eyes, behind the strain of searching.

How to turn away? Talk amongst ourselves? Disown the greed that seeks too quickly for the goal?

Everything is tucked away, no edges to betray the lair. Nothing stirs. The bustling world has gone. Occasional whiffs of past cooking in the air suggest a life that is no longer there.

Turn away! Find someone who can turn away! Conventional figments wander free, unhoused, without the habits of a known concern.

Who will turn away, show a face, allow the encircling sky to become a me?

A personal search

I have become so aware of the pains of the sort of search I have been involved within throughout my time as a psychologist and psychotherapist that I want here to explore this area of experience a little.

Among the most enduring experiences of my personal/professional life is my sense of searching for some new concepts or ways of understanding, that are somehow sensed as being *there* to be found. There have been moments and periods of clarity, new vision, sometimes bringing pleasure, exhilaration, sometimes personal disturbance that has shaken me with its intensity. This searching has demanded that I attend, hunt, labour, dig feverishly at whatever strands of fertile novelty are made available. Then it is back to waiting, preparing.

It will not be rushed. *It* has *its* own time-scale, which has often been very different from the one I've wanted. I have found difficulty in bearing the way in which *it* seems to have the upper hand, as if *it* knew what I was still seeking.

I have had a sense of knowing what I have been looking for and yet not knowing it in any way that can, initially and for a long time, be grasped and said. This knowing before knowing has allowed me confidently to recognize which signs are clues and what lines are dead, what avenue feels alive with possibilities and which trails have once more run into the sand.

This has been such a demanding servitude that I've found it hard to yield to it without resentment and bitterness at times. Yet when the promise shrivels and nothing is left, I am soon longing for that special joy, enjoyment, of the times when the silver threads of new ideas are spun from the tangled woolliness of my own mind.

What has struck me especially after years of struggle of this kind, with occasional and limited achievement along the way, is that I was utterly unprepared for anything like this kind of searching by any of my psychological education. Nothing there prepared me for the demands it makes or the special agonies it requires me to endure. Certainly it has been a relief, from time to time, to read of the analogous struggles of great artists or thinkers. The writings of Van Gogh or Kierkegaard spoke more directly of my experience than anything my professional discipline had offered me. But I was not one of them. I was an ordinary person enduring what must be an ordinary passion. It is this ordinariness that has seemed to me to make it specially worthy of attention here.

What kind of 'knowing' is this that I've been struggling with? It is clearly different from the more public and formal ways of approaching knowledge that psychologists are normally taught to employ. It is not primarily knowing of particular things, nor knowing how to achieve particular ends. It is more related to what I have elsewhere (Mair 1980) called 'knowing as lived personal experiencing' and which John Shotter (1984) has referred to as 'knowing of the third kind'. It is a kind of knowing that is intimately related to the knower and his or her involvement in the cultural and social world. It is owned and undertaken knowing through personal involvement, leading to a deepened understanding of issues. It may sometimes lead on to specific, verifiable pieces of public knowledge, but is more immediately to do with the frames within which our knowing of particulars is shaped and held.

In psychotherapy this kind of knowing seems essentially involved. It is often necessary for the client to sense and know themselves and their world differently, to undertake aspects of their own experiencing that they have known but not yet understood, to feel towards some deeper involvement in themselves or their world and undertake a different stance towards both.

A psychologist pursuing this kind of personal search is confronted by their own weaknesses and strengths, their own entanglement in the knowledge they seek and undertake. So also the client in therapy is involved in what to know and to ignore. Such knowing and ignoring is not, of course, knowing in the head, but comes when people begin to dare to experience what previously had been avoided or denied. In therapy, as in any personal search, this kind of knowing brings risk. It requires that you be given over to the possibility of loss as well as gain. It involves waiting as well as action.

Understanding some of the implications of this kind of knowing seems important if we are to be more honest in our search to create a psychology that both recognizes and respects the various forms of knowing that we variously employ.

Intellectual passions

Such is still the pervasive sense of impersonal blandness and formalized method characterizing the process of 'coming to know' in much of scientific psychology, that it can come as a scarcely intelligible surprise to find a philosopher of science who values the presence of passion even in the intellectual homeland of hard science. Michael Polanyi (1958) speaks with welcome delight of intellectual passions. Rather than the reiteration of homilies about scientific method, evidence, objectivity, hard data, statistical manipulation, and suchlike that seem to be the staple diet of fledgling psychological scientists, Polanyi speaks a surprisingly different tune. 'The affirmation of a great scientific theory', he says, 'is in part an expression of delight.' The theory, he suggests, has an inarticulate component which acclaims its beauty. This, he claims, is an essential contributor to the belief that the theory is true.

He goes further to suggest that a scientific theory which calls attention to its own beauty, and partly relies on this for its claim to represent empirical reality, is akin to a work of art, which directs attention to its beauty as a token of artistic reality. Nor does he regard 'scientific passions' as mere psychological by-products, but as having a logical function which contributes an essential element to science.

Since only a small fraction of all knowable facts are of interest to scientists, Polanyi claims, scientific passion serves as a guide in the assessment of what is of greater or lesser interest. He tries to show that this appreciation depends, in the last analysis, on a sense of intellectual beauty, and this he regards as lying beyond dispassionate definition, just as the appreciation of the beauty in a work of art, or a fine action, lies beyond precise analysis. Polanyi suggests that any inquiry not guided by intellectual passions would inevitably fan out and dissipate itself in endless trivia. Our sense of scientific beauty, he implies, helps us towards our vision of reality and also suggests the kinds of questions that may be reasonable and interesting to pursue.

In all this he had been talking of the *selective function* of intellectual passion. But our intellectual passions do not just affirm the existence of harmonies which foreshadow an unknown range of possible discoveries. They can also evoke intimations of specific discoveries and sustain our persistence in pursuing these through years of demanding labour. This he describes as the *heuristic function* of scientific passion, wherein someone's appreciation of scientific value can merge into their capacity for discovering it. Creative scientists, he suggests, spend their lives in trying to guess correctly and they are sustained and guided in this by their heuristic passion.

There is no suggestion in all this that the guidance of selective or heuristic passions guarantees that we get it right. Polanyi quotes Kepler to make it quite clear that these 'truth-bearing passions' are far from infallible. Intellectual passions may be quite misdirected, and often there is an interweaving of some intimations that turn out right and others that fail the test of time.

Polanyi illustrates how both Kepler and Einstein approached nature with intellectual passions and with beliefs inherent in these passions, which led them to their triumphs and misguided them to their failures. These passions, he says, were theirs personally, even though both of them held them in the conviction that they were universally valid.

Polanyi goes on to say that he believes that they were right to follow these impulses even though in doing so they risked being misled by them.

He also claims that what he, for instance, accepts of the work of these men today as true, he accepts personally, guided by passions and beliefs similar to theirs. In his turn he has the sense that his own impulses here are valid universally, even though he has also to admit the possibility that they may be mistaken.

Beyond the *selective* and *heuristic functions* of intellectual passion, Polanyi goes on to talk of *persuasive passion*. In order to be satisfied, he says, our intellectual passions must find a response. 'We suffer when a vision of reality to which we have committed ourselves is contemptuously ignored by others.' Unbelief on the part of others puts in danger our own convictions and our particular visions must either conquer or die.

In so far as a discoverer has committed himself to a new vision of reality, he has separated himself from others who still live within the old rules. It is here that his persuasive passion spurs him on to bridge the gap between his emerging view and others who have still to be converted. The advocate of a new framework, he suggests, may not even succeed in getting a hearing from those who still inhabit a different framework. He may first have to teach them a new language and this may be far from easy, since 'no one can learn a new language unless he first trusts that it means something'.

Proponents for a new system, suggests Polanyi, can convince their audience only by first winning their intellectual sympathy for a doctrine they have not yet grasped. Those who listen sympathetically will discover for themselves what they would otherwise never have understood. Such an acceptance as this, says Polanyi, is a heuristic process, a self-modifying act, and to this extent it is a form of conversion.

From all this we can begin to see the great difficulty that may well arise in the attempt to persuade others to accept a new idea in science. To the extent that it represents a new way of reasoning, we cannot convince others of it by formal argument, for as long as we argue within their framework we can never induce them to abandon it. Demonstration must be supplemented, therefore, by forms of persuasion which can induce a conversion. The refusal to enter on the opponent's way of arguing must be justified by making it appear altogether unreasonable.

Finally, here, Polanyi returns to one of his central themes, that the logical premises of factuality are not known to us or believed by us *before* we start establishing facts. They are recognized rather by *reflecting on the way we establish facts*. In science, just as with physical skills like swimming or cycling, we achieve and practise these skills without any antecedent focal knowledge of their premises. Indeed, insists Polanyi, the premises of a skill cannot be discovered focally prior to its performance, nor ever understood if explicitly stated by others before we ourselves have experienced its performance, whether by watching it or by engaging in it ourselves.

The frontiers of knowing

Those who do not enter the creative fire do not suffer the passion of knowing. Thus do we get a bureaucratic psychology, denuded of deep feelings of either joy or pain. We mostly create, amongst the many who do only what is expected of them, a view of science as a passionless activity, served by a passionless methodology, contributing ever more insidiously to a passionless view of life (as a domain of mechanical repairs, social skills, and procedural retraining). We insist on fostering technology and say little of creative involvement. We stress busy, behavioural doing rather than the passive actions of attention. We insist on manipulative mastery rather than being given over as servants and seekers.

I want, instead, to attend to the personal aspects of knowing as a corrective to the familiar stress on the impersonal and the formal. Our acts of knowing are acts of feeling. We reach out in our ongoing acts of feelings to touch and be touched, to give and receive messages in the darkness before we can yet see. Perhaps we tend to relegate feeling to a secondary place in the armoury of our competences because we are led by our cultural metaphors to conceive of 'feeling' as mindless perturbation, whereas 'seeing' is in the light of the higher intellect, above the ground, nearer to the gods. But all our actions are a seamless garment wherein feeling is an intimately important aspect of our multifarious involvements with a moving world.

In speaking of the passion of personal knowing I'm speaking of the basis of all our knowing. It involves an almost unspecifiable realm, only partially knowable. This level of human functioning is inevitably indistinct and inconclusive. That is its nature. We are on the boundary, seeking to know the *from* and *by which* we know. We can, perhaps, do this only by creating friendly metaphors to allow us to turn and look, listen to, and feel what we are up to or engaged within.

In speaking of the passion of knowing I'm concerned especially with the frontiers of personal knowing, before everything is converted into method and procedure, where things are still fresh and risky, and where you must approach with dedication and be given over to waiting, to feeling, to intimacy and isolation, wherein you are challenged and sometimes changed. It is a concern with the passion rather than the behaviour, methodology, conventions, techniques, impersonality, distance, or detachment with which we are professionally more familiar. This is a frontier place before conventions and rules become settled. These are green times, times of fire and reaching, the exceptional moments, the place of change where the obvious is transcended for a time. This is not a concern with formalized knowledge, but about persons in process, in being and becoming.

Essentially I want to stimulate you (and myself too) into a sense of newness, by conjuring up a place of possibility, choice, crisis. I want to put in question the settled routines of self and others and the framework of convention within which we grow and which constitutes who and how we are in the world. If I am to do any of this I will have to speak with all of me, reaching beyond where I am safe and able to justify, beyond where I know and live. I will be pretending and seeking thereby to predict how things may yet be.

Everything in my life is involved in this, all my lack and failure, my longing and loneliness. I wish to speak from the heart to the heart, and the head and the whole being. It is not a casual concern, but a cross on which my life is pinned. I am still, after so many years of struggle, squirming and begging that this cup will pass from me so that everything can be accomplished without pain and without trouble. But to go on in closed-in dread and resentful anger is to achieve nothing. There must somehow be rejoicing in the midst of pain. The dreadful dead times come again and again, but through these horrid spaces of emptiness and waiting something may yet become.

I write in the belief that we need (at least I need) to free ourselves from the tyranny of our present scientific rigidities. I don't mean that we need to free ourselves from the disciplines of proof and discovery, but from the aridity of mind that leaves us cripples in the realm of the intimate and sensuous.

Whether I speak only of my own crippled state or also for others I do not surely know. I do not believe that any simple abandonment of science is what is needed. Far from it. What I am seeking to say is, hopefully, within a more generous and more elaborated scientific philosophy.

I want to write without the binding Big Brother of empiricism looking immediately over my shoulder. I will try to speak as close to how I want and feel as possible, not to fit into the straight, unitary, flat world of logic and justified utterance. None of this is to abandon science but to reach more deeply into it for the sake of a credible psychology of knowing and ignorance.

People so quickly step in to say, 'Yes, but can you test the validity of anything you claim?' However valuable such a question is at some point and in some places, precipitate questioning of this kind shrivels up feelings, space, and thought long before it can know itself enough to know what is there to test.

The passion is to do with the waiting, the struggle, the suffering of knowing that does not know itself, which is beyond the reach of others to help. There is no simple external procedure that can put it right, make it clear, sort everything out, get things happily resolved. If you are the servant of what you know, yet do not know, you will often lose hope that it can ever be said.

It cannot be spoken without entering into the darkness more fully than has yet been possible, and that may not be possible for me. The darkness is not passively welcoming. You have to be capable of deeper darkness, not just be ready to stumble into something already there. It gets lost because I lose any accompanying self, I lose my sense of 'being of value to'.

Passion and relationship

Here I am in the midst of passionate waiting, despairing, emerging slightly from deeper despair to the hinted possibility of some light, thin flickers of pale possibility.

What sort of place is this? It has recently been a windless, lost place, a desolation, a place of dry bones, without sufficient humanity to conjure hope. It is a place that can change. Without destroying what was there it becomes different, sometimes easier, sometimes tightened towards fertility.

To live and search here is to be a seeker for communicable insights into the country and its people and places, rather than to be a programmed pursuer of what is public and solid. Somehow it is about being a different person, becoming arrayed differently to give recognition of a different world.

I hate its lostness, its hopelessness, the sense that it may never be resolved and that it cannot be sloughed off and easily abandoned.

I have somehow to get inside this place of passion and be given over to speaking my way into and through how it is.

When it becomes dead and desolate, there is no accompanying spirit — 'my God, why hast thou forsaken me'. Why am I left without a sustaining other, outwith a relationship, no longer between?

The dead lands wherein life itself becomes stagnantly unformed. Speaking it like it is can give a form so that alternatives become possible again.

If a form does offer itself it will make the whole thing a living activity and not a search for something that does not there-and-then exist.

I am afraid of every feeling, every flicker of life. Virtually none are left within reach. All are covered over, abandoned, excluded, left aside.

The passion of knowing is about relationship, the between, the deep conversation of our lives (surface and deep conversation should be distinguished). In the passion of knowing your ordinary self must be given over to waiting and listening to that deeper self, that more profound voice that surprises and eludes. The ordinary self, the superficial, the thought-thinking, logical self does not, however, want to be less than all important. It wants to be king-pin, the map of the known world.

The passion of knowing involves the lover and the loved, the caress and provocation, the gentle touch and the necessity of being available, attentive, understanding, concerned more for the other than yourself. It involves being given over and yet firmly there to be met and to be given to. To receive is hard when what the surface lover wants is to be the boss, to have everything in his or her control.

This passion draws us towards the sexuality and sensuality of knowing, the active and the passive, male and female, loving intercourse of knowing. May we yet be lovers and friends rather than masters and possessors of nature? May we yet be sensitive to the delicate touch, to the look and expression of the beloved eyes, to sense the breath of changing life, to be absorbed and to be faithful through barren and hard times? Or will we become resentful and close off, escape, insist on our rightness, and turn away into lonely isolation?

In all this I'm saying that giving yourself over to more intimate knowing means that we will need to move away from various familiar positions. We will have to move from invisibility to self and others, towards counting ourselves and others in. We may need to move away from bland officialdom towards raising a distinctive voice. We will need to move away from the repressing crudity of so many of our present concepts and methods towards a freedom to say. We will have to move away from institutionalized insensitivity and towards sensitive responding. We will have to move away from an abandonment of the intimately human towards a voice of life informing passion.

We may need to allow more into our experiencing so that we savour and taste and relish more. It is not enough simply to process our impressions in the most economical way possible so that we become efficient data-crunchers, machines of precision. Yet with the project of human rejection which still seems to inform many aspects of our scientific method in psychology, we are in danger of ending by saying (with all the scientific and technical developments neatly referenced to prove it) that the operation was successful but the patient died.

Passion and religious knowing

It is a form of action to be given over to receiving and waiting. The usual methods highlighted in psychology are mostly more obviously active. But if, as I believe, everything is already in motion, then it may sometimes be especially useful to undertake the less obvious activity of standing still, standing under, so that you may understand a little more of what you are engaged within. It becomes appropriate then to ask what 'distance' and 'impersonality' allow and do not allow us to know, and also what we can know through 'feelingful waiting'.

In the process of undertaking this kind of waiting game in psychotherapy, for instance, I have come to know (though I may still be mistaken in what I suppose I know) a number of things. I know that I will survive. I know that I will not often be at a loss. I know that if I wait and work and listen, some sense of pattern, of shaping motion, will emerge for me. I know that I must not expect some set pattern to be followed. I have to begin again and allow something new to emerge, now.

What I know in all this is of myself, how it will be with me. Perhaps all personal knowing is knowing of self in action, in motion.

In speaking of the passion of knowing I am drawing attention to a different path from the one trodden by the procedures of the experimental phase of science. It is not, though, a 'path less travelled by' since it has been used, in one way or another, for thousands of years. It is the path of sensed, felt, groped for knowing. It is concerned with the implicit, actively ongoing (though often stunted and disowned) activities of knowing from the inside rather than by objectification and formal public procedures.

Yet it is not just a concern with 'inside' as opposed to 'outside', but of *personal* knowing, which includes both subjective and objective. We have developed a hugely exaggerated attachment to objective and procedure-dominated, lowest-common-denominator knowing (anyone can do it if given the money, time and procedures — the cart-horses of knowledge rather than the eagles).

My claim is that we have lost more than we can afford in turning from 'religion' to 'science', even though we have gained many things too. In speaking of 'passion' I want to allude again to this 'religious' dimension which gets so easily excluded because many of us do not any longer accept the particular beliefs that cluster round, and obscure, the still important issues of knowing that were explored there. To know 'God', as that which is sensed as other and greater than yourself and yet 'speaking' to you and holding you within the mystery of a knowing that is not a knowing of something in particular, is not unfamiliar to scientists, artists, and creative people of many kinds. This kind of knowing is crucial to creative life and yet with our increasing estrangement from the religious contexts within which it was intimately explored, we have lost our means of acknowledging and recognizing something of its hidden ways.

This kind of knowing requires that you sense and inhabit, to some degree, a world of faith in what is invisible but more real than anything else in your life. This passion, this suffering and being given over to an emerging reality that is sensed and greater than ourselves, must be owned again if we are to create a non-reductionist, non-idolatrous psychology of knowing and ignoring. There is much in the life and writing of the religious traditions that is still of vital relevance to such a psychology, and we must be careful not to throw the baby of essential vulnerability out with the bath water of particular, and sometimes outdated, beliefs.

Perhaps I am seeking to make the structure of religious awareness available for non-religious concern. Ultimate concern does not surely have to be 'religious' in a traditional sense. What I am trying to say here is that the basic structures of knowing are far more like 'religious' knowing than the narrowly conventional views of scientific knowing.

Like so many more able people, I am trying to refound psychology (or what is involved in knowing) on personal grounds that are largely unspecifiable, rather than accept a strict and bounded account simply because it has the supposed virtues of being strict and bounded. Psychology should, I believe, become a meta-discipline, though 'experimental' psychology and other subdivisions might remain as disciplines within a meta-discipline of personal knowing.

Those things we are mysteriously involved in cannot be separated out and pinned down in objective form. We need to dig up the ground and attend to the fundamentally non-objective nature of what we live amongst. Those who insist only on objectivity must thereby do violence to themselves and others, and to the discipline they are supposedly serving. You must approach through the means that are sensitive to the matters in question.

Passion and being part of a greater whole

If I am being given over to attend and to be receptive to some things that I somehow know in the 'marrow bone' but would not otherwise come to know more clearly, this implies some acceptance of myself as being more than I normally assume. It may even suggest the possibility, as it often feels, of being 'whispered to', being made available to some active intelligence that is other than my ordinary limitations. This is where the issue of the boundaries of the self, and the importance of knowing on the frontier comes to the fore. It becomes necessary to raise questions of a kind that are often seen as religious, to do with the gods or muses.

Aware of the pain of being available for the possibility of knowing, I have had to ask whether you *need* a 'master', a larger being, a higher calling, an angel or a muse, your art or your god so that you can be held in place, held in allegiance by that within which your life is given and sustained. Otherwise what? In that place of special vulnerability, every disappointment may become a disaster without that wider perspective to allow some balance. Every reverse may become an instant threat of futility, final failure. 'God' or 'ultimate concern' or 'the ground of our being' may all be ways of talking of some such master, in relation to whom the seeker to know lives in active and creative service. It is a relationship of lesser to greater. It is, in the midst of many qualifications and avoidances, a relationship of demanding love.

Maybe it is almost impossible to sustain yourself in this place between known self and that which is beyond your familiar field unless you have some stability in a wider and bigger or higher calling. Unless you are held in being and handed over to something in the deeper reaches of the personal, beyond your immediate dimensions. Somehow, rather than being the tight little be-all-and-end-all of your life you may need to become a moving part within a greater calling, a larger being. To what greater fiction, larger self, higher calling might I be able to become any kind of willing listener, willing messenger, willing soldier?

How can you know what sort of calling calls you, what sort of being you may be a part of, what kind of ultimate concern may ultimately concern you? It can't surely be just an ordinary choice. Not if it is to have depth. Especially not when I've so often said in the past that something seems to be living my life rather than me, leaving me resentful and without my feet ever really touching the ground. How to create a suitably compassionate fiction of what and who you live within?

All my images may have to go, though they may have to stay for yet a while till I can bear to be alone and differently composed, without despair. How do you become a moving part of this larger whole, this compassionate and alluring figment of what is and may yet be? Over and over again your god will be too small. Over and over again your image of god must crumble. Over and over we must find in our living experience of our immediate lives that idolatry will not do. No graven image can be enough in this reaching to know who and what we are and are involved within.

Only by faith can this other world, these other worlds, be entered and known. If you radically disbelieve, you cannot go there because 'there' does not exist for you, and all doors have been barred. It also, thus, becomes clearer why too much cleverness, too much 'education' can readily become an impediment, and why the 'poor' in many senses are likely to be less hindered than the 'rich'. You have to begin to be there if you are to go there. This means that it can't be looked at from afar or known at second-hand.

There are many voices asking many different things. 'Quick, how can I be successful?' 'How can I be comfortably at peace?' 'How can I get by with as little trouble and effort as possible?' 'How can I be startlingly creative?' They are clearly incompatible and mostly drown out the much smaller voices which begin to try to ask those things that are 'buried deep' and are difficult to ask.

Schumacher (1977) suggests that for us generally these voices, infrequent as they are, are younger and still more uncertain, delicate, and tender in our human development than the more loud and ordinary. Such voices, he suggests, are in need of nurturing and strengthening, of being given space, protected for a time in a clamorous and more shallow world. All this makes good sense to me and gives a drop of hope, hope for the possibility of hope.

In giving yourself over to attend to what is beyond what you already know you know, you are attending to something different from that which is noted in more controlling, critical, or chosen attention.

How can you go about attending to this greater whole? Presumably by letting yourself become receptive, non-intellectual, and discriminatingly non-judgemental. You have to let yourself get out of your own way so that some 'feel' or 'sensing' beyond particulars becomes possible. In Polanyi's terms, you are dwelling in the particulars of the sensed situation in order to achieve a focal awareness of what the particulars point towards, what they mean.

This listening to the whole, with all of you (or as much of you as you can muster), is a crucial competence in psychotherapy as in many other creative activities. Psychotherapy is certainly one context in which at least the lower reaches of this kind of attentive, clue-searching, and combining activity can be tried and tested. Surely there is no reason to deny that some people are better at sensing wholes than others, penetrating through and beyond the world of particulars. It may also be possible to suppose that such sensing of wholes, when it works, carries with it 'self validation', a sense of wholeness.

The analytic study of parts, and the attempt to build wholes from an understanding of the working of parts seems to be the focal enthusiasm of ordinary science and technology. We have such a passion for 'parts' that these as intimators of 'wholeness' have been relegated to the category of mere fantasy by many. Yet it is not enough to seek only for 'wholes'. The identifying of parts and the understanding of ways-and-means is also crucial. What we need in psychology is not an either/or, but a seeking for the possibility of both so that they can separately inform each other.

We can become afraid to feel for wholeness, to feel the vibrations in self and situation. Often we have been hurt too much. We become less and less attentive to the possibilities of wholeness as we learn to ignore, to limit, to protect our smaller and more manageable selves. All kinds of pains will be accepted in our central thrust (as salmon seeking a place to spawn) to avoid the pains we cannot endure. Whatever pain we feel is likely then to be a reflection of the kind of pain we seek not to know. We know we could not survive the mother-pains of our deepest fears. We are mostly trapped within, and repeat, metaphors of misery. We array ourselves and our circumstances again and again to pose issues in the least painful way, to achieve some kind of mastery. Perhaps the mastery achieved is often a falsehood, based on looking intentionally in the wrong direction and seeking to solve the wrong problems.

Passion and personal power

We so much want to be in control, to have power over, to be in a strong position for defence and attack. We are afraid to be vulnerable, open, expansive, available, naïve, tentative, fanciful, feelingful. We attack and fear what is weak. It threatens our own weakness that must be hidden at all costs.

Weakness that is owned and offered to us as the weakness of another is accepted and patronized, cared for because it can allow us a sense of recognition, camouflage, and competence. It offers us relief that another is being humiliated, even as we work to prevent humiliation in a crudely apparent form. It is the open invitation of equals to bring us into our own and their own vulnerability, uncertainty, lostness, that angers us and unleashes the 'Doberman' response. We fear and despise the weak, except the weak who know their place and grovel to indicate that they know ours too.

There is a crucial issue of power here. We value, in science as in life, the means by which we can be protected and at a distance, in control, having power over the choices and destiny of others. Hardness is massively sustained by the rumbling tanks of the scientific methods we most value. We fear and despise and live in terror of our shameful weakness (though most of this gets hidden within the folds of our culturally sustained garments which help us to 'keep face' and cover our nakedness). Weakness is to be hidden at all costs, or used in ways that outsmart the appearance of strength. We cannot generally encourage the given-over, passive, listening and waiting aspects of personal knowing because all this celebrates 'weakness'. It encourages us to inhabit the flat lands of vulnerability where defenceless peoples can be slaughtered at will by the powerful intruders from the surrounding strongholds of conquest and cannon. Power for us is in the wielding of the means of destruction.

But to enter into the passion of knowing is to go beyond the realm of our ordinary, public rules of argument, logic, and proof. We are on our own and having to trust to our feeling rather than to shared evidence. We have to trust the pattern and the moving feel of things. We are required to respond differently. We are placed in the embarrassing position of having no simple recourse to the externalities of fact.

We are in the realm of *validation* and *invalidation* rather than proof and disproof. In the frontier lands where what may yet be realized is being sought, waited for, nourished, tended into independent life, there is no solid proof. Whatever evidence there is will seldom be enough to justify the steps we have to take beyond the known limits of our world. It is of the essence of this realm that we must sustain ourselves, or be sustained by the trust and relevant care of others, rather than protect ourselves from foolishness by the hard pellets of shared convention, tradable truths.

Validation involves being confirmed as real and of substantive value in the eyes of someone, even oneself. Invalidation may involve many specifics but is essentially to do with 'pulling the mat out from under'. You are saying 'You are a non-person, an unacceptable being'. 'You in your whole project are off-beam, not within the pale, outside the tribe, an outcast.' This is not a piece-by-piece rejection but a consigning of the all to outer darkness! You do not have to be taken seriously because you are 'way out', 'misguided', 'deluded'. You are on about something quite different from, and irrelevant to, the real concerns of those who matter, who are powerful, in the inner circle.

Over and over again in psychotherapy, the central issue is to help someone to build that fundamental cradle of self-regard wherein a person can begin to trust themselves, their own sustaining forms. So often people have been invalidated, disqualified, made worthless in their own eyes or the eyes they see in others. Within the therapeutic relationship they may begin to weave again the nets of self within which they can begin to dare to speak their own word, know their own ground, risk their own judgment. None of this is possible while they are unreal, unfounded, insubstantial, of no account.

Thus in validation and invalidation we are concerned with a person's essential maintenance procedures rather than with whatever aspects of the world can be attended to and put to the tests of proof. These have first to be risked and honed towards communal worth in the passionate trust of someone, who reached ahead because their sustaining forms were strong enough to bear the weight of their adventurous hope. These structures are so intimately of yourself (though also of the world), your stance in the world. If they are invalidated you, as a person and a worthy being, are put in question. These are the structurings from and within which we live the shape of who we are. They are our basic procedures for being able to claim any worthwhile standing in a world.

These procedures are likely to be close to what Kelly (1955) calls 'core role' relationships. If they are sustained, then the person can function as someone of value in the eyes of valued others (the value givers of that life). If undermined, then a person loses the capacity to trust themselves. They then have no means of entering *their* worlds since their basic postures are in question. They then may have to cling to some rigid façade or attach themselves to some other person's means of valuing. They no longer constitute the basis of a responsible and valid person and have to allow themselves to be inhabited by the demands and rules of others. They have to leave their boundaries open to the necessary support of whoever will provide the ground on which they can appear to stand.

These structures within which the person is constituted as a patterned being in the world are invisible. They are insubstantial and cannot be pointed to. They cannot be taken out for routine inspection since they are that from which the person lives. They have to be sensed and conjured up. We are here reaching out to touch and hold and give body to the sustaining forms of another person from which they live as disqualified cripples or as more worthwhile, self-confident, self-and-other trusting beings in a world.

No amount of objectivity will allow us to identify these shaping forms, these basic girders, these threads which allow the bounding of a world. We have to reach out to another to help us conjure into being the possibilities of form by which they themselves are in-formed. We have to seek for clues and signs of having understood aright. From such frail, but felt reality, the person can be immediate party to a sense of your reality and thereby, at the same time and of necessity, some possibility of the real in them.

This is a delicate and a testing time. Any old bets, well tried routines, will not do. But this is testing (not a matter of public proof and evidence for others to share and see, but in intimate relationship) in mid-air. It is a matter of fit and feel, of coherence and patterned adequacy. There is some place here for *verification* and *falsification*, but these are too concrete to be enough. It is pattern and shape, feel and fit that matter now.

I keep trying to make this realm more solid than it is, but it is inevitably insubstantial, liable to melt away, disappear, slip from your grasp. I still struggle to claim rights and securities of the kind that we are more accustomed to in accumulating evidence when we move from this insubstantial ground towards that which it allows us to see and hold. But all of this is an impossible task. We have to find another way of really undertaking this alternative level of inquiry. Perhaps it is a realm that only exists when it is lived and can be shrunk or made invisible at will. Caring for what is so, at this level of our ways of knowing, is to do with the quality of good faith in our inquiry. It is not to do with the more familiar levels of claims, justifications, buttressing of self, protection rackets, deceptions, the manufacture of appearance, face saving, the official line. Here we need to speak what cannot objectively be known or proved.

Poetics and passion

If we deny ourselves access to what we know we shrink our capacities, since what v .now guides all our scientific and other forms of creation, even though we do not yet know it to be true. To allow ourselves to say something of what we know, long before we may be able to claim that it is true, we need poetic licence. A bias towards a poetics of experiencing is needed to allow us to become available to ourselves in ways that may touch us profoundly, but which are not accessible to prosaics and particular proofs. If we are to speak with feeling of that which we are involved in knowing, speak of our passion, we need to be free to speak the form and style and manner of how it is. We must persistently refuse to let it be boiled down to what is not so.

I'm not here attending to knowledge that can be itemized and traded as specific end products. Rather am I speaking of knowing as being and becoming party to possibilities of sensing, feeling, thinking, beyond the limits of your former state. It is to do with changing the limits of the self, and with changing the consistency of self (to be more or less alive, open or closed, bubbling, aroused). I'm talking of making available that which can be sensed but not seen. We close and open, become more or less permeable, looser or tighter. Our ways of being are in motion. We become more and less and differently aware of being and events.

If we are to speak more truly, rather than speak crudely and falsely, as is often required in the most arid conventions of our prosaic selves, we need to question the very ground which sustains us, the depths of our embeddedness. We need to speak with loosened and yet obedient tongues.

If we destroy whole worlds of experiencing, destroy the infrastructure on which they can grow and achieve recognition, then they will not exist. Needs can disappear. We can come not to need or to recognize what could otherwise have been. We could become devoid of poetic passion. We could become carefully groomed constructions of factory-made components, not voices in pain.

Michael Ignatieff (1984) completes his unusually interesting book, *The Needs of Strangers*, with words that are apposite here.

We need justice, we need liberty, and we need as much solidarity as can be reconciled with justice and liberty. But we also need, as much as anything else, language adequate to the times we live in. We need to see how we live now and we can only see with words and images which leave us no escape into nostalgia for some other time and place.

We need words to keep us human. Being human is an accomplishment like playing an instrument. It takes practice. The keys must be mastered. The old scores must be committed to memory. It is a skill we can forget. A little noise can make us forget the notes. The best of us is historical; the best of us is fragile. Being human is a second nature which history taught us, and which terror and deprivation can batter us into forgetting.

Our needs are made of words; they come to us in speech, and they can die for lack of expression. Without a public language to help us find our own words, our needs will dry up in silence. It is words only, the common meanings they bear, which give me the right to speak in the name of the strangers at my door. Without a language adequate to this moment we risk losing ourselves in resignation towards the portion of life which has been alloted to us. Without the light of language, we risk becoming strangers to our better selves.

Yet, isn't all this talk of passion, of waiting, of being given over as a servant rather than a master, all too self-effacing?

While a certain radical humility is involved in the passion of knowing there is also a necessary arrogance. Only when I am able to enlarge into the arrogance of being eligible to speak is it possible to listen and to enter into what is between. There is a necessary pride which enlarges to a magnitude that is capable of giving and receiving. Only then can anything be said. To be a nothing and a nobody is to be empty and closed. There has to be some essential assumption of power.

You cannot, I think, endlessly disown your worth, shrink and belittle everything you are, and still be large enough to contain the glories you may have to bear. If you make yourself smaller than you are, you may render yourself unfit for service.

Yet it is not just blind arrogance. It is an arrogance which dares to walk, to strut if necessary, and wear with boldness the costumes and the colours you were meant, perhaps, to bear. In despair and depression, I endlessly become too small, too mean. Almost always I am too shrunken to bear the fruits of my own possibilities of spirit. To enter and endure the passion of knowing requires a certain size, daring, confidence, generosity of spirit. Too often, like many of my clients, I am reduced to small-minded self-flagellation which destroys what could have grown and blossomed.

When I am involved in other things, in work, meetings, visits, holidays, scattered things, then we have to go wandering. We divide and lose whoever it is we are sometimes, together, able to compose. Only sometimes when we are together is it possible to feel the mystery of the ordinary world. Only sometimes does the ordinary, silent world whisper in my ear. Mostly we are apart, divided, lost from each other. Only gradually is it sometimes possible to come together for a time, to listen and to sing.

Now is a time of scurry. It has been so for months. Perhaps we have been gathering different things which we can share. Perhaps we have been finding what, together, we could never know. Perhaps we have been forgetting even the little that we sometimes feel.

Whatever we seek is other and greater than I am. Whatever we seek may only be possible if we can come together so that we can together surrender who we are, not to leave stragglers believing that it can be done alone.

Settling into an easier way will not do. Comfort and convenience will not create the song. What I seek is beyond what I am. It is what holds and shapes us all into who we take ourselves to be.

Something like the awful adventure of prayer may be what is required of me. Not in the sense of cosy fireside chats with a knee-sized god, but in some more naked wandering in the wilderness, beyond the rush of ordinary things. Perhaps it is a task of shedding much of the imagery of our supposedly familiar gods, so that we can venture out alone and learn as best we can within the deeper conversation, still available to some, amongst the moving and mostly hidden interstices of our times.

Chapter ten

Speaking from within a world

How we 'speak together' is how we live. I want to conjure a different manner of attending to our speaking. We often seem content to go about our everyday affairs, even in psychology, with little attention to what and how we say, to where we are speaking from and what we affirm in what we seem to question.

Everything tends to take us outwards and to the surface. On almost every occasion we tell each other lies so that the useful collusion of convention can smoothly run its invisible way. Mostly we do not want to know. We prefer what is easy and comfortably false. If we try to speak the world afresh we have to 'begin again', speak now, attentively, with an ever to be renewed honesty that mostly will not comfortably own its claims.

Unless we can speak of our worlds, how are we to begin seriously to ask questions of where and how we are?

Speaking of speaking

Perhaps I have to start with my own failure to belong. I have to live with failing to belong. I am among the homeless of our time, those whom cultural crises have displaced, who shelter still in transit camps, shanty towns, clap-board houses of the mind. Nothing quite fits. Everything is provisional.

There are many displaced persons unable to belong to the beliefs and customs others still call home. Often we do not belong even with each other, but some do speak to some amongst the ruins others do not see.

I am a conjunction of worlds that do not fit. These worlds need each other but require work by me if they are to resolve their differences and allow a transitory place of fertile cohabitation. I am a place of meeting and non-meeting. In me worlds are at war. They do not know themselves till they are known by me. I do not know myself till I know something more of them. They cannot meet till they meet in me. They cannot speak till they speak in me.

We are the children and the parents, the fruit and the roots of worlds in the making. Worlds are silent except as they are sometimes, and to some extent, spoken by us.

This speaking is no simple *description* of our worlds, but arises from and in itself expresses how our worlds are. This sort of speaking gets something out in the open, for good or ill, rather than continuing the secret struggles in the underworld of the unacknowledged and the not yet owned.

Speaking in this sense is at the forefront of knowing, of the more open society, of the community rather than the oppressive institution of our selves. But speaking is dangerous because it lays us open to responsibility and blame. Yet the 'open society' is itself a myth. Everything fails and falls. It is not the end but the journeying that we inhabit. Final answers are never to be ours. We live on the move, preparing tomorrow's mistakes from today's achievements.

Between psychology and psychotherapy we need a *discipline of discourse* to speak of our speaking. We have to speak, not just speak *about*. We have to attend to speaking, not just to what we speak about. Everything we express in word or deed is a way of saying, as well as whatever else it draws attention to or from.

Speaking is the essentially human form of action. It is not an extra by which we add decoration to what we already do. Speaking together in whatever variety of ways is constitutive of who and how we are. Caring for how we speak in all our actions is caring for who and how we are together. This is not just a matter of concern for poets, writers, or moralists, it is a daily, practical necessity.

At times, no doubt, actions do speak louder than words, but they do *speak*. All our dealings together are conventionally articulated forms of speaking, expressive of what we mean. In language, our community and culture spins cocoons for the shaping and nourishment of generation after generation of its offspring.

I am reaching here for a greater concern for what we say in what we do, and what we are doing in our ways of saying. My concern is with meaning, held and shaped in the cultural conventions of our times, and the personal ventures involved in composing new meanings, new conventions, new forms of life.

It is speaking with care and passion that I am concerned with first of all. It is speaking with feeling, inventively, astringently, playfully, faithfully, that I want to encourage. Only secondarily am I concerned with reflection on and exploration of what and how we speak and listen. I do not want to foster just another arena of analysis that leaves practice in the shade. It is part of a discipline of discourse, *a conversational psychology* that starts in practice and involves reflection thereon, that I seek to encourage here. Speaking and living are to be held in close proximity.

We crucify what we somehow know but cannot say. We trap and poison our elusive possibilities. We are held hostage by the struggling crudities by which we tell each other of who and what we know. I want to write below the level that I ordinarily know, to speak deeper in, before the ordinary words begin. Mine is a shadow life in and amongst the often unspoken habits of my time.

But I am bounded by what matters to me. If that is too little then I am too. I stand huddled in the congregation of my time without the right to know that this or that or anything is so. Only those who claim the right, grasp the right, can gain the right to know.

Our society encourages us to settle down, fit in, and before all else be blind. You must not know more than you ordinarily say. We can so easily be covered by the syrup-balm of parochial success. I certainly am coated thick in blindness and the conventions of ordinariness, local style. I cannot afford to accept that muffled comfort. I am infiltrated by the false morals of a minimal quest, questions that do not require a life. Toys and decorations of asking stand proxy for a more serious morality of questioning. There are so many questions that are only for answering, and there are questions that have to be lived.

I want to see and say, hear and say, ordinary life. It is not a theory that I want to exemplify but a way of speaking which raises possibilities of life where previously they were hidden or absent. It is a psychology for the frightened, the lost, and the alone, that I am involved within. The loud and brash, successful and powerful are beyond my ken. They are likely to ignore those I seek to know. There is a bias towards the poor of a certain kind in what I have to say. I have to try to speak from within their worlds from within my own.

Everything encourages you to become external, scarcely more than a cypher of your place and times. How then to speak for the poor, the lost, and frightened?

To seek to undertake a conversational psychology, to be a 'go-between', an intermediary, is surely to be concerned with identifying the realities that constitute worlds in place and time and with making them sharable, capable of being personally known. If there is to be such a cultural discipline then its material has to be spoken into recognizable form.

An intermediary psychology of this kind has to be poetic, must be conversational and cannot but be steeped in the cultural web. This kind of psychological activity is frequently lost sight of, quivers and shrinks away because our more investigative approach adopts the enduring strength of impersonality, of rule and method. Everything in the intermediary mode of psychology depends on you and me, on who we are and are willing to try to be and do. It requires that we begin again and again. We have to find ever renewed ways to refresh our vision, see and feel beyond the ordinary appearance of things. Even ways of beginning become so easily routine. You long for some rule to follow, some place to freewheel, but this kind of psychological activity requires that we reach and search anew. This freedom is frightening. When you lose your nerve, you lose everything. It disappears.

It is a passionate, moving attentiveness that I seek, that believes and lives its right to say, to see, to touch, to express, to share. (There are so many times when we cannot afford a primly pedantic fearfulness that must wait on proof and only values what is filtered through a particular method.) If this is even partly to be possible, I need real belief in feel and flow, recognizing and following understandings that come through hints and pores. It is not going to be enough to look endlessly over your shoulder for respectability in external support or just speak diligently as others have already done.

It is clear that this approach is difficult and will remain essentially incomplete. It cannot answer questions in any conclusive way but is an investment in taking the commitment and understanding of the inquirer to a different level. I panic at my own superficiality and obvious limitations but unless I put faith in myself and the 'angel' who occasionally touches me, nothing can grow. It may all come to nothing much, but without trust in my own possibility of vision, nothing can survive. It is easy to fall away through despair when things get difficult. Everything becomes too big. Everything will surely fail if I am not willing to put faith in the possibility of my vision, however faltering and dim it often seems.

I am, it begins to seem, under a spell and the right words have to be spoken by the right one to set me free. The wizard has to be found.

It will matter who says the words and how. The words have to be fitting to some other world that I already partly know, but do not yet surely know I know.

We are rooted in what we cannot say. Our language is the magician and the jailer, the castle, and the dragon of our living in the world. The words said fair, just so, precisely how it has to be, can untie the knots, loosen and dissolve the ties, can quite surely set us free. Words and the speakers of words are the magic looseners of souls. The science of the mind is in using the instruments of precisely disentangled fears. In the beginning was the Word and the Word was with God and *the Word* was God!

It is not that all knowing has to be spoken in words but that we are tangled into what we are knowing *by* and knowing *from*. We mostly seek to know ourselves by looking in the wrong direction, away from where we are. Words are necessary at times to set us free.

We are tangled in amongst where we come from. The umbilical cord of our inarticulate life ties us still to the past, to that which shaped and sustains us. We are trapped in webs of unnoticed assumptions which ground us as surely as chains or roots. Unless these roots are dug out, or dissolved away, they cannot be left behind. Roots are anchors which hold us still and keep us from being blown to and fro by the whim of circumstance. They are also channels of sustenance, ways of being woven into the world. They allow us to draw the necessities of our human life from beyond our limited experience, our little selves.

We are woven together by metaphor. We are sustained as persons through the webbing of invisibly inherited roots, traceries of intention long since lost to individual attention. Human reality is composed through woven make-believe. The substance of our culture-dependent lives is in the invisible ways in which we undertake the conventions of our time, and how we are informed in the ongoing conversation of where we find ourselves to be. We are each, by our rootedness, accredited for certain kinds of worlds. If we are to journey to other worlds our securing ropes have to be untied. We have to draw sustenance from previously unfamiliar soil.

Perhaps the conversational psychologist is specially concerned with helping us to know the ground on which we stand and helping us to stand on ground that seems to have changed. Perhaps this kind of psychologist has the dual role of both putting in question the accepted world and also making us more familiar with what is frightening and still unknown. Both questioning the orthodoxies that kill and sustaining the mysteries that bring new life are involved. A conversational psychology is concerned with putting the accepted world of ordinary common sense in widening and changing circles of understanding made visible through an attentive speaking of extraordinary moments of all but convincing vision. These moments are so easily ignored in a world where 'replication' is taken as the hallmark of trust. Through a conversational psychology we would seek to know how we compose and are composed by worlds, how we can postulate new worlds, and sometimes travel to inhabit them.

Easiest of all is to speak the conventions of our time and place. There is safety there, acceptance, cover, camouflage. To speak more personally is lonely and can be threatening. You may then be rejected as an outsider, beyond the range of understanding in your tribe. The terrible punishment of being ignored and regarded as beyond the pale is immediately to hand.

In the struggle to find a personal voice there is the danger of being dismissed as bad or mad. To struggle for a view of what we are normally held within is liable to be dangerous and costly, and yet this is, in essence, the same adventure that leads us to explore the stars. Surely we have to find ways of knowing and recognizing the worlds we are implicitly and unquestioningly living within. We have to learn to move outside the cultural conventions of our locality to understand something of what they allow and do not recognize at all, the geography of constraints that they contain.

Trying to speak more personally is demanding and requires sensitivity as well as nerve. Reaching beyond or behind the comfortable steadings of our cultural homes is a venture, not yet a tourist trip. It requires moral courage and endurance. It often arises out of desperate need, a sense of nothing fitting, of not really belonging to what seems so easy for those around you. It is a venture that clients coming for psychological help are often unwillingly undertaking. They come to be accompanied, encouraged, and sometimes guided along some of the way.

I want to try to attend more carefully to our 'speaking together' so that we do more of many things that are often kept apart in different disciplines. Amongst these concerns are at least the following: looking 'upstream', to the worlds which shape our questions as well as 'downstream' to the particular answers we temporarily achieve; attending to the manner and style as well as to the content of what we say and do; caring for the stories we are telling as stories, as well as to what they claim to tell; seeking to recognize the contexts of constraint within which our stories are told to meet the cultural rules of what is real; trying to delineate the ways in which our stories are composed to place us in the best light for whatever our purposes may be; drawing into view the cultural colourings that determine many of the broad but unnoticed ways in which our taken-for-granted realities are shaded into substantiality; seeking to become more aware of the ways in which our experience is shaped and textured in how we constitute and share it; becoming more appreciative of the different ways in which we speak together as well as the ways in which we distance ourselves to speak about them.

All of this points towards a recognition that we inhabit particular and composed worlds, not a single place that obviously is so. We speak ourselves into and out of existence. Mostly we are parasites and prisoners of our cultural web. If we are to step free, even to a small degree, from the gravity-pull of our constituting worlds to see ourselves with renewed eyes, we need to bear loneliness with whatever courage we can muster. We must surely learn to give each other compassionate support in the venturing we undertake.

In all of this there is implied a changed location for our sense of self. Conversation becomes primary and personality is derivative but crucial. We still often deceive ourselves as to our separateness because we seem to be physically apart. Psychologically we are more 'together' than we seem, and grow from amongst the conversational practices of our time. We start and mostly live our lives in complete embeddedness. If we are to speak a more personal word from time to time, we have to sense creatively what is available to and through us and shape ourselves and it into intelligible form.

I have to start again from my own dishonesty. The trick is to try to slip past the obvious prejudices of my nature and culture. I am steeped in Protestant aspirations and self-flagellation. Neither will take me far here. They cannot be abandoned, since they are mostly what I am, but they can sometimes be danced around so that for a moment a hint of something slightly different becomes possible.

Everything I reach towards saying is shaped by where it comes from so that it longs towards platitudes that are surprising only in their familiarity after so much pain in struggling to be free. What I struggle towards saying is not summed up in how it is shaped by who and when and where I am. It is this hope that something reaches slightly round and beyond where it comes from that lights me on my way. Yet this too is just a conventional hope from whence I come. It is the kind of thing I may need to recognize and discard, even though it will then cling to some other part of what I do.

There is such a gap between my occasional aspiration and what is generally the case for me. The more I speak, the more the lie is bloated. The speaking here is a 'longing towards' from one who is still 'mired deep' in fear and laziness and much else besides. If I was seriously to seek to speak more of the invisible world between us I would be in immediate danger. I would be hurt and assailed by all the pent up hatred that lurks everywhere waiting for its chance to kill. I would be exposed and made to suffer total insecurity. There would be no comfortable place to hide. I would probably be unbearable to those with whom I tried to speak my sense of what was true. I would be found crass and stumbling, remarkably inadequate, revealed as the ignorant, clodhopping fool I already know and fear.

My familiar greed is wanting to grab for a conclusion and a visible production. In so doing it again blots out all my sensing of what wants and needs to be reached towards.

In trying to speak from within my world I am going to speak in stories, parables perhaps, poems, songs. I cannot just give the most mundane, convention-bound descriptions of something supposedly separate from myself. New form has to be given to what we feel or sense or know.

A conversational psychology seeks to realize something of our worlds in how we speak together. This is a radically different kind of work from that which seeks mainly to divide and count. Its concern is to speak of our worlds from which we know and in which we know. It seeks to speak something of the invisible and the taken for granted. It seeks, in George Kelly's (1977) term, to 'transcend the obvious', the way things unquestionably are, out there, plain to see. There is a fundamentally different format in this poetics of experiencing. We have to conjure into living form the invisible world between us. If we don't do this, but merely live in the conventional world of our given place and time, we are slaves, no more.

In speaking of a conversational psychology I want to make as strong a claim as possible for the recognition in psychology of a story-mode to complement the more familiar statistical-mode of knowing. I don't want this to be accepted only as a poor relation of a 'more scientific' elder brother. The boot is rather on the other foot. The 'scientific' mode we currently employ is already held and shaped within a story-world that we mostly seek not to tell.

To speak the world, rather than just speak about, implies community rather than division. It has to do with attempted good faith rather than speaking always with divided tongue. We speak our world, however tight or harsh or warm or generous it may become, into being between and amongst ourselves. We live in webs of partially shared worlds. Every new meeting creates something of a shared world, a place of habitation. These places of human habitation, wherein old and newer forms of life may survive or even flourish, are constituted in the conversational practices of our speaking ourselves together.

Mostly we speak *at* worlds we do not belong in and do not constitute. We are on the outside of most worlds. To speak worlds we need to participate imaginatively within them, rather than address them from somewhere else. In speaking about an 'assumed world in common' we assert stability and discourage questioning. By creating a psychology of answering we confirm and continue this conservative policy. By turning towards the possibilities of many worlds in the making we need to undertake a psychology of questioning which seeks radical alternatives, a questioning of roots.

If this kind of conversational psychology is to be sustained we will have to create contexts of caring within which forms of life can be given the necessary space and challenges. The 'easy life' will not always be enough. Warrior knowledge will require discipline and will demand endurance.

A conversational psychology will have to be rooted in practice and will involve a variety of ways of reflecting thereon. Our ways of speaking together are therefore of primary concern. This means that such a psychology is essentially a psychology of living rather than a description of parts and impersonally formulated processes. It is concerned with our living together and apart.

It is therefore a moral discipline that is being conceived, not an ethically neutral commentary on *homo sapiens*. Inevitably it will be a basically compromised discipline (rooted, if you like, in 'original sin') since we all start and continue in total immersion within the wider culture and the local, silent shaping of our family ties. We learn to speak ourselves by speaking the language already prepared for us. We have to become agents as we struggle to free ourselves from mere servitude, unquestioning carriers of a particular culture. To undertake responsibility for ourselves we have to venture into 'the wilderness', through the tools and conventions available to us, towards some degree of separated belonging. It becomes quickly clear why the great prophetic voices of any time have so often felt themselves to be outsiders, very much alone. It is by being to some degree outwith the herd that the possibility of a personal voice is to be found.

A conversational psychology is, therefore, in the first place, an enacted discipline. It is not something frozen in publications or remembered in solid monuments. It has to find a refreshing way between the dangers of self-flattery and the stultifying gaze of endless self-reflection. In being lived or partly lived it requires creative speaking, speaking with care, caring enough to speak. It is a form of life that will be freed by necessary discipline. It is a way of life that requires a willingness to be given over to speaking together, listening as well as saying.

You can only know what you undertake yourself. Personal knowing requires your life, not just your willingness to talk about involvement. There is a basic moral demand here. You must live what you are to know. In the last resort, at least, you must put your life where your words are, and *vice versa.*

No simple minded do-gooding will do. Everything we undertake is liable to turn out differently and other than we naïvely imagined. Chance, as well as the hidden meanness and double dealings in what we claim, will sooner or later catch up with us. Our apparent 'goodness' will be converted into something else as often as we care to reconsider where we were and where we are. A conversational psychology is then to be a lived discipline, not just something put on or taken off at will.

Our places of human habitation are mostly invisible. We will have to conjure out of invisibility the worlds that we inhabit. To do this we need a poetic imagination to speak of our experiencing within the ongoing conversation of our lives. To speak of what we know and do not know takes artistry, the startling uncertainty of new ways. The familiar narrative forms of 'behavioural science' will not do. Such plain style might be enough if we only wanted to explore 'single and accepted worlds' but this manner of speaking cannot seriously put worlds in question.

There are conversations within and through and across many conversations. Our worlds are cross-webbed in conversations of so many kinds. Voices cut in and out, point and counterpoint. There are many tones and styles, manners and angles of preference spoken together in the multiple communities we are constituted by.

We live in many more flimsy and transient habitations than we are accustomed to suppose. Even within 'ourselves' we constitute our selves as many different social worlds. Between our selves we are so much at the mercy of what is allowed to some and disallowed to others in the implicit conventions by which access is granted and rejected. Often in our very trying to say, we are trapped in impossibility by seeking to speak from silent but enacted falsehood.

Our momentary habitations are already shaped in the ways we carry with us and mostly do not know. Within such a world as this it is not easy to speak afresh. Even so, it seems to me that we must not retreat from whatever grain of attempted truth we may have to say. We should not apologize for the discomfort that it brings, though we may again be tempted to do just that, and pretend we do not begin to know.

Questioning our selves

If I am to speak something of what shapes our experiencing, I have to speak elliptically. A direct, logical down to earth, honest to goodness bluntness will not do since all of these are only appropriate for speaking of the world we already assume and live. If this structuring of assumption is itself to be questioned, in a way that does more than confirm its own prejudices, something of an alternative world has to be realized. If it is simply talked *about* in the manner of the world I already inhabit in my everyday affairs, this very manner of speaking will betray the felt-for world I sense but do not clearly know.

An alternative world has to be conjured into sufficient reality to offer potential habitation for particular lives. In trying to do something of this I will have to reach from and beyond my own experience in the hope that something of what I am sensing towards has a chance to speak to some similar strain in you. I have to try to tell stories that hint at possibilities, that weave sufficient warp and woof to provide the minimal texture of a possible world, or at least a sieve to catch the coarser grains. I have to imagine and try to make believe. If you wish to entertain the possibilities conjured here, you will also have to enter what I seek to say with imaginative compassion rather than coldly critical rejection.

Much of the world I sense and grope towards is held beyond my reach by the very manner of my present groping. How I am presently arrayed to face and feel the world is antagonistic to what, in part of me, I reach towards. I want here to hint at something of the cultural roots which bind me and the more bitter fruits they allow to grow in and through me. I will then jump forward to imagine, in 'ideal form', the kind of person I would have to resemble more if I were seriously to undertake the world I seek.

None of this would matter much if, in this, I spoke only for myself. I do not believe that this is so. I have more in common with others of my cultural kind than the shades of difference which distinguish us. To some degree I am a representative of my time and place, and the manners and concerns of these speak through me. The shaped concerns of our times in science and religion (and much else besides) speak through me and are nourished and held in place by similar roots. We are all part of that mythical tree of the knowledge of good and evil which Adam had some dealings with.

That 'tree' multiplied and spread its domain over large tracts of the world, bearing many fruits, some sweet, some very sour. I gradually came to recognize myself among the branches of those hardy specimens that managed to survive on the north-east coast of Scotland near the beginning of the second third of the twentieth century.

The culture from which I have been grown is one corner of Western civilization with deep, dark roots, long since grafted into the Christian tradition, pruned back hard by the Protestant Reformation, and now running to seed, growing wild. The family from which I come was rooted in the land and in the church. My parents were honourable, devoted, church loving, hard working, education valuing, kind and caring people. A pure strain of Protestant values flowed through them for good and ill. The life thus bred in me has both served me well with values and strength of purpose, and cost me dear in loneliness and moral pain.

Science, religion, art, poetry, philosophy, psychology, psychotherapy and myself, all these seem to be amongst my concerns. Perhaps science and religion have been my most persistent cousins, tantalizing me with worrying concerns. Both speak so powerfully of where I am growing from. Both are concerned with *knowing*. In different ways they say that their own routes to knowledge are worthy of particular trust. The tension between these very different claims to knowledge has especially engrossed me, mostly in inarticulate ways. Even as I went faithfully to church I could not stop myself from asking and doubting. I had to find my own ground to trust what I might claim to know, and could not take anything at second hand. Thus did I move from the world of religious caring to that of scientific hubris as represented in the mainstream psychology of the time. Gradually I realized that I did not fit comfortably in either world, as they often seemed to be.

Only very slowly did I come to sense something of the same manner of concern in both these worlds. This style is inevitably a part of me, but is what I was increasingly able to put in question as I moved towards psychotherapy with its open invitation to intimacy and caring, knowing without often being known. Within this sheltering context it became more possible for me to feel and say, to touch gently a place of private pain and stand firmly in a land I did not know about but somehow knew.

I began to grasp something of these felt-features that percolated through both the church I knew and the science that I came to live. The Protestant world that straddled both has much in it that I value and admire, but I became aware of a *style of being* that might be called *the separating self*. What is he like, this pervasive product of that puritan world?

He is angry, hard-edged, driven, and often because of this, hard working. Being good is related to doing well, being a success in the world. Long ago he set out on a course of questioning and objecting to authority while still being quite authoritarian about it. His questioning tended to undermine beliefs of many kinds and undercut much of the religious ground on which he stood. This led to him becoming a pure scientist so as to channel his passion for work and questioning. Through time he built a new home, a cathedral of impressive proportions, the church of science. He is critical of others and critical of self. This constant criticism makes his own life hard to bear but contributes powerfully to his scientific competence. Within his new faith of science, research is at the core, and the pervasive posture towards others in the context of psychological research at least is one of unbridled criticism.

There is a distrust of feeling about all he does. He relies on doing, and this again feeds into his scientific style (and leads in psychology to behaviourism, which is behaviour-held-in-the-grip-of-circumstances rather than meaningful action). Pleasure is suspect and so, in quite crude forms, becomes either guiltily or rebelliously prized (self-gratification becomes readily accepted as the vehicle of change in behaviourism's early formulations; self interest, seeking pleasant things and avoiding unpleasant ones, still without regard to meaning).

There is a harsh quality in the relationship of the *separating self* and his world. This relationship tends to be sombre and colourless, or crudely lurid. Loneliness is endemic for the *separated self* since each self stands alone, initially before God, and increasingly before nothing at all, as his protestations against authority cut away credibility from any ultimate father figure. This harshness of protest also leads often to a rigidity of stance, in or out, black or white, with me or against me, up or down.

The *separating self* wants to divide and rule. His concern is with analysis rather than synthesis. His manner of dealing with events and people is to demand proof and the pursuit of sanctioned method. His talk is limited. He distrusts what cannot be said simply. He would rather count than say. He insist on plain and simple style, to the point of preferring crudity to care, in his insistence on the plain unvarnished facts behind the fanciful impressions others still enjoy.

If the transitory and invisible worlds between us are to be entered and known we *have to* speak and feel with greater care. There has to be a change of manner, not just a change of means and ends. We will need a different style to inform our expectations of how to behave 'appropriately' to know the worlds between. The grimly prim, tight, straight, businesslike, clipped, hard, precise, critical, comparing, measuring up, and chopping down ways of the *separating self* will not do.

In this 'New Reformation' that I am suggesting still lies hidden in the Protestant tradition, how might a more adapted self be arrayed?

She will surely be a more generously questioning soul. This questioning will reflect the tradition from which it comes but will be less harshly interrogatory. It will be more open, less defensive, more ready to be given over to genuine encounter with a loved world than seeking to achieve mastery and controlling power.

Questioning will become even more important than before, but in a different way. The new self will be a *conversing self*, involved in turning round to see and sense the other side, other points of view. In seeking to know, she recognizes that she must also become changingly known. Even with the most ordinary things, her manner seems to say 'You matter. You are special. You have your own beauty and strength. I am prepared to know something of that through the changes you may require of me.' Hers is not, however, a naïve, passive posture of submissive saintliness. She is secular and worldly-wise, realistically rational, loving, caring for herself as well as for others. She is 'ecologically caring' you could say.

Her primary concerns are to live with herself and others in ways which will allow us to know and be known more fully, to understand our place and condition more. She also tries to undertake something of the moral demands entailed in sustaining contexts for creative living within the dangers that will always threaten who we are or try to be. In seeking to know herself and others more, it is important to recognize that 'knowing' for her includes enjoying and playing with, participating in, enacting, as well as finding out about and saying how it is. This knowing has to do with living together amidst understandings and misunderstandings, rather than abstracted knowledge used for some other and more distant ends.

This *conversing self* has a different sense of personal security in that she has become more able to bear the fears that made the *separating self* stay well away, out of touch with feeling and vulnerability. She is more secure because she lives closer to her knowledge of pervasive insecurity. She knows we are always at risk, open to many threats. To some degree, she is able to undertake these fears rather than smother them in hard crusts of knowledge or by remaining isolated at a safe distance. She is less aggressive and domineering than the *separating self*, less concerned to seek victory for her own favoured point of view. At the same time she has strong enough boundaries to ensure that she is not blown out of shape by every wind of difference. She has shifted ground as regards the basis of relationship with others who differ in their views from her. She starts with the assumption that cultures differ and individuals within them differ too (however wide and pervasive their hidden similarities may be). She begins by assuming that individuals differ in their construing of events. This is *a given* for her, so she is not being repeatedly surprised by differences in others. She starts by assuming that she has to begin by trying to understand the concerns and way of understanding of the other. She does not see apparent difference as a threat or regard it as an open invitation to no-holds-barred missionary work.

Of course she is not always like this. Her toleration varies. Her willingness to feel and know is limited by what she has to ignore. Hers is not an all-things-to-all-men-and-women policy with no points beyond which she will not go. Hers is still a world of ever likely and often present confrontation. Pain, bafflement, betrayal, suffering, anger, wounding, tragedy are everywhere involved. Within all this, however, the *conversing self* is given over to trying to understand. She tries to construe the constructions of others and is quite often willing to suffer the personal pains of being changed in her struggle to understand the other person's (culture's, party's, profession's, partner's) point of view. It's not that, having understood to some degree, she will necessarily go along with them. Yet, this commitment to try to understand, even if a little and too late, the point and structure of viewing of the other is crucial to her way of being in the world.

This inevitably involves a different kind of willingness, from that undertaken by the *separating self*, to deal herself in. She more often tries to attend to her own mixed and often fearful, obscure, tangled, compromised, and dubious involvements in affairs. She recognizes that things don't just happen 'out there' but that we are ourselves imtimately involved and are always party to what is created or destroyed between us. She knows that we are already implicated from the moment of our conception in much that we did not choose (within our culture, country, family, class, race, ability group, sex, history, language, and biological inheritance). She knows that rejecting this will not resolve any issues. It is unfair, but that is how it is. Her world is not a place of security and often becomes too much, and has sometimes to be rejected.

This *conversing self* starts from a position of attentiveness to self as her major way of being attentive to others, and to others as a vital way of also being attentive to ourselves. She recognizes that unless there is meeting of some kind there can be no personally important knowing. All knowing is to do with being encountered, confronted, reflected back, made somehow aware at some level of what we are engaged within. Attention to this self/other ground of meeting is essential for her sensing of her world. We are all versions of market places and assembly rooms, pubs and parties, communities and institutions of many kinds. We are, she senses, places of meeting, not separate identities in the sense that the *separating self* used to suppose.

This sense of herself as places and manners of meeting, rather than a separated entity, helps her to recognize that knowing herself is already a deep involvement in knowing self/other. Knowing and caring for other is then more clearly sensed as a part of being oneself. She recognizes that we would not be 'self' without the community and culture of meeting that becomes possible in our social existence. Much of who we are remains the presence of others in our midst, rather than being intrinsically our own. In her world there is a need for other words since talk of 'self' and 'other' is recognized as misleading. She knows that it is always some version of the infinite variety of 'self/other' and 'other/self' that we are dealing with. Sometimes, for example, it is useful to speak of a 'you-I-me' or a 'they-you-I' experience.

In all this it is being recognized that few of us ever speak as a single unity, a coherent 'I'. We are created socially as a variety of amalgamated voices, and others are always involved in whatever 'I' say. We step into and out of many selves, many places and positions, as we meet and undertake the demands of different situations. Experiencing from both within and without (which is, of course, within somewhere else) is important and basic to the *conversing* self. She recognizes that outside knowledge and control will not be enough. Both 'indwelling' and 'breaking out' of our intimate experiencing is required, lived into knowing, as well as knowing about this or that.

The *conversing self* assumes and accepts that we have access to the 'inside' as well as the 'outside' of the world. We are intimate with reality, coextensive with it. She senses that we have access to our worlds through our experiencing and not just by seeing it 'out there'. While the *separating self* was afraid of feeling and relegated it to a secondary role, the *conversing self* lives her life as a continuing education in feeling. For her, feeling does not of course replace reason because she knows that our many acts of feeling are fundamentally involved in how we know. She knows that 'feeling' is a term we use when we are exploring our world more intimately, often when we cannot see or hear or taste what may be so.

There was a definite, hard edged quality to the *separating self's* way of being, and a more clear cut belief as to what constituted right and wrong. For him, morality was still largely given by outside sanction and authority, even though his questioning had eaten away the earlier foundations of credibility in the given rules. For the *conversing self* there is a more tentative quality on the one hand, and a more sure-footed sensibility on the other. While she is more ambiguous and tentative, more willing to approach and open up issues, she is more intuitively sure-footed in matters of right and wrong. She senses that what is 'good' and what 'evil' is a serious matter, but open to repeated question. The whole area of morality is important for her but not in the sense of some injunction requiring unquestioning obedience to some unquestionable rules.

This openness to and concern with the nature of 'good and evil' is perhaps one of the defining features of the *conversing self's* world. Since external authority is no longer the guiding convention, she is more fully required to tackle personally what she considers to be good or ill. The questions of morality have become large and important once again, in that rampant separateness and greed had all but brought destruction. Social and personal morality is taken as a serious matter of concern in daily living. Old notions of 'virtue' have been laid aside since they no longer had the coherence of their earlier cultural disciplines of honour. New ways of valuing self and other have had to be created in being lived.

George Kelly (1969) suggested that our central concern should be 'the fullest possible understanding of the nature of good and evil'. The *conversing self*, as a humane inquirer rather than a self righteous protester that the *separating self* often became, may have a posture to living that allows the openness to future knowing that Kelly's approach generally implied. Her life is one of quest and questioning, seeking to understand through speaking together in word and deed. As she looks back on what she once called 'good' the *conversing self* sees that things change and change again. She struggles to understand how 'good' becomes variously transformed to 'evil', and *vice versa* too. It is because the *conversing* world is a world of radical and compassionate questioning that the moral realm is so much to the fore.

Perhaps, therefore, it is worth considering some of the more obvious values in the world of the *conversing self*.

She has a commitment to *honesty*, or attempted 'good faith'. This is not a simple following of rules but involves a probing concern that insistently tries to find a way amongst the deceptive, ambiguous mysteries of our selves and our being in the world.

She is committed to a sensing of *self-other-world as an intertwined and interdependent composite*. She does not have a commitment to any notion of self as a separated entry, nor even to some notion of self-and-those-accepted-as-of-the-same-tribe-as-self. Hers is an ecological view which takes concerned note of our human involvement with each other and all other aspects of our world. In the human realm this view recognizes that we can know from 'within' as well as 'without' and the necessary conversation between them, and that we have a special duty to care for our possibilities of understanding. Only we can come to know what human understanding and misunderstanding may yet achieve or fail to realize.

Special value is placed on *experiencing*, on knowing through personal involvement rather than simply knowing from a distance. This requires the development of ways of knowing more of how to talk, explore, and experiment within the territory of experiencing. In the development of a more adequate psychological science, more articulated experiencing has come to accompany more sensitive experiment.

The *conversing self* clearly attaches great value to *trying to understand*, to talking together, negotiating, learning to live together, caring how we meet. In this, conflict is not minimized. Frustration, pain, and fear are repeatedly experienced, but attempts are made to create contexts of caring to allow sufficient safety and support. By seeking to survive both knowing and being known the *conversing self* is in even greater danger of being precipitated into reactions of destruction and fear. It is not always an easy life she lives, even in many contexts of greater care.

Because of this, *courage* is valued and required. Any willing approach to greater openness to self or others requires nerve and steadiness of purpose. Pains and fears have to be faced in being alone and in more intimate involvement with others.

Knowing is valued, but it is a more rounded and extensive kind of knowing than that pursued by the *separating self*. It is a lived knowing that involves being known as well. It is a responsive and responsible knowing that is prized more than impersonal knowledge-in-the-head or in theory only. Questioning is valued, but again it is questioning that carries the weight and price ticket of a cherished life that holds sway.

Great value attaches to *creative living* and the issue of living is much more articulated than simply being a 'success' or a 'failure' in some easily measurable way. How we live together is in how we speak together in everything we do. Learning to speak more fully and imaginatively is of especial importance for the *conversing self*.

I can see as I spell out a little of the lives of these cousins of mine, the *separating self* with whom I am uncomfortably familiar, and the *conversing self* who I rather fear and admire from afar, why I am closer to the former than the latter. Both can be seen as offspring of the Protestant tradition. For each of them the web of their habitable world holds and sustains them where they are. Whatever 'selves' we become, we are woven from the fibres of particular worlds. Our worlds and our selves are woven together, but worlds are born out of worlds just as people are. Both worlds and people change, and some little part in that is through what we aspire towards and are willing still to realize.

Speaking our worlds

Every self presupposes a world. Every self is created in relation to another and in the necessary context of a world. Everything is created to mediate between what we imagine and what is somehow so. Every self must somehow be related to another self. This starts in relation to the mother and other close figures who lay the foundations of selfhood and are part of the context of a world. As we grow and change we move into other worlds which draw forth other selves composed to meet the fears and challenges of each supposed, sensed, and acted from world.

We are born into worlds of physical nature, culture, language, family, locality. Everything is in contexts and these contexts are not bland containers but precisely relevant challenges and opportunities which we sense and in relation to which we compose ourselves. The context of every self, of every action, of every symbol needs to be sought, if it is to be understood. The contexts of our living have to be understood as essential aspects in any exploration of persons. We have to speak of selves and worlds, persons and worlds together.

A world sustains and shapes the life within it. No wonder people feel they are stepping off the edge when they risk new moves of a personally significant kind. Worlds are more basic than selves. In becoming selves we must assume worlds of certain kinds in order to inform ourselves to meet them. To change ourselves we may then have to put worlds in question. We may have to postulate and dare other worlds, with the possibility that they may not support us. If we are to be on the move we have to develop the means of surviving for a time between worlds. People sometimes get lost in the dark void of nothingness between worlds when they have left one place of habitation and cannot find another to sustain them.

The creation of selves is our attempt to describe and survive in worlds. All the time we are attentive of worlds even though in being so we more often attend from than to them. Psychology, then, is directly related to physics in this regard, that it deals with 'worlds'. It however deals with worlds through the medium of our creation of selves which know and live from worlds.

We are living postulants of worlds. We reflect and assert worlds. Even though this may be so, it is not easy to attend through 'selves' to the 'worlds' they imply. We are more accustomed in psychology to attending to 'self' and 'personality' and leaving the necessary worlds from which they grow implicit, out of sight. If you sense very different kinds of worlds then what you attend to and create will be very different too. To criticize a production of world A from an unrecognized stance in world B may result in unrecognized confusion. We may need to learn to compare like *with* like, and like *from* like. We need to recognize more clearly what we attend *from* and not just what we attend *to*.

It is not just our assumptions about worlds that I'm trying to attend to, but the fact that our worlds are constituted by and through our assumptions. It is not that we stand separate from 'a world' and make assumptions about it. Our assuming constitutes us as well as our world. Our hidden assuming is the living means by which we-in-relation-to-world are held in being.

For us there is no world separate from a world maker and sustainer. Everything is in the darkness between self and world. We are part of the consciousness of being. Self is the inside of world. We create, through our assumptions, a stable world, but a habitable world is not a specific entity or physical place but a relationship of lived context. There are many habitable worlds even for a single person. We live in sheafs of worlds. In saying this I am not speaking of *the world*, but our endless possibilities of envisioning habitations.

We know that we learn visual constancy in a world of motion. Even as we move around we learn to make the world seem still. Within our selves we also learn constancy to varying degrees. We come to keep some sense of stability in the midst of the moving of attention and intention. As we stretch we learn to suppose a stable base. We take ourselves as referents and stand guard to keep some version of ourselves/our world in place.

We are often trapped by worlds that we implicitly act to sustain ourselves against. We commit large parts of whatever we are and have to holding up huge boulders that seem to threaten us, even though we would see from somewhere else that they were not there at all.

It is important to recognize that we are in the dark. We are postulating worlds within the dugouts and bunkers of our threatened existences. We are blinded to ourselves as persons in worlds by the competence we have as animals in a physical world. Our education tends to stop before it tells us much of ourselves as 'person/worlds'.

It is not isolated world makers, each in his or her own corner, that I assume. It is rather that we are held and made within communities of intention. It is between and amongst ourselves that we are shaped and braced. It is the active shaping by other selves that structures us. We are shaped and given our limitations which we have to endure or circumvent. We breathe within the given atmosphere of yester-years. We shrivel or grow in history.

The world needs to be broken up. The world is a figment of many imaginings. We tend to assume, within our culture, that we know how *the world* is. It is as in photographs rather than in paintings. By our partly shared conventions, we hold ourselves within a certain quality of reality. We have to recognize more clearly, however, that worlds are created in our manner and modes of meeting. We are always and at all times constructing worlds between us. *We* are fundamentally implicated in *world.*

Other worlds are not just abstract possibilities. They are everywhere. We live in and assert them at all times. We endlessly misunderstand and seek not to credit, to warrant, worlds other than the ones we ourselves inhabit.

Within ourselves and between us and our environment we live through differing and mostly unnoticed conversations of our times. Mostly we do not stop to identify the participants or the assumptive world within which they exist and hold their sway.

A conversation seeks to establish a shared world and takes place within an assumed world. Often the assumed world is asserted and built implicitly into the tone and stance of the participants. Some conversations are hard and full of misunderstanding when the participants assume wrongly that they share a mutually valued world. Conversations often do not have any satisfactory flow because the world being asserted is not adequate to the needs of one or other of the participants. Because of this we need to ask ourselves and others what worlds we are offering and allowing. What kinds of worlds do you live within in your dealings with yourself? What alternative worlds do you variously inhabit and have available to share in the ongoing conversation of your life with others?

To sense a shared, indeterminately fertile, world is deeply satisfying. Worlds that are shared and lived from allow creative meeting, but many do not share a world with anyone. In psychological therapy, of course, we seek to compose shared worlds. Usually this means the therapist attending to the client's worlds and gradually offering access to a possibility of sharing. The therapist offers a world that, in being shown, is already in practice, and is to a degree, one that the patient may already recognize as related to his own.

We share worlds within the limits of trusting. There is a boundary of risk and danger, of chanciness, beyond which we fear to go. Sometimes we mistake the amount of sharing that is possible. We share too much or too little and suffer hurt or impoverishment.

There are worlds within worlds. All psychologies, for instance, postulate worlds. Each of us lives within different worlds, sometimes with almost no bearing on each other. Within worlds it is not just persons or selves that matter. Our attention should also be drawn to atmospheres, kinds of nourishment, light and dark, the changing seasons, desert and mountain, open spaces, and the stinking slums. We are here concerned with a human geography of knowing.

Conversation is concerned with the making and destroying of habitations, places of life and places of varying kinds of destruction and death. In speaking of worlds I am trying to refer to the lived context in any particular human transaction. Language in use composes many such worlds, places, and kinds of human habitation. Heidegger (1971) spoke of language as 'the house of being'. Wittgenstein (1953) considered 'language games' to be forms of life.

I start from a deep sense of being left out, of being on the outside of the psychology I was taught. It requires me to act on knowledge brought *in* from *out* there, rather than, sometimes and also, brought *out* from within my own experiencing. I was not encouraged to dwell on my own possibilities of experiencing and little encouragement was, and is, given to developing one's own ways of sensing more or less or otherwise.

Gradually I sensed that I have access to more knowledge and understanding than I ordinarily recognize. It is, however, not just a matter of taking in or drawing out knowledge, but of recognizing more surely that I already participate in and am shaped by the ongoing knowing, permeated and informed by the ongoing conversation of my world; I enact some of the knowing and understanding of my culture. Through me there must therefore be access to knowing that we often do not know we know. I participate in knowing, and as a psychologist at least, need to gain fuller access to those ways of being which shape our competence and blindness too.

Like everyone in their somewhat different ways, I have found myself cast into a world in a particular place and time. I am the inheritor, in a radical and total sense, of much of my wider culture and the particular shaping of that culture within my own family of origin. I am taught to understand and not to understand through my culture's and my family's concerns. I am encouraged to approach and avoid what it and they have already undertaken or fear to know. I, and others before and around me, without having any way of questioning, are woven up into what is to be attended to and what attended from, and what is just left silently aside.

It is because each different person has a slightly different vantage point, and our culture is itself composed of almost endless local variations, that we each can have some chance of becoming more or less aware of a little of what we are born amongst. Some learn to know more explicitly something of what shapes and holds us. Many learn little or nothing. Some do not acquire any spelled-out knowledge, but through their lived understanding may be especially good at riding the implicit waves that carry and contain us.

Much that I am is quite unknown to me. There must be many possibilities still untapped in the mystery natures we inherit. Beyond what we yet know must lie much more that we do not yet even imagine. This seems likely to be true across the centuries as well as in the span of particular lives. We are shaped in ways which reflect the practical competences of our tribe. Had we been born into different tribes, different possibilities would have been found and realized. It is this scope for enacting something else and other that we try to gain access to in psychological therapies and many other disciplines of transition in our society.

Most of what we are is beyond the reach of words, but our only means of understanding our lives is through language, how we speak and are spoken to, the conversational practices and opportunities of our place and time. All our knowledge and understanding is shaped by the structure of our language and the ways in which we are able, or are allowed, to use it in practice. It is in speaking, and in other more formal uses of language, that we create the realities and the possibilities that we know. Language does not just mirror some real state of affairs beyond words, it constitutes what is real and possible for us. When our ways of speaking to our selves and others change, our reality and our possibilities of feeling and being real change too. As we discover new (or old and forgotten) ways of entering into living conversation, so does our understanding, knowledge, and sense of reality change, shrinking or expanding, twisting or variously transforming.

In speaking here of 'speaking', 'language', and 'conversation' I am referring to more than the use of words. All our social life is structured with conventional ways of enacting and symbolizing our communal concerns. By 'language' I am referring to all the patterned, conventional ways in which we implicitly and explicitly order our affairs together, 'say' what we mean and come to mean what we 'say'. In this complex world, our verbal language probably shows more clearly than our other ways of 'speaking together' many of the issues involved in much that we do together. It is likely to be limited too, and much that is important in how we enter into the 'conversation' of our lives may be structured in ways that distinguish it from the use of words and syntax.

What we take ourselves to be, how we experience our selves and our worlds, what is real for us (including our own reality) is intimately related to how we speak together. Who and how we are is in how we speak together. We are conjured into being in the conversational opportunities in our lives, and can be conjured out of being, disintegrated, and otherwise destroyed by change and decay in these possibilities. How we organize our conventions of meeting and parting shapes who and how we are. If our understanding and knowledge of ourselves and others is to be changed in significant ways we have to change our ways of speaking with each other. Only as we create, protect, and sustain appropriate conversational contexts for the nourishment of certain forms of life can we hope to come to know possibilities that lie beyond our present ways of being in relation.

We are not, however, merely compositions of the present. We are historical and prehistorical as well. We are formed implicitly in structured ways of relating which can endure in spite of all general influences in later life. These early ways of relating can constitute our basically assumed world that is then beyond easy alteration. It may only be in 'total control' methods like 'brainwashing' that some of these patterns can be made available for change. Many forms of chosen help may be ineffective since the person may not be able to choose to engage in manners of engaging that are themselves prescribed.

It is important to recognize more clearly that the conversational practices by and within which we seek knowledge and understanding themselves contribute significantly to creating their own realms of reality ('reality' being a protean fiction, a way of speaking of the multi-faceted mystery within which we live and have our being). In each such 'creation' there are regularities to be 'discovered' by the practices we use to shape their discovery. There are new or different ways of valuing people implied within the practices and perspectives on ourselves and others contained therein. There are politics of power and the organization of particular ways of life in every kind of conversational practice that we can undertake.

We will repeatedly destroy or put in question the conventions and syntax of former realities (ways of speaking together) by new approaches which break the old rules. Metaphor is a rule-breaking procedure that can allow us access to new versions of reality and may offer us scope for new fashions and styles of living. In a wider sense also, new conversational practices of many kinds can break with the means and manners by which old worlds were sustained.

This means that different ways of inquiring and different manners of dealing with each other (enshrined in different cultures, theories, forms of asking and answering) are *essentially* incomparable. They create different worlds, different realities, that may sometimes be compared in terms of some of their products, against some chosen measure, but often this will not sensibly be so. This is perhaps why old systems in psychology seem to fade away rather than get disproved or built upon. Fashions change, and the worlds of active endeavour change their garb and move elsewhere. Sometimes they are able to pick up old themes, but often not. It is noticeable in psychology that most work does not refer back beyond a few years, and most psychologists do not refer to work beyond the boundaries of their own tribal loyalties.

In adopting the manner of inquiry of the early physical sciences, psychology encouraged its investigators to learn to stand in new and special ways in relation to other people who were to be their subject matter in scientific study. They were to stand over against their subject matter in such a way as to be able to specify and observe aspects of their visible or recordable behaviour. Experimental psychology was then to be the outcome of this way by which psychologists set themselves apart from their own kind. They were to treat others as observable 'outsiders' rather than understanding, inquiring and communicating agents in the bosom of culture, just like themselves.

Their version of psychology was then to be a creation outside history or ordinary social conventions. New conventions were being created in the conversational practices that were enshrined in its new methods. The discipline was thus to grow in the realm of reality that these procedures conjured into being and allowed. This new realm of 'data', acquired through means of communication that largely denied or obscured many of the normal assumptions about meaningful communication, was to be promoted to the level of 'scientific' fact. It was thus accorded a cultural invulnerability from ordinary criticism and allowed to cast spells of enchantment over many who wished to undertake its ways, or were trapped in its web without knowing what was being done to them.

In being encouraged to stand over against the experience and subjectivity of others, we were similarly encouraged to become outsiders even to our own experience. Just as others become the *objects* of our scientific interest, so do we become objects even to ourselves. In doing this we are taking a particular way of standing and being arrayed in relation to our own experience. We are accepting certain ways of asking and answering as the crucial and desirable ones in our conversational practices as scientists. Eventually this makes us increasingly sense ourselves as outsiders in the world as well. In this way we have increasingly lost access to the kinds of sensibilities that were more properly part of a different world of conversational practice.

Many of our ways of being in relation to events that involved us being 'in the midst' rather than 'set over against', personally committed rather than impersonally detached, have tended to be downgraded and left as suspect relics of a bygone time. Yet it seems likely that this haste, on the part of psychology at least, to separate off from the older, traditional ways, was too brashly done. We may have thrown away some of what was vital to human understanding and the pursuit of knowledge of more intimate aspects of human affairs. It may be that unless we can learn to marry the true spirit of scientific endeavour (combining courage, persistence, honesty, sensitivity, attentiveness to hints and clues, intuition, and evidence) to that special kind of conversational courage whereby we allow ourselves to 'live in and amongst', we may be deprived access to worlds of reality that are specially rich for human understanding. In fearing and fleeing from superstition and mouldering religious dogma (which were once filled with new life and a spirit of genuine adventure) we may also have abandoned certain vital ways of 'being in the midst' so that we can listen as well as speak from personal participation in what we sense and feel.

I can sum up what I have been saying in a single, bold assertion. *We create realities by and through the conversational practices we are involved within and undertake.* These 'conversational practices' are not just in our use of words together, but also in how we organize, signify, and enact our meanings. Thus the experimenter in a psychology experiment, for instance, already before beginning, is speaking of the kind of event this is and is not in every detail of the setting as well as the manner and method of addressing his subjects. By restricting their rights of reply or protest, by limiting their choices of answering, by ruling out of court almost everything they might be feeling, their ordinary worlds are shaped into something of another kind.

This implies that different ways of going about the business of inquiry themselves create the realms of fact and possibility that they then explore. The ways in which we speak together constitute the realities that we know of ourselves and of our worlds. This is not necessarily to say that reality is all in the mind, but how our 'mind' is constituted composes what we take reality to be. Whatever limits to our capacities there are, we can be sure that any radical revision in what and how we know will cost us dearly. We will have to leave our present, comfortable 'homes', to wander in a 'wilderness' perhaps, towards 'fertile habitations' still beyond our ken. In all this, of course, our ways of speaking together may themselves be crushed or crippled by physical and social worlds beyond our capacity to control.

What I am suggesting is that the ways in which we enter into conversation actually create the realities that they then offer for further inquiry. In this way the very manner, tone, style, shaping, context, and surrounding structuring of how we speak together constitute potential realities that we often claim were already there and waiting to be found. Our usual way of dealing with this has been to focus on getting our methods 'right' (be they scientific, humanistic, or whatever) and then focussing on the special material we attend to by means of these ways of asking. We have tended to suppose that if we act in a certain way to each other (such as by means of 'the scientific method') we will have specially worthy access to the way things 'really are'! All other ways of inquiring are then downgraded because they don't 'really' get at how things 'really' are. Other ways of speaking together are relegated as variously being too subjective, contaminated, biassed, or of some other less than worthy kind.

The understanding we generally now follow is that certain *methods* are specially worthy of trust if we are to be *scientific*, for instance. We tend to regard them as being better *on the same dimension* and *in relation to the same reality* as other methods of discourse or inquiry we might employ. What I am suggesting, though, is that *our favoured methods are only favoured in relation to the world of reality that they create and offer for exploration.* They are just like many other methods in relation to the worlds which they variously, by their use, create and offer for exploration. Within our society we have somehow chosen to ascribe the greater worth, for our communal purposes, to some ways of speaking together and organizing our affairs, and less to others.

This is not, of course, a simple state of affairs. What it draws attention towards is, however, quite different from the focus of our attention in much of present day psychology. This perspective encourages us to be attentive to *our ways of speaking together* rather than giving very special status to certain methods of inquiry and the 'facts' that are constituted from within that kind of method-governed world. It means that we have to stop claiming unique rightness and become more 'ecumenical'. Every culture of conversation allows access to and creates the possibilities of its own reality. We should not rest content with ignoring or downgrading all but a chosen few.

This suggestion draws attention to our conversational *practices* rather than giving priority to our theories or our claims about the nature of reality or the worth of different methods. We have to develop means of attending to conversational *practices*, to what is going on in our ways of speaking together (not just in words but in our conventions of dress, hierarchies, decorations, possessions). As we act differently, understand differently, listen differently, allow different possibilities for openness or protection, learn to use words differently, so will we actually, there and then, constitute local realities whose further reaches may still be well beyond what we imagine.

This, though, will not be just a matter of observing 'behaviour', the more easily noted and recorded shell of what we say. It is *conversational* practice that we are to learn to give attention to, not movements or biological changes. This focus takes us beyond notions of 'relationship' and 'interaction' or even 'system' to the meanings and intentions, as well as the 'pragmatics' of communication and community conventions. It requires that we come to understand more of what is involved in 'conversation', not just as a verbal exchange between individuals but as the moving web of cultural practices that we live amongst. It takes us into and beyond the study of 'language' (which is a formal abstraction and systematization) and towards *speaking* together. It requires that we come to attend more to how we compose our rationality and irrationality through the conventions we inhabit and the rhetorical devices we are capable of employing in our thrust towards persuasion.

In all this I may still miss the point in what I am still feeling towards. I do not have ways of conceiving of conversational practices that yet allow much scope for new action. I still seek ways of talking about our ways of talking, and the manner in which both kinds of talking may be done. This is no easy matter, as many others have pointed out, since we are then trying to use the very competences we are seeking to conceive of in trying to specify something of their form. Direct linear, logical thought and method will not be enough. Being more able to step out intuitively and figuratively will have a centrally important place, allowing us sometimes to conjure up senses and patterns of where and how we are arrayed.

We need ways of construing conversational practices. These will have to be new kinds of conceptions which focus on this 'joint' or 'communal' action of speaking together. We will need conceptions that speak of this new focus, not ones which divide conversational practices immediately into the interacting of separate blobs, or focus on the frequency of use of certain categories of phrase. These sorts of concepts derive from our present atomistic and analytic way of cutting into complex unities, whose coherence may rather need to be conceived and sustained.

There are many worlds of realities shaped and constituted in our manners, intentions and contexts of being in conversation. There are worlds within and around worlds. There is no single world that we all have access to (or if there is we do not have access to it). We live, though, within a powerful fiction which allows us the assumption (very useful for the natural sciences and very harmful for the social sciences) that we all live within the same world, but sometimes see it more or less differently in minor but correctable ways. I want to challenge this and to encourage an awareness that this bland view of regularity is not a necessary fiction. Nor is it a helpful fiction in trying to understand our personal worlds. We live, rather, in multiple and changing worlds, varying in texture and possibilities, themes and colours, clustered within each other and being everywhere reconstituted and disappearing. In a precise sense there is no continuing human world, no worlds that ever exist again. There are instead many families of worlds which maintain some more or less stable forms of life, for a time while they evolve, distort, shrink, or bloom. Worlds die daily, every moment of every day. Worlds that might have been remain unborn.

Telling our stories

We come forth from within the conversational 'soup' of our times and place. We grow in conversation and absorb many unspecified messages. We live into being the many patterns of convention that, in being absorbed, become who we blinkingly take ourselves to be. We are patterned cross-currents of argument and assertion, expostulations and platitudes. Almost everything in this culturally primordial soup is analogical and has to be teased out in threads, as wool from the tangled skein. We have to separate out the yarns that we will tell ourselves and others. Mostly we remain tangled within the threads of the story lines spun by others before and around us. We are held in ways we do not own or control.

There are many voices and many incipient stories too. There are stories that have been inherited and passed from others. Many stories are begun, but never clearly end, remaining ragged and inconclusive. Seeking a strong story line occupies much of many lives. Mostly we have to make do with fragments, bits and pieces of conventional wisdom, odd comments, well worn rubrics of our culture.

Only occasionally are we asked to provide an authorized version of who we are. Mostly when this is required it becomes an expurgated version with many of the juicy bits left out. An authorized version of who we are is for public presentation of some kind. It is like a communiqué after an international conference. Every phrase is weighed and blunted till it tells little of the life that it supposedly recounts. It is honed towards an acceptable communication of what we are willing to appear to be. It is likely to leave many loopholes so that we have escape routes readily available from commitments we might not wish to honour.

It is easy to attend to the line of the story and forget the conversational net in which it is a necessary strand. Every story is a story in time. Some reach beyond particular times to speak of many places and many times, with more universal appeal. Often the voices in which we tell our stories will not tell it like it is for us, but adopt a given, sanctioned way. There are many people around us and voices within ourselves who do not have the right to speak, many voices within the voice who do not know what rights they have. We are compositions for many voices, some of whom make mouth and body music only.

Everywhere and on every occasion we make up stories and tell tales of many different kinds. Sometimes we find ways of telling that speak afresh in new surroundings. Some of our story telling is to convince ourselves and others that we have found the *true* story, the way things really are. Mostly we are wrong of course and other ways will still be found.

In every generation new stories are needed, and new ways of retelling old stories so that we can trust them and ourselves anew. We are born into ongoing stories and breathe in our parts in the air and food that nourish us. These inherited characters are often undertaken as the way things unquestionably are for us. All our attention is shaped by the real life 'plays' in which they have some place. We know by feel and long apprenticeship what gestures, attitudes, actions, opinions we are allowed to have. We quickly learn to know what fits and what just will not do.

Some of our stories have enduring themes. Some are more closely bound to the fashions of a moment. We invent new ways of researching our story lines. We conjure up new characters, new explanations of motive, new angles of modernity that put the old ways out of style. Surely we are a society grown frantic to tell our stories. What anguish we experience, those of us who are not able to be heard, for whom no obliging ear makes time for us to say our piece. Many come for psychological treatment, supposing themselves to be approaching madness because no one listens to what they mean, so they fear they don't mean anything. Mostly we feel we do only mean something if we mean something to someone in the stories that we share.

Perhaps it is even worse to have no way of telling, no way of understanding what part we play, what stage we walk, what script we follow, what plots we are party to. If we do not understand the language in which our inarticulate pains cry out their own sad song, we can be brought to despair. We listen to others seeming so easily to tell how it is with them, little knowing that they too tell lies. More often than we naïvely imagine they merely mouth the parts they believe they are expected to inhabit, leaving their own more intimate tales struggling with disqualifications that they have not been allowed the means of recognizing, far less overcoming.

Stories are necessary to weave a web of meaning within which we can live. We all live in story worlds. They create for us the atmosphere of understandability that seems necessary for ordinary survival. Sharing and participating in popular stories is how we can reduce the basic anxieties we feel when events are beyond the limits of our individual story lines. Many of our stories cover our nakedness which would otherwise leave us unbearably vulnerable. They cover our tracks so that it looks, to ourselves and others, as if we know what we are up to. Children who cannot provide stories that have some ring of truth get punished. They learn early that any story is better than no story, and it is better to stick to a feeble story than to admit that you just don't know!

All our stories are expressions of ourselves even when they purport to be accounts of aspects of the world. We are deeply implicated in the very grounds of our story telling. The conventions within which we compose our tales are given us in our culture and speak of our place and time (for those who can eventually recognize that this is so), even when we think we are being free of our own society's bias and limitations.

All our stories are self stories of our place and time, not just of some abstracted wraith. Even the obscuring of self that is favoured in our current 'objective' stories are still speaking of a particular posture to self. All stories are located social events. They speak towards ends and in some ways that are considered relevant by the people in question. All stories are told by someone in relation to some audience of relevant others. In this context all stories are ways of trying to assert a particular view and set of rights to hold certain positions of perspective. They are claims made over against someone or some others, and are varying kinds of rehearsals for or participation in human conflicts.

Stories only make sense within the ongoing conversation of their times. They are given credibility by the language and customs, beliefs and limitations of particular times. Without the conversational flux within which they arise they would not be possible and would not be intelligible. Conventions of conversation give local credence to some ways of telling and not to others. The local ways of giving credence allow some ploys to be given special weight in some tribes which would be totally inadequate in others. Within the psychoanalytic tribes, for instance, certain mythologies and ways of collecting material for stories are used that are never considered of even passing worth by the radical-behaviourist tribe.

Stories serve many functions. One of the most important is to provide the context of normality within which members of the tribe live out their lives. Stories that form the backbone of a culture are normative in providing the party line that spells out the place of freedom and opportunity for some, and the lines beyond which the deviants and dissenters live. Stories specify the boundaries of the acceptable, the normal, the usual, or the strange. Presumably all tribes have stories which speak of what is beyond the pale of understandability within that culture. These help to keep in place an awareness of what is beyond the tribal limits. They keep people 'in' and provide a cultural borderline where even those who roam 'out there' can be recognizably strange, within the accepted strangeness of the tribe.

One of the major concerns of our society is with developing means whereby the stories that we tell about ourselves and the world around are worthy of wide belief. We have developed ways of composing our stories (such as investigative journalism and scientific experimentation) that require us to follow certain approved procedures for testing the worth of our stories. We weave our preferred themes through the markers that we are given and often do not recognize that many different stories could have the same characters and the same testified events.

It is very noticeable in our scientific story telling that there are fierce conventions as to how the stories have to look and sound. They have to be logical and make a convincing claim that A did lead on to B and then to C. It is still not so very widely recognized that most of this logic is put in after all the other work on the story has been done, and is part of the final rhetoric of the scientific story teller's art. Even with the most rigorous conventions, the passionate writer's pet themes still appear, woven through whatever landmarks of socially confirmed evidence are mandatorily there. Like salmon seeking their place to spawn, it is not easy to stop a person or a tribe telling the story that they want to hear.

How a story is told can be of such importance. Even a logically shaky construction can win the day if told with feeling. Some of us insist on our stories being simple and matters of attested fact. Some would prefer the colour of a good romance to humdrum ordinariness as the way their story should be told.

Stories are social events, not individual things. Even when we tell ourselves stories (and we do this all the time in many noticed and implicit ways) a whole army of silent watchers is there to sanction us in speaking as we do and understanding the significance in what we say. Stories are our way of weaving ourselves together and driving ourselves apart. If our stories are repeatedly rejected by those around us, we are likely to become non-persons, outcasts.

Do stories speak of a reality beyond themselves? Clearly in our culture we believe that some do and others don't. We believe in the value of the distinction between fiction and non-fiction, and between non-fiction and scientific tales. We seem often to believe in the worth of distinctions between different kinds of stories, even to the point of not recognizing that those at the scientific end of our scale are still in the category of 'story'. Psychologically, it seems to me important to bring them all back clearly within the story-world and then explore the different ways in which we use and abuse, compose and recompose, research and conjure out of our feelings, the stories that we tell and value. A psychology of stories has, though, to be explored within a psychology of conversation, part of a discipline of discourse.

In times of extremity it can become more clear. Every act of saying, every telling of a tale, is an act of war. We have to fight for our existence, for our place in the sun. In our acts of speaking, as in all our other actions, we are battling for and constituting our way of existing, our forming of life. We do not live in a static and placidly enduring world that we can describe at our leisure with words that quietly picture what is there before us. We do not copy the world in our words without interference or influence. We fight to survive. Every word, every gesture, every silence, every way of saying, every manner of expressing what we mean is an act of struggle. Each is part of the lifelong campaign of informing ourselves, our others, our worlds. Man is a form of motion and that motion is in forms of struggle.

When we speak of ourselves we give ourselves marching orders. We outline formations for battle. More than this! When we speak of ourselves, personally or professionally, we are already at war. Our words are in the thick of action. Sometimes they are foot soldiers in the dirt, sometimes long-range bombardments, sometimes aerial surveillance or the strafing bullets which wound from the sky.

What we say is active in leaving out what we could have said but did not. Everything that we say is a bulwark against what could have been said. What could have been said, and how it could have been said, is especially dangerous. All that we are not capable of being, all that we know and fear, all that we long for but cannot bear, all that lies beyond even the camp fires of our local imagination, all that lies out beyond what we did not manage to say, is held at bay by the particular words we wield and the particular manner in which they are arranged and said. Beyond what is said is the known and beckoning, and also the unknown and terrifying. Mostly this latter is kept so far off by the familiarity of what we say that we do not even know that the wilderness begins just beyond the pallisades of our particular words.

More even than this is involved. Our speaking is a defence and an assault on others in the human world. Everything we say, even to ourselves, is an engagement with others-in-self, self-in-others. Every time we speak we are displaying our plumage, making gestures of intended threat. We struggle to carve out, maintain, and protect psychological space wherein some kind of living can be composed. When our words change, our space for living, our very form of life, changes. Our words and stories are staves and arrows, wattle and branches. The culture and customs of our tribe are enacted in our worlds. Our ways of speaking stand against the other worlds that are denied a chance of birth, and the worlds that are realized in the spoken claims and speaking practices of others who are also fighting to maintain their ways to be, other cultures of cohesive exclusion.

One problem is that if we speak too readily we can kill and do harm to the very issues involved. Once an issue is wrongly worded it takes on a life of its own. It becomes an 'it' towards which floating meaning is sucked, leaving only denials that themselves do harm, and qualifications that should not be made since they encourage respect for what is already said and wrong. It is so easy to do damage to what is and is not yet known to be so (and will not be availably so unless realized with care).

We tell stories to our children and create story worlds in which to dwell. The kinds of stories we tell sometimes see us through and often fail us when things don't turn out the way we have been led to suppose. When a story and the associated story world fail then we may be in difficulties. Our essential stories are not just casual entertainment. It is as children ourselves that we speak and listen. We are thrust into the darkness of the universe. We try to create worlds to live within and to spin our stories through time so that we and our world are constantly being recreated, retold, revised. We are creating ourselves and being created in our stories. They are not just about others and spoken from afar.

Psychologists to some degree, but psychotherapists more especially, trade in the unknown and the almost unknown. We develop ways of helping people to tell and live their stories, understand their experiences, risk new undertakings, or the re-examination of old ground.

Psychologists and psychotherapists, like everyone else, are creatures in culture but, more than most, are near the edge. We have to live within the culture and also draw ourselves out of and away from the ordinarily accepted conventions and conversational practices of our time. We have to live within the rules and yet come to know and sometimes challenge the rules when that is needed.

Many of our clients come to us because they are trapped and confused. They are frightened by the rules of the worlds within which they live. Our task is to help them grow a new culture around and within themselves so that they have freedoms and possibilities that previously were denied. Almost all our professional ways of entering into conversation introduce them to new cultural norms, new conventions that we offer as potentially normal, liveable, acceptable. This is no easy matter since conventions are deeply grounded and persistently supported in and by the social world of the person's every-day life and upbringing.

There are special problems for those who seek to listen to the stories of others and help them tell new tales, change and divert the story line. You have to live a double life (even more persistently than most). You have to live in the public world of ordinary convention and also in the underworld of secrecy and dread. We are as spies, secret agents, and sometimes double agents, living between two worlds.

As spies we are expected to bring back secrets from the other side as well as listen to and make use of the secret side of our conventional culture. To some degree you do not belong. Many who become psychologists and psychotherapists do so as a means of somehow belonging within the ordinary world while making special use of their outsider understanding of a culture they know mainly by exclusion. In this way they may sometimes be especially acute perceivers of the ordinary world of appearances that must take things to be the way they seem. Those who do not quite belong may see more clearly than those who effortlessly fit into the common mould. To be this kind of psychologist is to be stretched, to be uncomfortable, to feel almost alien to those who lead a single life within the fold.

We are paid outsiders who are allowed inside because of what we can contribute from this dual perspective. We are not altogether trusted or accepted though. We continue to be regarded with some suspicion and fear. We hear too many secret tales, and may be sensed as threatening to the established order of things. We are in the realm of secrets and deception, pretence and cover stories. We act in part as pressure valves within our culture whereby appearances can be saved.

We do not only trade in the secrets of the public world. We are merchants and carriers of strange tales from many worlds. We are made privy to other worlds, other ways to live and love. We are cultural adventurers, being amongst the traders, travellers, and soldiers of our times. Some of us even fall under the dangerous delusions of being cultural missionaries, saviours, shapers of destinies.

Psychotherapists occupy a remarkable position in society. We daily have access to the secrets of our clients, and therefore of the society of which they and we are part. We are secret agents, being told what others try to hide. We probe and listen behind the mask of ordinary appearance.

We are ambiguous and liable to be suspect by many in the ordinary world. For some we may become the focus of fascination because we have access to the hidden world, to double dealings behind closed doors, improprieties that dominate private lives and must be hidden from the public gaze.

We live between the overworld of conventional appearances and the underworld of fear, anxiety, passions, and secret dread, of lives lived in the threatening shadow of discovery. Some of the suspicion in which we are held is because it is not always clear whose side we are on. Are we the paid agents of the public world, doing duty in tidying up and returning the deviants to a conventional role? Are we subversives who are a threat to decent people, to conventional society, because we put in question ordinary moral standards, undermine authority, infiltrate dangerous ideas into the minds of those who need to be corrected rather than believed?

We participate in both worlds to varying degrees and in our own ways. Mostly we seem to assume that we are paid to keep our mouths shut. Many seem to act under the power of a ruling mythology of care which suggests that secrets are to be *treated* rather than *understood* or used as 'intelligence' that might point a way to some different ordering of things.

Mostly as loyal citizens of the public world which pays our wages we 'forget' the secrets we are told, or know for ourselves in the dark places of our own lives. We do not want to be considered traitors to the way things seem to be. Perhaps we do not want to be too closely associated with the murky depths or the underbelly of our society. We want to be legitimate professionals, respected in the world of bright and light. We want to be chartered and registered, sanctioned and approved, fully paid up members of the legitimate realm.

We don't want to be thought to know too much and yet we are drawn towards knowing by the needs and secrets of our own lives. Professionally we seem to try to keep our hands as clean as possible. Perhaps, then, it is no wonder that many clinical psychologists espouse the professional myth of being 'applied scientists'. Secrets of *nature* are considered legitimate game in our society. Even secrets of human nature are relatively safe provided they are treated as a part of nature.

Secrets of *society* are a different thing! The thought of these being held and transmitted at often unacknowledged places of contact (lies having been told to workmates and family to cover tracks) raises qualms, an uneasy feel. This begins to verge on the political and the socially dangerous. Fears about the disaffected and those who have failed to live as the régime seems to require begin to stir. This is a more doubtful business altogether, not cricket, don't you know!

So we must fight harder to keep our hands appearing clean. We must keep ourselves apart, keep our knowledge and our clients at arm's length. Experimental methods, impersonal knowledge, objective facts, statistical and public procedures, all these may keep the dangers at bay. If we don't get too close, don't get involved, don't allow ourselves to be thought to be a 'weak link' or a 'fellow traveller' with the poor and the afraid, we will be safe. Don't let it be thought that you might bite the organizational hand that feeds you!

There is a great deal to be said for keeping well away from secrets. If you don't know them, or can pretend you don't, and do nothing to pass them on or encourage their exchange or decoding, then you may be safe from social condemnation. If you take a view of your discipline as being concerned with individuals and the study of behaviour, or something else equally 'real', then you may be considered suitably safe. You may be promoted to positions of public power, however murky and unresolved your own secret worlds may be. If you attend to formal and specially constructed 'experimental' situations rather than enter the ordinary social world; if you attend only to small time-spans and very limited ideas; if you have no truck with history and culture; if you act as if you were uncontaminated by the enveloping assumptions, values, preferences, blindnesses, fears, and intentions of your times, then with all this you may just be safe from the dangerous world. You may be able to ignore what has thereby become invisible and intangible, everything that lurks still in the darkness beyond the tribal fires.

It is more difficult to live an 'ordinary' life if you acknowledge and then get sucked into the secret world under the stone. Everyone knows that you will get *sucked in* if you meddle in that sort of thing! Once they have a hold on you they never let you go! No good can come of it! We mostly, therefore, live an ambiguous life both inside and outside ordinary society. Some of us struggle to remain insiders to society and largely remain outsiders to our clients. Some try to be insiders with their clients and are in danger of becoming distanced from society.

There must, it seems to me, be great danger here. Psychologists, for instance, have struggled so long (through experimental psychology, clinical psychology as an applied science, behaviour therapy, etc.) to be 'straight'. We have even had phases when we persecuted and reviled those secret grubbing, sex and aggression mongering, Freudian Jews! They seem to have survived though, and as traders in human secrets have mostly made a pretty good thing out of it. They were perhaps clever to camouflage themselves in our capitalist society by adopting high-price, private enterprise as their way of doing things.

Not only this, but as early practitioners in the secret realms which society disowned, or was disgusted by, they found a different way to appear clean. Both in theory and in the practice of many who followed Freud, therapists maintained a distance from those who came for help. In practice this came to mean increasingly long, expensive, esoteric, uncomfortable rituals of decontamination, cleaning of the hands. Through personal analyses it is supposed that their own profound involvements in the secret worlds would be dissolved, or safely skewered, available for private scrutiny and control. Ordinary mortals would continue to be sucked down and held for ransom in the cellars of the lost, while the purified few could walk through fire and still survive.

There were also further practical ways in which this separation of secret agents from the underworld were enacted. Patients were not spoken to directly but were debriefed lying on their backs, speaking they knew not what to a hidden but listening ear. Contact is in code. Few clues are given to reveal the human identity of the listening ear. He sits behind the patient's head, out of sight, giving as little as he can away.

In theory too, a distance was and is maintained. Unlike the customer the patient is always in the wrong. Everything she says is cast in doubt. Everything is made a projection of her own needs and fears. The conceptual language the professional uses makes it clear that the patient is the one in need. The theory is a tool, an armoury of protective and often penetrating power. If she says that he is angry, it is she who is *projecting*. If she does not know, it may be that the knowledge is *repressed*. If they disagree, she is *distorting*. If she suddenly changes tack, she may be *splitting*. If she or he feels warm or cold towards the other it is not how it seems, it is *transference* of a positive or negative kind.

All these are ways in which secret psychoanalytic agents have managed to work and yet be free. The freedom here is of a different kind from that acquired by scientific distance, but it is freedom through distance still. The professional 'spy' allows the continuance of a particular craft by trying to claim immunity in the public eye. These different kinds of claim by the objective scientist or the psychoanalyst receive different degrees of favourable regard in the public world.

We have no option but to tell ourselves stories of what we know and what we seek to know. We have to tell stories to conjure ourselves into being as creatures in culture rather than dumb beasts in the grip of necessity alone. We live in time and have to spin yarns to link now and then, self and other, what we hold in common and what is beyond the pale.

We are born into story worlds which already have a place for us; where we already belong is some kind of changing scheme of things. We are taught and have to learn our lines, the parts and characters others have prepared for us. What they do not know, and we may have great difficulty in coming to know, is who and what we are and may yet choose to be.

We are told stories from the moment we are born. All kinds of stories decorate and populate the world of what we might become. The most telling stories may be figments of the mind, not direct accounts of how things supposedly are. We are told many kinds of stories all at once and all the time. We are told stories in words and in ways that tell a very different tale in the manner of the telling. Every manner, context, style, tone of telling, tells its own silent tales.

We are told many stories that are not true, many that are true only in some other sense than how they seem. We are often told that we must seem to know what is so, even when much that we have been told is lies, figments, fantasies, comfortable fictions of former times. We are told different things that do not seem to 'gel'. We are given different accounts of what it's all about, what really is the way things are. We have a right to be confused and yet are judged especially harshly if we do not seem to know who or what or where we are.

People need to be able to find some place within some of the stories of their times, but sometimes people feel they don't fit in. Some try to fit into stories in dull obedience or against the grain. They give up their rights as authorizing their own life. Others struggle to be free, to walk out, clear of at least some of the cloying stories laid upon them, into another that is sought and undertaken by themselves.

We are inhabited by stories we know by and do not know about. We are peopled by story lines, characters, plots, endings, and styles. We have to pull ourselves free to some degree from the ongoing givenness of our lives. I am mostly dumb and deaf, insensitive to touch, incapable of sight. In this darkness, only dimly lit with words I grope for contact with another who might see or hear or taste or touch whoever it is I am and may yet be. Our conversational practices are shaped within and shape the stories that we live amongst. Apart from them I do not know who or what I am, none of us do. We do not know most of what we do. We spin yarns, tell tall tales to sew the world together, make it whole.

There are multiple meanings in everything. Beyond words everything is indefinitely uncertain and yet before and beyond question. Telling it is a way of catching a handful of air, laying a claim to primeval lands, fencing off a patch of desert. Words are our way of appropriating, laying claims, drawing bounds, insisting on particular cultivation.

Reality is created in our conversational practices and spoken into some form of being in the conversation of our lives over and over again. Reality is moment by moment on the run. Moment by moment the extraordinary is seen through the patina of convenience we cover over all the unknown world so that it can become a story world. It is unknown world that is our quest, not just the repetition of familiar story worlds. We stand always within the unknown world that we are also constituted of and by. We know more than we can say and have to learn sometimes to say what we do not know. 'Telling it like it is' has been shaped for us so that we tell it in the style of our roots, but we are always on the edge, the frontier of what we may yet know. How do we reach by our words into the heart of the possible? There is no method and no frauds will do.

Poets in science and art and every other sphere of life are forever nibbling at the world beyond what we can say. Occasionally there are larger conjurings from the void. When new stories are told, new listeners have to be there to realize their possibilities amongst us.

References

Allport, G. (1968) *The Person in Psychology: Selected Essays*, Boston: Beacon Press.

Aristotle, (1932 edn) *The Poetics*, Cambridge, Mass: Loeb Classical Library, Harvard University Press, London: Heinemann.

Bachelard, G. (1964) *The Poetics of Space*, Boston: Beacon Press.

Bachelard, G. (1969) *The Poetics of Reverie*, Boston: Beacon Press.

Bakan, D. (1966) *The Duality of Human Existence: Isolation and Communion in Western Man*, Boston: Beacon Press.

Bannister, D. (1959) *An Application of Personal Construct Theory (Kelly) to Schizoid Thinking*, unpublished PhD thesis, University of London.

Bannister, D. and Mair, J.M.M. (1968) *The Evaluation of Personal Constructs*, London: Academic Press.

Barfield, O. (1928) *Poetic Diction*, London: Faber and Gwyer.

Cupitt, D. (1985) *The Sea of Faith*, London: BBC Publications.

Eliot, George (1965 edn) *Middlemarch*, London: Penguin.

Gombrich, E.H. (1972) *The Story of Art*, Oxford: Phaidon.

Happold, F.C. (1973) *Mysticism: a Study and an Anthology*, London: Penguin.

Harré, R. (1979) *Social Being*, Oxford: Blackwell.

Harré, R. (1983) *Personal Being*, Oxford: Blackwell.

Heidegger, M. (1971) *Poetry, Language, Thought*, New York: Harper.

Hobson, R.F. (1985) *Forms of Feeling: The Heart of Psychotherapy*, London: Tavistock.

Ignatieff, M. (1984) *The Needs of Strangers*, London: Chatto and Windus, The Hogarth Press.

Jung, C. (1963) *Memories, Dreams, Reflections*, ed. Aniela Jaffé, New York: Pantheon Books.

Kelly, G.A. (1955) *The Psychology of Personal Constructs*, vols 1 and 2, New York: Norton & Co.

Kelly, G.A. (1969) *Clinical Psychology and Personality: The Selected Papers of George Kelly* (ed. B. Maher), New York: Wiley.

Kelly, G.A. (1969) 'Sin and Psychotherapy' in B. Maher (ed.) *Clinical Psychology and Personality: The Selected Papers of George Kelly*, New York: Wiley.

Kelly, G.A. (1977) 'The Psychology of the Unknown' in D. Bannister (ed.) *New Perspectives in Personal Construct Theory*, London: Academic Press.

Kopp, S.B. (1971) *Guru: Metaphors from a Psychotherapist*, Palo Alto, California: Science and Behaviour Books.

Krishnamurti, J. (1972) *You are the World*, Wassenaar, Holland: Servire.

Lomas, P. (1981) *The Case for a Personal Psychotherapy*, Oxford: Oxford University Press.

Mair, J.M.M. (1970a) 'Experimenting with Individuals', *Brit. J. Med. Psychol.* *43*, 245–56.

Mair, J.M.M. (1970b) 'Psychologists are Human Too' in D. Bannister (ed.) *Perspectives in Personal Construct Theory*, London: Academic Press.

Mair, M. (1977a) 'Metaphors for Living' in A.W. Landfield (ed.) *The Nebraska Symposium on Motivation: Personal Construct Theory*, Lincoln and London: University of Nebraska Press.

Mair, J.M.M. (1977b) 'The Community of Self' in D. Bannister (ed.) *New Perspectives in Personal Construct Theory*, London: Academic Press.

Mair, M. (1979) 'The Personal Venture' in P. Stringer and D. Bannister (eds) *Constructs of Sociality and Individuality*, London: Academic Press.

Mair, M. (1980) 'Feeling and Knowing' in Phillida Salmon (ed.) *Coming to Know*, London: Routledge & Kegan Paul.

Mair, M. (1985) 'The Long Quest to Know' in F. Epting and A.W. Landfield (eds) *Anticipating Personal Construct Psychology*, Lincoln and London: University of Nebraska Press.

May, R. (1975) *The Courage to Create*, London: Collins.

Polanyi, M. (1958) *Personal Knowledge*, London: Routledge & Kegan Paul.

Pollio, H.R., Barlow, J.M., Fine, H.J., and Pollio, M.R. (1977) *Psychology and the Poetics of Growth*, New Jersey: Lawrence Erlbaum Associates.

Richards, I.A. (1936) *The Philosophy of Rhetoric*, Oxford, New York: Oxford University Press

Rimmon-Kenan, Shlomith (1983) *Narrative Fiction: Contemporary Poetics*, London: Methuen.

Rycroft, C. (1985) *Psychoanalysis and Beyond*, London: Chatto and Windus, The Hogarth Press.

Schumacher, E.F. (1977) *A Guide for the Perplexed*, London: Jonathan Cape.

Shotter, J. (1984) *Social Accountability and Personhood*, Oxford: Blackwell.

Smail, D.J. (1978) *Psychotherapy; A Personal Approach*, London: Dent.

Smail, D. (1984) *Illusion and Reality: The Meaning of Anxiety*, London: Dent.

Smail, D. (1987) *Taking Care: an alternative to therapy*, London: Dent.

Stead, C.K. (1964) *The New Poetic: Yeats to Eliot*, London: Hutchinson.

Thomas, L.F. and Harri-Augstein, E. Sheila (1985) *Self-Organised Learning: Foundations of a Conversational Science for Psychology*, London: Routledge & Kegan Paul.

Watzlawick, P., Beavin, J.H., and Jackson, D.D. (1968) *The Pragmatics of Human Communication*, London: Faber & Faber.

Wittgenstein, L. (1953) *Philosophical Investigations*, Oxford: Blackwell.

Index

DATE DUE

FEB 27 '96		
OCT 28 '96		
NOV 2 3 2000		
AP 8 04		

Demco, Inc. 38-293